Exploring Women's Suffrage through 50 Historic Treasures

D1257736

Exploring America's Historic Treasures

About the Organization

The American Association for State and Local History (AASLH) is a national history membership association headquartered in Nashville, Tennessee, that provides leadership and support for its members who preserve and interpret state and local history in order to make the past more meaningful to all people. AASLH members are leaders in preserving, researching, and interpreting traces of the American past to connect the people, thoughts, and events of yesterday with the creative memories and abiding concerns of people, communities, and our nation today. In addition to sponsorship of this book series, AASLH publishes *History News* magazine, a newsletter, technical leaflets and reports, and other materials; confers prizes and awards in recognition of outstanding achievement in the field; supports a broad education program and other activities designed to help members work more effectively; and advocates on behalf of the discipline of history. To join AASLH, go to www.aaslh.org or contact Membership Services, AASLH, 2021 21st Ave. South, Suite 320, Nashville, TN 37212.

About the Series

The American Association for State and Local History publishes the Exploring America's Historic Treasures series to bring to life topics and themes from American history through objects from museums and other history organizations. Produced with full-color photographs of historic objects, books in this series investigate the past through the interpretation of material culture.

Exploring Women's Suffrage through 50 Historic Treasures

JESSICA D. JENKINS

ROWMAN & LITTLEFIELD
Lanham • Boulder • New York • London

Published by Rowman & Littlefield
An imprint of The Rowman & Littlefield Publishing Group, Inc.
4501 Forbes Boulevard, Suite 200, Lanham, Maryland 20706
www.rowman.com

6 Tinworth Street, London SE11 5AL, United Kingdom

British Library Cataloguing in Publication Information Available

Library of Congress Cataloging-in-Publication Data Available

ISBN 978-1-5381-1279-3 (cloth: alk. paper)
ISBN 978-1-5381-1280-9 (electronic)

♾™ The paper used in this publication meets the minimum requirements of
American National Standard for Information Sciences—Permanence of Paper
for Printed Library Materials, ANSI/NISO Z39.48-1992.

*For Karen and all the resilient women
of today, yesterday, and tomorrow.*

Contents

List of Illustrations

Preface

Several years ago, I gave a talk on women's suffrage at the local museum I worked for at the time. After the presentation, one of the museum's board members approached me—what ensued was a lengthy and lively conversation about the impending centennial of the ratification of the 19th Amendment. We chatted about the history of the movement, the impact of the legislation, and the historic objects scattered in countless public collections that piece together the story of suffrage. While the discussion kept me at work much longer than planned, I didn't mind. In all honesty, this particular board member was someone I secretly looked forward to in-depth conversations with. As a historian of women's history, and a passionate advocate for women, she had earned my adoration and respect long before that day. As we talked, she expressed concern to me that the centennial would come and go without the level of attention it deserved. To her it was an event worth the highest level of recognition. As we closed our conversation and prepared to part ways, she urged me to encourage museums, curators, educators, and individuals around the state to begin thinking of ways they could do justice to the complex milestone looming in 2020.

With the commemoration still several years away, my life and work took another path before it could arrive. I moved out of the state and began new curatorial opportunities at another institution. Still, the conversation from years before would occasionally surface in my mind. It popped up like a nagging feeling that I had forgotten to do something or left a task half-finished. Often when it happened, I contemplated those "historic objects in countless public collections." My former board member was right; items telling the story of suffrage are scattered in every corner of the nation, and across the middle, sometimes in the places most expected and other times in the least likely. They can be found in museum collections, at public libraries, and on university campuses. They may also take the form of public art or a historic site itself.

When I found out, in 2017, that the American Association for State and Local History planned to launch a new book series a light bulb went off. After years of gnawing at my subconscious, I finally knew how I would play my small part in commemorating the suffrage centennial. The book you now hold in your hands is the result of that "ah-ha!" moment. It can be difficult to bring items from far-reaching locations together physically and travelling the nation to see one object here and one object there is simply not feasible for most people. Picking up a book is much easier. From years of working as a curator, I also knew that people connect with recognizable items. While nineteenth-century garments may not look a lot like today's jeans and T-shirts, the simple fact is, everyone understands clothes. You pick them out, you put them on, and you wear them every day of your life. Using these types of familiar items as the driving force behind the book, suffrage is presented in an approachable manner, bringing related objects together in one place. For museum and historic site fans, this creates an opportunity to "visit" sites and objects they may not otherwise be able to see in person. It also allows access to items not fully represented online and takes away the burden of sifting through countless websites and collection databases to find images of "the real thing."

The story of suffrage is not just for historians, history buffs, or feminists, however—it is for everyone. It is a story of inspiration and perseverance, as well as a story of discrimination and hardship. It is also a story of both women and men. As the centennial has inched near, the topic of the women's suffrage movement has become more visible to the general public. The 2015 film *Suffragette* brought the fight for British women's voting rights into theaters and homes. In 2016, the US presidential campaign created an interest in the suffrage story in the United States as female candidates from both major political parties vied for nominations during the primaries. Since then, new books on the topic have hit bookshelves and more are on the way. While women's suffrage has deep and broad published literature, much of it is written for an academic audience, limiting the topic's accessibility to the general reader. On top of these formal approaches, the topic itself (which is steeped in the history of politics and legislation) can quickly become complex and difficult to process, creating further barriers.

As an alternative to these models, *Exploring Women's Suffrage through 50 Historic Treasures* approaches the topic of women's suffrage in the vein of books such as *The Smithsonian's History of America in 101 Objects*. Unlike the Smithsonian's publication however, which only draws on items from its own collections, this book brings together a group of highlighted objects from multiple public repositories and locations across the country. As the title implies, each of these objects is truly a historic treasure. To be a treasure, not every object must be rare or plated in silver and gold. Rather, what makes these items treasures is their historic value. Each one also provides an entry point into exploring various aspects of the larger suffrage story. And in this instance, every item is available for the public to access. While many fascinating items are held in private collections around the country, each item presented here is owned and cared for by a public entity; making each one not only valuable but available to all people—a truly universal treasure. Without these tangible relics of the past, our understanding of history would not be as deep or meaningful. Likewise, because each of these items holds importance and usefulness to historians as well as the general public, they deserve not only our appreciation but also attention toward their continued care. Without the ongoing advocacy and preservation that public institutions provide, their value runs the risk of being lost.

Definitions aside, flipping through the pages of this book, readers will see treasures as small as lapel pins and as large as an entire historic site. I believe it important to highlight not only archival items and traditional museum objects in this volume but also historic buildings. Like so many museum and preservation organizations have reminded us lately, historic buildings are important objects worthy of preservation. These structures can tell us just as much about the past as a letter or published pamphlet, so they, too, should be elevated as treasures. While it may not be obvious at first glance, every item in this book is in fact connected to suffrage and has a part of the story to tell. At the same time, some of the objects have a historical value obvious from the time of their creation. For others, it was not until much later that the importance became apparent. Selecting only fifty treasures to include was not easy, however. To help guide the selection process I identified nine broad themes I felt would present readers with a well-balanced picture of the suffrage movement. I then began the tedious and enormously fun task of identifying objects that fit within those categories. The process led me back to some "old friends" and introduced me to new historic items along the way. I identified many more objects than could fit into the pages of this book, and the field had to be narrowed.

Wanting to make sure the sheer volume of the book did not become burdensome to the general reader, fifty objects seemed like an appropriate target—enough room to explore varying angles, but not so little information that the reader was left only asking questions. In deciding which items to include, many factors were considered. What story does the object tell? How does it relate to the other objects under consideration? Is the object representative of a national narrative, a state and local one, or both? What kind of repository does the item belong to? Where is it located? Ultimately, I put together a wide variety of objects from many regions of the country to show suffrage did not happen in a vacuum; it was a movement that happened in every part of the country, touching all races and social classes. I also selected items from a variety of different sized organizations. While readers will see iconic objects from such prestigious institutions as the Smithsonian, they will also find local treasures that are cared for by small museums like the Whitley County Historical Society in rural Indiana. Similarly, some objects, such as a "Votes for Women" sash, display their connection to women's voting rights clearly, others, like a statue of Sacajawea, may not be as apparent at first glance. These choices were intentional, to encourage readers to consider the complexity of history and the items around us. Like people, all objects have multiple stories to tell, and it is always worth looking deeper to find out more.

As the reader flips through the pages of this book, they will find full-color images of all fifty objects that made the final cut. Many more could easily have been included or swapped for the ones appearing here, but practicality came into play. Following an introduction providing a brief summary of the US Constitution and its ties to female voting rights, as well as additional social context, the objects are arranged into nine thematic sections—Early Years; Organizations; Symbols; Consumer Culture; Allies; Roadblocks and Setbacks; Tactics and Public Demonstrations; Milestones; and Legacy. Each of these thematic sections contain between four and eight chapters, each highlighting one of the treasurers and their story. Like the highlighted items themselves, I arranged and rearranged these sections more than once, looking for the best presentation. While I considered a purely chronological delivery of the objects and stories, I ultimately determined that the thematic groupings made a bigger impact in understanding the overarching ideas of the movement. The order presented here will hopefully provide readers with information that builds upon itself, allowing them to see the multiple connections between the sections and objects.

Because this is not intended to be "THE" book on suffrage but "A" book on suffrage, each chapter has been kept short, so readers can easily move through its content in a single sitting. Hopefully, general readers will come away with a broad understanding of the national movement, some insight into the suffrage work that happened at the state and local levels, and an appreciation of how the actions of suffragists still have impact on the world today. It is always the hope of an author that her book will spark further curiosity and readers will be inspired to learn more about the topic in the future. For museum professionals or volunteers who pick up the book, I hope it will provide a model for thinking about objects, the variety of stories they can tell, and how to consider the complexity of the suffrage stories in their own collections. At the same time, I hope that the reader will see the interconnections of national history with narratives on the state and local levels. In many instances, and especially in the history of suffrage, the three are connected in many ways, and you cannot tell the story of one without the stories of the others.

While the information has been researched using a variety of primary and secondary sources (including some written for young adult readers, which serve as exceptional models for accessibility), readers will find that some specific language choices have been made in this book. For instance, you will find both the historic term "woman suffrage" as well as the more contemporary term "women's suffrage" within these pages. In the nineteenth and early twentieth centuries, the singular term "man" was used to personify and stand for all men (e.g., rights of man). Therefore, when "man suffrage" was achieved and further defined with the passages of the 14th and 15th Amendments, suffrage leaders turned to "woman suffrage" as a way of expressing their desire for the female vote. But "woman suffrage" did not encompass all women, rather it was an exclusionary term referring specifically to suffrage for white women. As you will discover through the chapters of this book, suffragists did not all look the same. While many were white and wealthy, many were black or representative of the countless immigrant communities and socioeconomic levels seen across the nation. Therefore, in these pages you will find the singular "woman suffrage" used when appropriate to reflect its historic use as an exclusionary term. Moreover, you will find "women's suffrage" used when referring to the broad movement for all women's rights, no matter race or social status. This is a conscious choice because, in fact, suffrage is a story involving *all* women—something that should not be lost in the semantics of one word.

No book is the be-all and end-all of a topic, no matter how hard it tries. Hopefully, *Exploring Women's Suffrage through 50 Historic Treasures* will provide readers an enjoyable introduction to the history of the suffrage movement. Filled with stories representative of the actions and experiences of suffragists around the country, it is my sincere hope that something new, interesting, or thought-provoking can be taken away by those who pick up this volume. The objects, public art, and historic sites highlighted in its pages are the heart and soul of the book. And as Dr. Lynne Templeton Brickley (the wise board member) once reminded me, the individual narratives of each are only strengthened when pieced together to tell the larger women's suffrage story.

Timeline of Objects

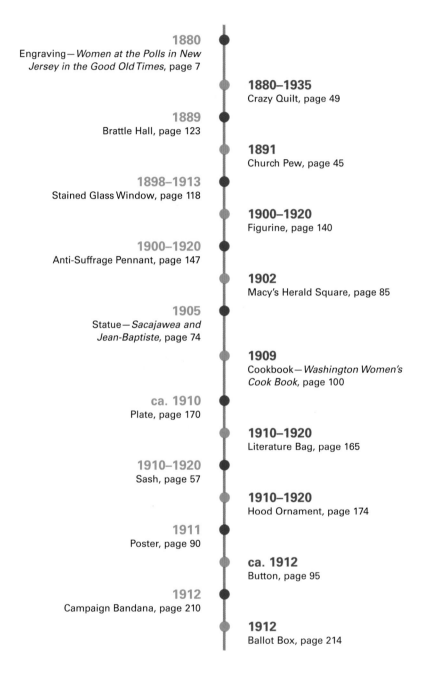

1880
Engraving—*Women at the Polls in New Jersey in the Good Old Times*, page 7

1880–1935
Crazy Quilt, page 49

1889
Brattle Hall, page 123

1891
Church Pew, page 45

1898–1913
Stained Glass Window, page 118

1900–1920
Figurine, page 140

1900–1920
Anti-Suffrage Pennant, page 147

1902
Macy's Herald Square, page 85

1905
Statue—*Sacajawea and Jean-Baptiste*, page 74

1909
Cookbook—*Washington Women's Cook Book*, page 100

ca. 1910
Plate, page 170

1910–1920
Literature Bag, page 165

1910–1920
Sash, page 57

1910–1920
Hood Ornament, page 174

1911
Poster, page 90

ca. 1912
Button, page 95

1912
Campaign Bandana, page 210

1912
Ballot Box, page 214

1913
Norwegian Headdress
and Vest, page 192

1913–1920
Banner, page 61

1914
Banner, page 128

1914
Photograph of National Women's Life-
Saving League members, page 188

1914
Photograph of Scandinavian Woman
Suffrage Association, page 41

1915
Movie Advertisement—"*Your Girl
and Mine*," page 105

ca. 1916
Shoe, page 219

1916
Photograph of Theodora Youmans
wearing suffrage tunic, page 183

ca. 1903
Top Hat, page 223

1917
Convention Ribbon, page 31

1917
"Jailed for Freedom" Pin, page 198

ca. 1918
Anti-Suffrage Stamps, page 66

1919–1929
Broadside, page 237

1920
Letter, page 229

1920
Suffrage Victory Map, page 157

1920
Sculpture—*The Portrait Monument*,
page 257

ca. 1920
Banner, page 178

Acknowledgments

Women's suffrage has long been an interest of mine—probably stemming back to my obsessive watching of Winifred Banks proudly wearing her "Votes for Women" sash in *Mary Poppins*. As I grew out of my childhood fascination stage, I came to understand that one woman did not drive the gargantuan task of moving the needle forward in terms of voting rights for the female sex; countless women and men all played a part. And they did not just work for one movement, but many around the globe. Without all the players, from the largest to the smallest, their goals might not have been reached. Likewise, I cannot take credit for creating this book alone. The writing of history is by nature a collective task. Historians, curators, and researchers must rely on the documents created contemporary to their topic of research. They then consult the work of others, carefully learning what has been written before. The many words they encounter help shape their analysis and interpretation of the ever-fluid thing that is written history. With each new perspective, bits and pieces of the researchers, historic figures, and societies that came before show through in the final product. My gratitude to the suffragists, historians, museum professionals, journalists, and researchers who have dived and continue to dive into the story of suffrage is immeasurable. Without their work, this book would not exist.

Specific thanks must also be given to the late Dr. Lynne Templeton Brickley. From the first time I met Lynne, she was generous of her time, knowledge, and enthusiasm for women's history. Over several years, I had the opportunity to interact with her at the museum where she served as a board member, and where I worked on the staff. Whether it was collaborative work on a museum project, or simply conversations about current events, Lynne always encouraged me to share the importance of women's history with others. At the same time, a debt is owed to the many teachers and professors who trained me not only in the skills of research methods but also in the art of looking past the paper trail to discover the three-dimensional objects, historic structures, and landscapes that are just as important in telling the stories of history.

Beyond my own research and the inspiration of published sources, I have relied heavily on the help and knowledge of others during the creation of *Exploring Women's Suffrage through 50 Historic Treasures.* For providing creative insight, assistance in exploring possible artifacts, and making suggestions for objects and stories, I extend my thanks to Susan Berning and Asantewa Boakyewa, Woodrow Wilson House; Dr. Patricia Cunningham, Ohio State University; Thomas Dublin, Binghamton University; Kenneth Florey; Amy Hague, Smith College; Linda Hocking, Litchfield Historical Society; Linda Lopata, The National Susan B. Anthony Museum and House; Rich Malley, curator extraordinaire; Doug Misner, Utah Division of History; Kathleen Pate, Arkansas Women's History Institute; Dr. Heather Prescott, Central Connecticut State University; Alan Rowe, IU Medical Health Archives; Ellen Shea and Diana Carey, Schlesinger Library; Louise Smith; JoAnn Staab; and Shirley Wajda.

Over the nearly two years it took to prepare the manuscript, I also worked with many talented and dedicated professionals at a variety of organizations and businesses who provided additional resources, research assistance, and photography services. In many cases these same people fulfilled the endless stream of image requests I submitted around the country—keeping their good humor as I juggled dozens of such requests and correspondence at one time. For this support I wish to express my gratitude to Alcione Amos, Mariam Doutriaux, and Susana Raab, Anacostia Community Museum; Eric Paff and Victoria Singer, Architect of the Capitol; Doreen Crowe, Loraine Jones, and Kate Stewart, Arizona Historical Society; Erica Hague and Jena Jones, Atlanta History Center; Madeline Moya, Austin History Center; Michael Lange, University of California, Berkeley, Bancroft Library; Leslie Martin and Angela Hoover, Chicago History Museum; Danielle Davis, City of Portland, Regional

Arts and Culture Council; Eisha Neely, Cornell University, Carl A. Kroch Library; Mindy A. Leisenring, Cortland County Historical Society; Stephanie Lucas and Donna Braden, The Henry Ford; Jim Janke; Nikaela J. Zimmerman, Matt Renick, and Nancy Sherbert, Kansas Historical Society; Pally Polhemus, Knox County Public Library; Ann McShane, Library Company of Philadelphia; Michael North, Kelly Dyson, and Alexis Valentine, Library of Congress; Dana Puga, Library of Virginia; Alex Dubois, Litchfield Historical Society; Jacqueline Roshia, Rona Dixson, and Michael Roets, Lorenzo State Historic Site; Sofia Yalouris, Maine Historical Society; Adam Taylor and the Library Permissions Team, Minnesota Historical Society; Dennis Northcott, Missouri History Museum; Margarete Ordon, Kendra Newhall, and Lori Ereth, Montana Historical Society; David Corrigan, Museum of Connecticut History; Christine Pittsley, Connecticut State Library; Jennifer Krafchik, National Woman's Party; Lauren Murphree, Camille Tyndall Watson, Ashley Yandle, and William H. Brown, North Carolina Office of Archives and History; Eleanor Gillers, New York Historical Society; Ashley Hopkins-Benton and Robyn Gibson, New York State Museum; Nadine Sergejeff, Newark Public Library; Kay Peterson and Debra Hashim, National Museum of American History; Doug Remley and Carrie Feldman, National Museum of African American History and Culture; Sarah Biller, Oklahoma Historical Society; Jo Ellen Mack, Old State House Museum; Victor Sanders, Portland Parks and Recreation; Ann Lowder, Robbins Hunter Museum; Kiki Smith and Stan Sherer, Smith College; the staff at Untapped Cities, LLC; Eileen Price, Washington State Historical Society; Aaron Mathieu and Dani Tippmann, Whitley County Historical Society; Frederick Stipe and Tim Hodgdon, Wilson Library at University of North Carolina, Chapel Hill; Scott Roller and Lisa R. Marine, Wisconsin Historical Society; and Andrew Phillips, Woodrow Wilson Presidential Library and Museum.

My deep appreciation also goes out to my editor at Rowman & Littlefield, Charles Harmon. He not only guided me through the publication process, but also provided valuable feedback along the way, answering my many, many questions. Bob Beatty, John Marks, and Rebecca Shrum, my editors at AASLH, all played vital roles in helping to form and refine the manuscript, both in its very earliest stages and the very last. To my friends and family who have provided unlimited support during this project I cannot say, "thank you" enough. Especially to Cathy, Linda, Liz, Megan, Jess, and my former Seminar for Historical Administration classmates who all sent more than one email or message telling me, "you've got this!"

From the time I was still in a stroller, I remember my parents taking my sisters and me to countless museums to explore art, history, science, and nature. They encouraged my love of history and put up with my nerdy childhood reading and dog-earing of pages in our home encyclopedia set. Without their nurturing and encouragement, I'm sure I would not have had the courage to tackle this project. I know in the past two years I have also missed many family functions and visits with sisters, nieces, and nephews. Thank you to them for understanding why I needed a little extra time in my home office.

And last, but not least, thank you to Karen—my constant source of energy, my in-house editor, and my sounding board. Not only did you take the brunt of making sure the cats and I were fed, the house didn't burn down, and the laundry was done for the past two years, but you've also shown me endless love and encouragement. You always know the right time to remind me to calm down; the times to let me freak out; and the moments to give me that gentle, "Don't worry, you're doing great." To you, the largest debt is owed. I thank you a million times over.

Introduction

The vote is the emblem of your equality, women of America, the guaranty of your liberty. That vote of yours has cost millions of dollars and the lives of thousands of women. . . . Women have suffered agony of soul which you never can comprehend, that you and your daughters might inherit political freedom.[1]

When the September 4, 1920, issue of the *Woman Citizen* came off the presses, these words of Carrie Chapman Catt greeted readers. As a long-time leader of the National American Woman Suffrage Association, Catt had invested countless hours of her energy, sweat, and tears into working for the suffrage movement. After witnessing the ratification of the 19th Amendment—the modification to the US Constitution providing women the opportunity to vote—she wanted to ensure that female citizens at the time, and in the future, understood the significance. To Catt and her peers, the vote symbolized more than just the ability to slip a ballot into a box. For them, it also signified a major shift in the legitimate citizenship of American women.

As Catt implied in her words, the concern about women's equal representation in the US government was nothing new. In March 1776, only four months before the Continental Congress declared independence from the British monarchy, Abigail Adams wrote a telling letter to her husband, future-president John Adams. Knowing that her spouse and other leaders would soon be drafting laws of the new nation, Adams wrote:

I long to hear that you have declared an independency—and by the way in the new Code of Laws which I suppose it will be necessary for you to make I desire you would Remember the Ladies, and be more generous and favourable to them than your ancestors. Do not put such unlimited power into the hands of the Husbands. Remember all Men would be tyrants if they could. If perticuliar [*sic*] care and attention is not paid to the Laidies [*sic*] we are determined to foment a Rebelion [*sic*], and will not hold ourselves bound by any Laws in which we have no voice, or Representation.[2]

Eleven years later John Adams gathered with the other Founding Fathers of the nation to draft the US Constitution—setting forth the framework of the nation's government. Despite his wife's earlier words and warnings of potential consequences, the framers continued to exclude women from participation in the new system.

When it was ratified, the Constitution reflected the experiences of the white middle- and upper-class men who wrote it, as well as the experiences of the lower-middle-class men who had been heartily involved in the revolution. While it did not explicitly welcome women as voters or take particular account of them as a class, what it left unsaid was just as important as what it did spell out. Generally, the document refers to "persons" and rarely used the generic word "he." Women as well as men were defined by the Framers as citizens, but no voting requirements were established, leaving it up to the states to set up voter qualifications. Early on, the state of New Jersey even experimented with allowing single female property owners to vote—a practice that was quickly abandoned in favor of male-only voting. Notably, the document also kept intact the authority of husbands over wives. When married, any assets belonging to the wife passed to the husband, leaving most women with no legal claims to property—often an entry point into voting rights and other recognized legal actions. Likewise, without the vote, women could not serve on juries. As citizens however, they were entitled to trial by a jury of their peers. Surely, a jury of their peers should have included women like themselves.[3]

Despite the hurdles created for women by the Constitution, the Founding Fathers' words left considerable room for interpretation and refinement through the amendment process. For decades, many supporters of women's voting rights hoped additional states would follow New Jersey's early example and experiment with voting rights for female residents. Ultimately, none of the male-run governments made that move until after the close of the Civil War in the 1860s. Even then, it was a rarity. The decision by these few states and territories to extend the vote to women came at a turbulent time for women's suffrage advocates, however. As the Civil War brought the issue of race to the forefront of American government and society, the nation's governing body amended the Constitution to address the legal standing of the countless blacks who found themselves freed from the institution of slavery. As set out in Section 1 of the 14th Amendment, in 1868 citizens were defined as "All persons born or naturalized in the United States, and subject to the jurisdiction thereof."[4] This broad definition allowed both women and blacks to see themselves reflected in the definition of citizenship. Section 2, however, muddied the waters. Where the sex of voters had not explicitly been called out before, supporters of women's voting rights now faced more direct language that stated:

> But when the right to vote at any election for the choice of electors for President and Vice-President of the United States, Representatives in Congress, the executive and judicial officers of a State, or the members of the legislature thereof, is denied to any of the male inhabitants of such State, being twenty-one years of age and citizens of the United States, or in any way abridged, except for participation in rebellion, or other crime, the basis of representation therein shall be reduced in the proportion which the number of such male citizens shall bear to the whole numbers of male citizens twenty-one years of age in such State.[5]

If the inclusion of the word "male" in Section 2 of the 14th Amendment had not been enough to squelch the hopes of women's voting rights supporters, the 15th Amendment (added in 1870) wiped out any questioning of its meaning when it guaranteed the vote to all men despite race or previous condition of servitude. With the addition of the single word "male," the US government made it clear where they stood on the issue of female voting rights.[6] Supporters now found themselves divided about where to start. Should they lobby for female votes in their individual states? Or should they push for yet another amendment to the federal Constitution providing the vote to women as well as white and black men? Many white female activists also saw the granting of voting rights to newly freed black men as a betrayal to their perceived white superiority and entitlement—leading to decades of ugly and ingrained racism within their movement. For black women, the extension of the vote to African American men served as the first step in their communities' quest for equality under the law.

With these constitutional definitions established, generations of American women watched as individuals advocated for both state and federal governments to provide female citizens with the opportunity to vote. Many of these women stood to benefit from the vote. Others opposed it because they believed they stood to lose, while some were simply indifferent. Throughout the lengthy and contentious campaign, words like "suffrage" and "franchise" were used interchangeably and in varying forms. While common terms to Americans in the nineteenth and early twentieth centuries, in the twenty-first century they can appear foreign or possibly leave individuals unsure of their meanings. Although no longer used frequently, the terms are quite simple. Boiled down, "suffrage" and "franchise" both refer to the right to vote. Ironically, "suffrage" can also sound similar to the word "suffering," but the two should not be confused or connected. Even though suffrage activists endured many long, agonizing years working to secure the vote, it is only coincidence that the name of their movement sounds like a term so apt of their own experiences. In reality, the modern word "suffrage" was borrowed from the classical Latin term "suffrāgium," also referring to the right to vote.[7]

No matter the words chosen to describe the circumstances, motivations, and outcomes, the journey of black and white Americans toward securing female voting rights had many ups and downs. They also did not struggle alone. Globally, other nations saw similar campaigns surface at the same time—some granting the vote to women before the United States, while others did not come onboard until after. As early as 1893, New Zealand had enfranchised its female citizens, and in 1906, Finland became the first European nation to do so. Even before the United States ratified the 19th Amendment, Australia, Norway, Denmark, Canada, Austria, Germany, Poland, Russia, the United Kingdom, and the Netherlands all extended voting rights to women. Since then, many other nations have continued pushing for greater female equality, with governments extending women's suffrage in all regions of the globe, including Spain in 1931, Brazil in 1934, China in 1949, Algeria in 1962, Oman in 1997, the United Arab Emirates in 2006, and Saudi Arabia in 2011.[8] Like many of these other countries, the American movement, whose modern roots stretch back to the eighteenth century, evolved over time. As supporters gained steam in the late 1860s, they began a roller-coaster ride toward ratification of the 19th Amendment in 1920. Rather than screech to a halt after ratification, however, the momentum of activists carried them into the next phases of work for broader women's rights, inclusive suffrage for minorities and people of color, and placing more women in political office.

While the work of American suffragists and agitation for broader equal rights for women ultimately played out across the entire nation, the organized national suffrage movement began in the northeastern United States, where a broad range of social reform was underway in the 1840s. What had largely been a region dominated by agriculture only a few decades earlier now felt the economic and social shifts brought on by expanding railways and canal systems, and the resulting increase in manufacturing and commerce. With new business also came growth in population, immigrants, and a more urban society. As the white native-born residents' sense of familiarity and community faded (or at least changed), they formed organizations ranging from religious and civic, to educational and social to sooth their anxiety. Ultimately, many of these groups would assist in helping many white Americans reframe their way of thinking about, and being part of, the newly emerging American society. At the same time, free blacks, as well as immigrants, also bound themselves together to not only establish like-minded communities but, in many instances, to work to secure and protect their own rights in the United States.[9]

By the late 1840s, groups advocating for social reform related to antislavery, health, education, consumption of alcohol, and labor conditions were thick on the ground. Through these organizations, many white middle-class citizens, as well as a smaller number of free blacks and immigrants became participants in wider social concerns than ever before. In addition to concerned male citizens, reform movements attracted middle-class women. Without a voice in politics, social reform appealed to females looking for ways to become involved in molding the issues of society. When many were denied the right to fully participate or hold roles of leadership however, some began speaking out for women's rights. They demanded changes in the social, moral, legal, educational, and economic status of the female sex.[10]

In 1848, the first women's rights convention in the country was held in Seneca Falls, New York, kicking off a string of similar meetings in various regions of the nation. Over time, interest in expanding women's rights spread, and the women and men concerned with female voting began focusing more and more on the issue of suffrage. Then in 1868, the US Congress adopted the 14th Amendment introducing the word "male" to the conditions of citizenship and voting rights as defined in the Constitution. Two years later the 15th Amendment extended the vote to black men. The adoption of these two pieces of legislation prompted some women's rights leaders to see the vote as their most important goal, and a separate women's suffrage movement was born.[11]

During the next fifty years, various organizations dedicated to suffrage formed around the nation. At the national level, competing groups came into existence in the late 1860s. By the 1890s, the two organizations realized that compromises must be made in order to merge into one stronger unit. This did not come easily, however, and disagreements over issues such as race relations, tactical methods, and whether to push for state or federal support continued to plague the movement for years. At the same time national groups were forming, countless people founded suffrage clubs at the state, county, and local levels as well. While momentum was slow at first, in the late 1890s the nation experienced a surge of volunteerism among middle-class women.[12] Over the next twenty years, a new energy was building in the suffrage movement, and by the 1910s, suffragists hit their stride.

Just as the suffrage movement was growing and changing, so was the nation. If citizens in the 1840s thought they experienced rapid change, the explosion of national growth in the last half of the century certainly felt like an earthquake in comparison. During the 1860s, Americans battled each other in a devastating Civil War. During the ensuing bloodshed, the 13th Amendment put an end to slavery, President Lincoln was assassinated, and the Industrial Revolution pushed forward like never before. As manufactured goods poured out of factories, Americans developed an appetite for consumer products. In the 1870s, the bicycle captured the attention of the nation, while Thomas Edison introduced both the light bulb and the phonograph. With the growth of cities and industry, the United States saw an influx of immigrants from around the world that only seemed to increase from year to year. By the early twentieth century the United States looked drastically different than it had only a few decades earlier: automobiles could be seen on roadways, airplanes had taken flight, and the United States had become a melting pot of unique and interesting cultures and nationalities. With a booming middle class, department stores allowed citizens to indulge their desires for new and exciting home goods. While only twenty-six states existed in the nation in 1840, by 1900 the total had reached forty-five.[13]

Much like what occurred earlier in the nation's history, with expansive change came a desire by some citizens for major reform. Stretching from the 1890s to the 1920s, the Progressive Era produced widespread social and political activism on a scale never before seen. The citizens and politicians involved targeted political machines and corrupt lawmakers—hoping to remove them from office, creating a purer democracy. They also focused on eliminating the perceived problems blamed on industrialization, urbanization, and immigration. At the same time Progressives sought to promote equal competition in business, and many favored the prohibition of liquor. Often fueled by fear of "the other" and the unknown, in many ways Progressivism touched all aspects of life. It promoted modernization, scientific method, Americanization, and efficiency at work, at home, and at play.[14]

For suffragists, these major social, political, economic, and lifestyle changes proved beneficial. In a world where everyday citizens experienced rapid change, suffragists' desire to alter women's enfranchisement seemed less radical than it had a few decades earlier. Activists also had new tools available to spread their message. As modern newspapers proliferated, more and more people had access to information promoting suffrage. And for those hungry for mass-produced goods, suffragists could now easily churn out a variety of brightly colored and inexpensive goods promoting their cause. As more and more Americans saw the need for social reform, proponents of women's voting rights hoped they would lend support to them as well. At many times, they did. In all areas of the nation, many women and men who supported progressive reforms such as pure food and drug legislation, protection for workers, and the ending of child labor believed women's votes would help them reach their goals. This belief led many Progressives, both female and male, and both citizen and lawmaker, to lend their vocal support to female voting rights. When indirect support was not enough, women of all backgrounds joined suffrage clubs looking to secure votes for progressive laws quicker.[15]

As suffragists' activities became more visible and membership in their organizations exploded, activists hoped the government would take notice of the growing support. Eventually they did. After decades of encouragement from suffragists and allies, the US Congress passed the 19th Amendment, providing women the opportunity to vote. The path to victory had been long, and many women had sacrificed countless amounts of time, energy, and resources to make it happen. As Carrie Chapman Catt so bluntly pointed out in 1920, the women who had done so, "suffered agony of soul" during the process. Indeed, the process had been torturous at times, but in securing the 19th Amendment, activists hoped they had proven women were legitimate citizens of the nation, entitled to the same rights as their male counterparts. As time passed however, women realized that while they had taken a major step in expanding women's rights, the work was not done. The 19th Amendment did not create the idealized equality some suffragists dreamed of. Instead, as Catt noted, this important step in women's rights provided female citizens the opportunity to inherit the political freedom needed to continue pushing boundaries. It is that freedom that has allowed them to expand upon the work begun in the past and carry it forward into the future.

Part I

EARLY YEARS

When asked for the birth date of the women's suffrage movement, the year 1848 often comes to the lips of historians and teachers. That summer, a women's rights convention took place in Seneca Falls, New York, and began the first substantial fight for women's voting rights. While this event may be worthy of being called a birthday, in reality, the seeds of suffrage had been planted many years before. Long before 1848, women thought about how to improve their lives and roles in society, and following the Revolutionary War, New Jersey even experimented briefly with allowing women to cast ballots. Despite this failed attempt at more inclusive suffrage, early women's rights proponents showed little interest in focusing their energies solely on the vote. Instead, they questioned the centuries-old assumption that women belonged in the home and nowhere else. Through writings, conversations, and actions, they looked to expand their educational opportunities. They fought back against the concept that gender or race automatically made them inferior. Although the itch for female voting rights had started to stir in some women, even after the Seneca Falls Convention suffrage did not exist as a singular goal of female activists. They also worried about women's lack of control over property and earnings, legal status, and rights regarding divorce and guardianship of their children. Even women's freedom (or lack thereof) due to fashions of the day received their attention. It took many years for suffrage to break out as its own fight. Without this broader work for women's rights, however, the suffrage movement would not have been the same. Before the push for voting rights became its own cause, these women laid a strong foundation, and their path guided early suffragists on a long march to victory.

1

Laying a Strong Foundation

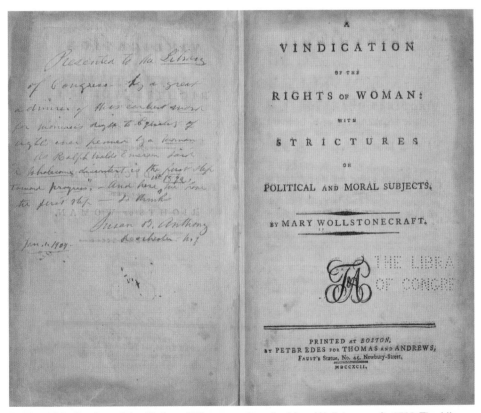

Book—*A Vindication of the Rights of Woman*, written by Mary Wollstonecraft, 1792, The Library of Congress, Washington, DC, http://www.loc.gov

Nestled among the millions of books filling the shelves and storage rooms of the Library of Congress of the United States are nearly four hundred items donated by Susan B. Anthony. In 1903, the world-renowned social activist and suffragist donated her personal library to the institution—arguably the largest repository of its kind in the world.[1] Although small compared to the total number of holdings, Anthony's assortment of books, pamphlets, and scrapbooks provide insight into both feminist and antislavery literature. Additionally, through personal annotations written into many of the volumes, the collection serves as a window into the personality and life of Anthony the person, rather than Anthony the public figure. On the inside covers of the literature, library patrons will discover short notes about the activist's parents, her opinions on some of the greatest writers and orators of her time, and even short reflections on her travels. In fact, many of these personal notes were added when packing the library for shipment during the winter of 1902–1903. During the process, Anthony no doubt reflected upon her life while saying goodbye to the publications she had accumulated and referenced many times throughout it.[2]

While the collection is not limited to Anthony's work for women's voting rights, it does contain notable volumes documenting the history of the women's suffrage movement. In addition to late nineteenth-century titles such as the *History of Woman Suffrage* and Elizabeth Cady Stanton's reminiscences *Eighty Years and More*, Anthony also included an influential work from much earlier.[3] On the inside of the book seen on the previous page, Anthony inscribes, "Presented to the Library of Congress by a great admirer of this earliest work for woman's rights to Equality of rights ever penned by a woman." Published in 1792, *A Vindication of the Rights of Woman* rolled off the presses well before the suffrage movement took off in America. Although its English author, Mary Wollstonecraft, wrote the powerful work thousands of miles away, in the United States her book ignited the minds of many women leading the effort to expand the rights of females.[4] Through her words, a desire was sparked in many American women to consider social and political reforms that would improve their lives, as well as the lives of countless others around the nation.

When *A Vindication of the Rights of Woman* was published, Mary Wollstonecraft quickly became famous and infamous simultaneously. Some people considered her views visionary, while others saw them as extremely controversial. Either way, Wollstonecraft used her book to argue that women could achieve levels of moral, intellectual, and political merit equal to those of men.

To do so, however, both sexes needed to receive the same education and have the same political rights. Written at a time when women held few rights and became invisible to the law as soon as they married, this idea seemed outlandish to many people. Women's husbands took control of any property they owned, money they earned, and in cases of divorce, children they bore. Girls also faced limited educational opportunities, especially compared to today's standards.[5] For many people who lived in this setting and accepted these norms, Wollstonecraft's ideas of equality made little sense.

While many people saw no value in the ideas presented in the book, others saw common sense in the concepts. President John Adams even read earlier works by the female philosopher and playfully referred to his wife Abigail as a "Disciple of Wollstonecraft." In 1794, the presenters of commencement addresses at Philadelphia's Young Ladies Academy quoted and praised the book.[6] Despite these mixed reviews, Wollstonecraft had put down in writing the thoughts many women had experienced before and would continue to expand upon in the future.

The positive reception of the book, as well as the author's philosophy, soon took a hit, however. Only five years after its publication, Mary Wollstonecraft died at the young age of thirty-eight. To memorialize her, Wollstonecraft's husband penned a memoir as a tribute to his late wife. What began with good intentions quickly backfired. Rather than uplift her memory, the book instead tarnished Wollstonecraft's reputation. The shocking details he included about her affair and illegitimate child with an American diplomat, as well as their own premarital relationship, did not sit well with many readers in the 1790s.

Although the memoir hurt Wollstonecraft's reputation, the philosophy she laid out in *A Vindication of the Rights of Woman* continued to appeal to many women's rights advocates in the United States. Suffragists like Susan B. Anthony and leaders who came decades before her, looked to the book as a guide for shaping their own ideas about female equality. Like Wollstonecraft, some considered the need to advance women's education and political rights. Others pondered the moral virtues of women and how they could balance motherhood with civic duties. In a nation where laws varied widely from state to state, women of many backgrounds, and in many regions, found themselves working for pay equity, control over their own property after marriage, and custodial rights of their children after divorce. When women began campaigning for the right to vote, suffragists encouraged young women who had never heard of the author to read her book. As a tribute, suffrage pioneers Susan B. Anthony and Elizabeth Cady Stanton even hung a portrait of Wollstonecraft in the offices of their suffrage newspaper when it opened in 1868. By placing Wollstonecraft in a position of high regard, they confirmed their admiration for the woman and her early insights into women's rights.[7]

While it is not known when Anthony first read Wollstonecraft's book, she, like many other suffragists, considered the author and her work a foundational steppingstone for their cause. In 1906, she gave her last public suffrage speech. During her time on stage Anthony said, "I never saw that great woman, Mary Wollstonecraft, but I have read her eloquent and unanswerable arguments in behalf of the liberty of womankind."[8] Through words like these, American suffragists confirmed that they considered *A Vindication of the Rights of Woman* is a founding theory of their movement. While she wrote an ocean away and more than one hundred years before the ratification of the 19th Amendment, Wollstonecraft's words laid the foundation suffragists would march upon throughout their fight. In donating her personal copy to the Library of Congress, Anthony ensured history would note the importance of the work to suffrage, a cause her name came to represent.

2

Pawns of Politics

Engraving—*Women at the Polls in New Jersey in the Good Old Times*, by Howard Pyle, 1880, Special Collections Division, The Newark Public Library, Newark, NJ, https://npl.org/

For many years historians of American history brushed off an interesting event in the early story of women's suffrage—the fact that for a short time following the American Revolution, a segment of women held the right to vote in the state of New Jersey. In the past, the importance of this was downplayed as a simple oversight in the language of the state's constitution. Historians even argued that lawmakers never intended to allow women to vote. Therefore, it made perfect sense to many people that in 1807 the state amended its constitution to clarify its original intent and make sure women could no longer cast ballots at the polls. Lawmakers were simply course-correcting a previous error in wording. Over time, however, individuals studying suffrage have blown the dust off the incident and taken a closer look. In doing so, it became obvious the story is not that simple, and the actions of lawmakers in 1807 should not be quickly shrugged off. In 1880, *Harper's Weekly*, a popular magazine at the time, published the engraving seen on the previous page. The image depicts women one hundred years earlier peacefully casting their votes in the Garden State. Although this short-lived experiment in New Jersey's early years of statehood has been forgotten by many today, it is a significant event in suffrage history. In fact, its story further demonstrates that American women's desire for the right to vote stemmed back to the founding of the nation itself.

So how did women briefly gain the right to vote in New Jersey? And how had it been taken away? In May 1776, with the smell of freedom in the air, the governing body of the American thirteen colonies sent out instructions for each to prepare for their impending statehood. When New Jersey drafted its state constitution in response, it stood out from the others in one very specific way—it not only gave the vote to men who met certain property requirements, but it also extended the right to vote to some women, blacks, and alien residents.[1] As written, "all inhabitants . . . of full age, who are worth fifty pounds . . . and have resided within their county . . . for twelve months" held the right to vote.[2] Because married women could not own property in their own name that automatically meant only single women could cast ballots. Although female residents in New Jersey had not specifically asked for this right, they embraced it, and in the 1790s and early 1800s, large numbers of unmarried women regularly participated in elections and spoke out on political issues.[3] For married women, it was assumed the votes of their husbands represented their interests.

Unlike the argument swirling for many years however, this was no mistake. Lawmakers did not make a poor choice in wording, and they did not have an accidental oversight when preparing their constitution. Falling in line with their own liberal construction of voting rights, New Jersey's lawmakers intended for propertied women to have the right to vote; just as they intended for blacks and alien residents as well. If it happened accidently, they would not have spent from late 1775 through the first part of 1776 debating voter qualifications, adjusting the property requirements time and again, and finally deciding to set those guidelines to include a portion of the female residents. In fact, an early draft of the state constitution used the word "he" to identify voters; the language was then changed to be gender neutral.[4]

Even in their own revolutionary ardor of freedom, however, forward-thinking New Jersey did not know how to handle the rights of women. While single females held the right to vote right away, the young state's constitution went through many revisions in its early days. Soon after the adoption of the state's 1776 constitution, New Jersey's revisions in 1777 and 1783 altered the description of election laws using only the pronoun "he." Then in 1790, when the government amended the constitution again, a specific area of seven counties referred to voters as both "he" and "she." By 1797, revisions had occurred once more, and the constitution again described all voters in the state as both male and female. Throughout these changes, women cast ballots when they could, and from 1797 onward, they voted in large numbers and participated in political discussions.[5]

Why New Jersey's lawmakers decided to extend the vote to women has never been completely clear. Some people argue the revolutionary spirit of freedom and equality prompted the state to have a more inclusive view of citizenship and voting rights. Also, because they had just spent years battling for freedom from England, they wanted to ensure their own citizens experienced as much independence as possible, especially since women tended farms and businesses and acted as couriers and spies throughout the conflict. A similar argument was made by suffragists after World War I. Others look to the state's Quaker population for answers. John Cooper, an active public official and devout Quaker, served on the committee responsible for drafting the state's first constitution. With members of the religious community making up a large portion of the state's southern population, Cooper may have advocated for his religion's strong belief in the equality of women. No matter the specific reasons, by 1807 party politics came into play when New Jersey suddenly limited voting and women had the right taken away.[6]

Following Republican Thomas Jefferson's victory over Federalist John Adams in the 1800 presidential election, the Federalist Party began to worry that bloc voting by females benefitted the Republican cause. As towns that were previously Federalist strongholds began electing more and more Republicans, politicians feared it was due to the increased number of female voters voting en masse in support of the Republican Party. If true, then it seemed reasonable that they could reduce the numbers of ballots Republicans received by not allowing women to vote.[7] To do this, they needed to revise the state's constitution once again, but the Federalists' first attempt to do so flopped. Asking women to approve a measure disenfranchising themselves was not exactly an easy sell. In response, Federalists began a hard push to find a way to accomplish the goal by the presidential election of 1808.[8]

As it turned out, when the 1808 presidential election crept near, taking women's voting rights away was just as easy as it had been to grant them in 1776. By then the political power of New Jersey had shifted, and charges of voting fraud ran rampant. With politicians claiming white men exploited ignorant women and blacks to cast illegal ballots, Federalists and Republicans agreed it was no longer to either's advantage for all state inhabitants to vote. Using a recent corrupt election in Essex County as their reasoning, lawmakers claimed they needed to "clean up" politics. What ensued was not a widespread "cleaning up," but instead an act of the legislature to amend the constitution without public approval. In sharp contrast to their previous stance, lawmakers' amendment declared, "no person shall vote in any state or county election for officers in the government of the United States or of this state, unless such person be a free, white male citizen."[9] Without even having the opportunity to exercise their legal political voice, women, black, and alien residents had their voting rights taken away in the blink of an eye.

In the young nation, party politics had become a strong game. When politicians felt women no longer benefited them, they simply removed female voters from the equation. To make it happen, they acted under the guise of fighting corruption. Under modern standards it may be surprising that the retraction of female voting rights came without much public outcry. At the time however, a renewed focus on the importance of women in the home had emerged, making vocal opposition minimal. Although New Jersey's actions meant later generations would have to push against an injustice from many years earlier, the years following 1807 prepared women for the fight ahead of them. With their right to vote revoked, women in New Jersey increased their political voice in other ways. Through petitioning, they made their opinions heard—even if not directly from their mouths. They also became active in groups looking to change society through temperance, economic rights, and abolition.[10] When looking back on what lawmakers claimed had been an accident after the Revolutionary War, it is obvious that from the earliest years of the nation's history, American women saw value in having a political voice. In New Jersey, however, male lawmakers sealed the political fate of female residents. Rather than continue to model equality for the nation, New Jersey's male politicians defined women as nothing more than pawns of politics; an attitude that would linger for generations to come.

3

Change Begins with Education

Globe, made by William Barden, circa 1790, Litchfield Historical Society, Litchfield, CT, http://litchfieldhistoricalsociety.org/

Today, a quick internet search turns up scads of options for anyone looking to attend college.[1] In fact, the barrage of marketing materials starts well before it even occurs to many young students to think about life after high school. Almost the opposite of today, when Mary Wollstonecraft published *A Vindication of the Rights of Woman* in the 1790s, "limited" might have been the best description of educational opportunities for girls. In her book, the author even highlights education as one of the causes of female oppression.[2] Wollstonecraft was not the first or last woman to call for better schooling options for girls, however. Ten years earlier Judith Sargent Murray, an American advocate for women's rights, expressed similar ideas. Through their writings, Murray and Wollstonecraft grabbed people's attention, and soon many other women and men began grappling with the issue. Out of this enthusiasm, female education became one of the first aspects of women's rights to become a matter of high importance and receive attention from numerous women and men across many states in the nation.[3] Over the next several decades the educational opportunities for girls grew. This created a generation of young women who, along with their children and grandchildren, continued fighting for better education and expanded female rights, including women's suffrage.

After the close of the American Revolution, a new concept gained popularity in the United States, particularly among white women of means. Known as Republican Motherhood, it stressed the responsibility of women to provide the early educational and moral training of their children. According to the theory, because young boys would grow into leaders of the nation, their early education was crucial for the survival of the country. For the concept to work however, mothers needed to have a top-notch education themselves. While this placed women as the intellectual equal of men, no one saw it as a threat if women remained happy to limit the use of their newfound knowledge to the private sphere. Because women had not yet expressed an interest in joining or replacing men in commerce and politics, the push to advance women's education persisted, and women looked to use their minds at home and in schools to enable and support sons and husbands in the work they did.[4]

Students of Sarah Pierce, a pioneering educator who opened a school for girls (and a small number of boys) in Litchfield, Connecticut, in the 1790s, used the globe pictured on the previous page. What began as a small operation in her family home soon outgrew the space and required the construction of a separate academy building. During the thirty years after its opening, the Litchfield Female Academy enrolled more than two thousand students from seventeen states and territories, as well as pupils from Canada and the West Indies.[5] Through reputation and increasing enrollment, Pierce's academy thrived in the early nineteenth century. Not only did the school enable Pierce to support herself and her family, but it also established a model of education that valued the abilities of women and did not assume that their sex limited their potential for learning.

As an educator who fully embraced the ideas of Republican Motherhood, Pierce's school stood out from others at the time because of her approach to what and how her students learned. Like other girls' schools, Pierce offered a variety of ornamental subjects, such as painting, needlework, and music. While she knew these lessons provided useful training in practical skills such as stitching, and accomplishments in art and music carried the mark of a refined woman, Pierce was not content to offer her students these subjects alone. Academic courses made up a large bulk of her students' education. English, Ancient and European history, geography, arithmetic, and composition all played important parts in regular studies. In addition to those subjects, students could also explore Latin, moral and natural philosophy, logic, and rhetoric; subjects typically reserved for boys and men.[6] When they did sit down to work on artwork, Pierce required students to accompany their efforts with reading aloud or serious conversation. No time was given to ornamental subjects alone. In many cases the embroideries and paintings the students executed tied into their academic studies. The painting of beautiful maps and careful study of globes reinforced geography, while literary and philosophical subjects came to life in colorful embroideries. Without a doubt, the students who attended the school came out with a well-rounded education meant to launch them into the next phase of their lives.

While some of Pierce's students returned home, hoping to marry and start a family, many became teachers themselves—a tribute to the school's emphasis on Republican Motherhood. This great success was a double-edged sword, however, and it played a major role in bringing the Litchfield Female Academy to a close in the early 1830s. By that time, many of her graduates had not only become teachers but also established schools of their own. This created more options for families looking to educate their daughters and reduced the number of students attending school in Litchfield.[7] Sarah Pierce had started a chain reaction. As the next generation of educators struck out on their own, they expanded upon Pierce's ideas and formed their own groundbreaking institutions.

Idea Strong was just one of Pierce's early students who exhibited great potential. When the town of Middlebury, Vermont, approached Pierce to advise them on the creation of a school like hers, Pierce knew Strong would be up to the task. Strong based the curriculum for the school on Pierce's model and took on the role as head of the newly founded Middlebury Female Academy. The school would later be taken over by Emma Willard, who went on to earn her own place of honor in the history of women's education when she opened the highly successful Troy Female Seminary in Troy, New York. As time went on, schools such as Willard's served as important models for future high schools and successful women's colleges around the country.[8]

While Sarah Pierce and many other early female educators did not believe women had a place in politics, their schools, and the many that followed, produced prominent female reformers, including abolitionists and women's rights advocates. The famous suffragist Elizabeth Cady Stanton attended Emma Willard's academy as a young woman. And Henry Ward Beecher, a student of Pierce, became the first president of the American Woman Suffrage Association. Interestingly however, during their lifetimes many early suffragists found it beneficial to downplay the importance of these early pioneers of female education. When arguing women's state of oppression, it simply would not be beneficial to acknowledge the advancements that had already occurred. In reality, the remarkable education they received prepared many of those leaders to tackle the public debates and highly intellectual subjects they did. The work of Pierce, Willard, and other educators elevated the regard for women's intelligence. While the philosophy of Republican Motherhood did not encourage women to enter the civic or political world, time would eventually intervene. As more and more women earned advanced educations, it only made sense their worldviews would shift. If their intelligence was good enough to shape the next generation of leaders inside the home, why not shape the policies of the nation? To do so many women had to become leaders themselves. They put their minds to work, using their intellect to campaign for the right to vote—a necessity if they wanted their voices heard, and their education used to its fullest potential.

4

Created Equal

Declaration of Sentiments Table, 1800–1848, National Museum of American History, Washington, DC, http://americanhistory.si.edu/

Each day people interact with items in their homes, offices, and public spaces. Chairs are sat upon and pillows smashed and then fluffed again. With daily use, furnishings become commonplace, rarely getting more than a second thought. Much like the daily objects in private homes, the item seen on the previous page could easily be mistaken for just another old table. Upon further inspection of its unique history and story, however, this once ordinary object becomes extraordinary. While women spoke out in favor of expanding their rights well before 1848, many deem the Seneca Falls Convention the official birth of the suffrage movement. In addition to being the first convention for female equality held in the United States, the event also marks the beginning of coordinated support for women's voting rights.[1] This backing did not come easily, however, and the considerable attention the issue of suffrage received at the convention stemmed from a document titled the Declaration of Sentiments. Written on this table, the declaration put forth a long and bold list of demands from women that would expand their rights. By the end of the convention it had received considerable support from attendees—although at first the demand for voting rights almost derailed the whole thing.

A week and a half earlier, on July 9, 1848, a group of women gathered in Waterloo, New York, for tea. They ranged in age from early thirties to midfifties. As white women of the elite and middle classes, they did not endure many of the day-to-day hardships faced by women of other races and lower social class.[2] In fact, most of them saw issues of poverty, illiteracy, and menial employment as a foreign concept. Despite this lack of firsthand knowledge, they all shared an interest in the larger issue of women's rights, and their social standing provided them the ability to devote time to thinking about improving the lives of women. Most in the group, including noted abolitionist and women's rights activist Lucretia Mott, were Quakers; a religious sect noted for their belief in the equality of the male and female souls. One guest was not. Elizabeth Cady Stanton, an educated social activist, had moved to the area with her husband and children the year before and gladly accepted the invitation to gather with like-minded women. While not a Quaker herself, Stanton, like her companions, whole-heartedly believed in greater equality of the sexes. During their conversation that afternoon the women discussed many issues, including the injustices they faced. According to Stanton, "I poured out . . . the torrent of my long-accumulating discontent, with such vehemence and indignation that I stirred myself as well as the rest of the party to do and dare anything."[3] The time had come to expand the conversation beyond the tea table, so the women began planning a convention to tackle the topic of women's rights.

They decided to hold the meeting just ten days later, on July 19 and 20, in the nearby community of Seneca Falls. An advertisement was written and placed in the local newspaper, and Stanton began drafting a declaration to present at the meeting. On July 16, she met with four of the women again. At the home of Mary Ann McClintock, they sat around the circular mahogany table and revised the document. During their discussion, the women decided to model it on the Declaration of Independence. They titled their version the Declaration of Sentiments and changed the familiar opening to read, "We hold these truths to be self-evidence; that all men *and women* are created equal." The Declaration of Sentiments then went on to replace the grievances of the colonists with a list of ways women were repressed at home, in education, in church, in professions, and in government.[4]

Three days later the big event arrived. Unsure if anyone else would join them, the organizers made their way to the Wesleyan Chapel in Seneca Falls. An unexpected crowd and a locked door met them upon arrival. Undeterred, the crowd quickly hoisted a young man through an unlocked window. After opening the front door, they poured inside. To the surprise of Stanton and her fellow organizers, nearly 340 people joined them over the course of the two-day convention. Organizers who later chronicled the event depicted the crowd as purely white, except for Frederick Douglass, an influential black activist and abolitionist. More likely than not, however, other free men and women of color attended the meeting along with Douglass.[5]

On the first day, when only women could enter the convention, Stanton filled a large portion of the time with reading the Declaration of Sentiments. Going through the document paragraph by paragraph, changes were proposed and made by the females in attendance. On the second day an even larger crowd gathered, and men were welcomed to participate as well. When the time came, the edited version of the Declaration of Sentiments, prepared the prior day, was read, then discussed and debated in hopes of adopting it as an official call to action.

During the presentation of the document, it became obvious to attendees that it addressed a wide range of issues facing women, including moral, political, religious, legal, educational, occupational, and even psychological matters.[6] At the core stood twelve resolutions intended to promote women's equality. Overall, the declaration and its resolutions received considerable support from the men and women at the convention. One resolution, however, received more attention than the others, and many people pushed back on its inclusion in the document—the ninth on the list; it demanded suffrage for women. Viewed as extreme, many of the participants, including Stanton's fellow organizers, feared it would make them look foolish and undermine the overall call to action. Stanton stood firm behind the demand, however. Despite the initial outrage against its inclusion, Stanton, with the support of Frederick Douglass, insisted the vote was the only means to achieve their other demands. By the end of the day, the resolution for women's voting rights passed by a slim margin, and attendees unanimously adopted the declaration. Sixty-eight women and thirty-two men then signed the document to show their support.

The Declaration of Sentiments proved central to launching an organized women's rights movement in the United States. After its adoption as a guiding document, national conventions popped up annually between 1850 and 1860.[7] Women had captured the attention of the nation, but not without ridicule by many. Outraged newspaper editors denounced the convention as shocking, unwomanly, monstrous, and unnatural. The protest was so strong some of the initial signers of the declaration withdrew their names from the document so they would not be associated with it.[8] Nonetheless an organized movement had begun, even if unrealized at the time. When looking back decades later, it became obvious that more than anywhere else, the fight for women's right to vote began in Seneca Falls with the debate surrounding the Declaration of Sentiments.

In the end, the negative press in 1848 ended up helping both the broader women's rights movement and the future suffrage movement. As word spread of the Declaration of Sentiments and the Seneca Falls convention, women and men from all walks of life were exposed to broader views of women's rights. As individuals, black and white, rich and poor, read Stanton's words, they, too, joined the movement from all regions of the nation. Together with elite leaders, they formed the coalition needed to make the ninth resolution a reality seventy-two years after being written. Despite the long delay in achieving suffrage, some people saw the importance of the table used to draft the Declaration of Sentiments much sooner. When the significance of what had occurred became apparent, the owners gave the piece of furniture to Elizabeth Cady Stanton as a memento. In turn, Stanton gave it to Susan B. Anthony as a birthday gift, when her fellow suffragist turned eighty years old. After Anthony's death in 1906, the treasured table remained in the possession of the National American Woman Suffrage Association. To make sure its history remained intact, the group pasted a copy of the Declaration of Sentiments to the underside. The importance of this everyday object was not limited to suffragists, however. When the 19th Amendment passed Congress in 1920, the Smithsonian invited the organization to exhibit the furnishing at their museum.[9] By placing it on view, the institution made clear that this was not just another old table but an extraordinary piece of history.

"Ain't I a Woman?"

Cabinet Card of Sojourner Truth, 1864, National Museum of African American History & Culture, Washington, DC, https://nmaahc.si.edu/

Eyes fixed on the camera; the woman in the photograph on the prior page shows no fear. She sits straight and tall in a plain setting surrounded by a small array of objects.[1] A vase of flowers. A book. Knitting held in one hand spreads across her lap and her clothing is tidy, but not flashy. While the setting may seem ordinary to modern eyes, the woman and her story are far from it. Remembered as a straight-talking, authentic, and unsentimental woman in the twenty-first century, Sojourner Truth stands as a symbolic figure representing strong black women.[2] In her own time, Truth was no less remarkable. A strong voice and advocate for antislavery, she is also noted by many historians as one of the first suffragists of color.

Today, many people around the world recognize the name Sojourner Truth, but this was not the first identity she had. Born into slavery around 1797 in upstate New York, Truth's given name was Isabella Baumfree. Plagued by inevitable mistreatment, around the age of thirteen her first owner sold her, separating Truth from her parents. She later suffered continued beatings and abuse at the hands of slave holders, and like all enslaved peoples, she had no rights of her own. She worked long hours at the backbreaking tasks demanded of her, with no reward for her efforts. The white men who owned her, along with the government of the nation, even withheld her basic human rights. In 1826, after enduring years of mistreatment, Isabella did something radical. Her owner had promised to free her ahead of a state law requiring it. When he failed to do so, Isabella, with her infant daughter, walked away from his New York farm in protest. Soon after the incident, she took her owner to court in an attempt to claim her son who had been sold illegally to another man in Alabama. As an African American and a woman, the possibility of succeeding seemed nearly impossible. To the surprise of many, however, she won the case, making her the first black woman to ever win a court case against a white man.[3]

Although successful with her legal proceedings, when Isabella gained her freedom in 1827 she was destitute. To support herself she worked as a household laborer in New York City, making very little money. In 1843, another chapter of her life began when she experienced a religious conversion and began spreading the word of the Bible as an itinerant preacher. She also took a new name. Leaving her old life behind, Isabella Baumfree became Sojourner Truth. As her name suggests, she traveled, spreading the truth about Christian values, as well as the atrocities of slavery and the need for women's rights.

By 1851, Truth's reputation had grown, and she was recognized as a leading African American speaker and abolitionist. That year she attended a women's rights convention in Akron, Ohio, making a spontaneous speech that still defines her today. On the first day of the meeting, Truth entered the crowded church where the event took place. Making her way to the front of the room, she seated herself on the steps of the pulpit where white activist Frances Gage presided over the meeting. Sitting quietly, Truth listened to the speakers and what they had to say. While she did not utter a word, her presence in and of itself created a stir in the crowd. Surrounded by a sea of white conference attendees, many of the women in the audience thought that if Truth spoke it would distract from their cause and turn the meeting into one about abolition rather than women's rights. Despite their concerns, on the second day of the meeting Truth returned to the same spot at the front of the room. As the day got underway a group of male ministers dominated the discussion and debate. After listening to their arguments about women's inferior abilities Truth slowly rose to her feet and approached the podium—Frances Gage gave her the floor.[4]

When Truth began to speak the room grew silent. Disregarding previous attempts by many of the white attendees to keep her quiet, Truth spoke on behalf of all women that day, rousing the crowd with her eloquence and conviction. According to Gage, she stated in her deep voice, "I have ploughed, and planted, and gathered into barns, and no man could head me! And ain't I a woman? I could work as much and eat as much as a man—when I could get it—and bear the lash as well! And ain't I a woman?"[5] After finishing her passionate speech comparing her own abilities and worth to those of men, Truth quietly returned to her seat and the audience burst into a roar of applause. Through her words, she had brought tears to eyes and squelched her critics. Although the phrase appears in publications as early as the 1830s, and was used by female antislavery societies, in the years following Truth's speech, "ain't I a woman?" became a phrase unquestionably attached to her. Today, it continues to appear in history books as a mantra of women's rights—particularly for black women. In 1981, author bell hooks titled her own groundbreaking work on black feminism, *Ain't I a Woman*. Today the book still rings true for many women of color as they continue to struggle with the social, political, and economic conditions caused by racism and sexism during slavery.

Knowing the story of Sojourner Truth makes it easy to imagine the sitter in the photograph at the beginning of this chapter uttering the call, "ain't I a woman?" As she gazes into the viewer's eyes, the phrase almost seems to trip off her tongue. In reality, Truth may not have ever said the famous words that have become firmly linked to her. Looking more closely, the possibility of

Truth using such a phrase seems slim. Born and raised in upstate New York, Truth's first language was Dutch, not English. These facts make it unlikely that she spoke in a dialect often used to portray southern blacks at the time. Just as problematic is a transcription of the speech published just one month after Truth delivered it. Nowhere in that version do the words, "ain't I a woman?" occur. In fact, it was not until twelve years after the conference, when Frances Gage published her own version of the speech, that the iconic phrase appeared. In Gage's telling of the events, the speech's theme is very similar to earlier versions. Setting it apart however, the phrase "ain't I a woman?" is liberally scattered throughout, and the dialect altered to fit the stereotype of the time. Even though Gage's version was enhanced and altered, many have come to regard it as the original.

The issue of whether Sojourner Truth ever used the phrase, "ain't I a woman?" has taken a back seat to the phrase's ability to inspire women and evoke the passion Truth had that day. Although unable to read and write herself, her words are often quoted, and mainstream suffragists included her name in their history. Despite the recognition given to her by white suffragists, Truth's work took a different path than theirs. While they could more easily afford to participate in speaking tours by staying with friends or by funding their travels through their family's financial means, it remained a continual burden for Truth to afford her travels and speeches. To support herself she turned to commercialism. With the help of family and friends, Truth dictated her life story and had it published. She also had photographs taken of herself and copyrighted in her own name. She carried copies of her book, *Narrative of Sojourner Truth*, along with photographs, like the one at the start of this chapter, with her to public appearances. With these commodities sold in person and through the mail, Truth paid her way.[6] Often printed with the phrase, "I Sell the Shadow to Support the Substance," Truth let her customers know she controlled her own life. Where she had once been bought and sold as a commodity for whites, in her freedom she turned her own image into a way to support herself. Sojourner Truth's efforts to end slavery and expand the rights of blacks and women represent the work that exploded in the years before a separate suffrage movement formed; a time when many causes, such as abolition and women's suffrage, overlapped in the work of early reformers. In Truth's case, she represented many of the other African American women who felt just as strong about the need to expand their rights and secure the vote but did not have their names recorded in history books.

Dressing the Part

Bloomer Costume, 1851–1855, Cortland
County Historical Society, Cortland, NY,
http://www.cortlandhistory.com/
PHOTO COURTESY OF CORTLAND COUNTY
HISTORICAL SOCIETY

Sweatpants, leggings, shorts . . . these garments are go-to comfort clothes for many girls and women.[1] In fact, numerous clothing companies would argue that nothing is easier to toss on than a pair of jeans when the weekend rolls around. Even at work many women opt for pants over skirts and dresses. While the norm today, the Bloomer costume pictured on the previous page would have shocked many people in the 1850s. In Homer, New York, Meriva Carpenter, a successful portrait painter, owned this particular outfit. Although known around town for her "artistic" personality, a woman wearing pants was such a foreign concept that many people probably considered it downright scandalous.[2]

For many decades social activists tackled a wide range of women's rights issues. From education to property rights and voting, women looked to improve any aspect of their lives contributing to their inferior position in society. In the late 1840s, female reformers even claimed that fashion held them back.[3] Attacking the popular silhouette of the time requiring women to maintain a cinched waist and wear many layers of heavy petticoats beneath their skirts, a small but vocal group of critics argued that the look was detrimental to women's health. These opponents contended that tightly laced corsets, although fashionable, made it hard to breathe and move. Furthermore, they argued that long skirts and heavy petticoats limited the ability of women to move freely. And if that was not enough, they also pointed out that long skirts gathered and held dirt and grime from unclean streets. For these critics, being healthy simply made more sense than being in vogue. In that vein, they urged women to wear shorter skirts and throw off their corsets and tightly bound clothing.[4]

For many women's rights activists, not only did these improved aspects of comfort seem appealing, but they also believed this change in fashion could alter gender roles, and with greater range of motion women could tackle many of the tasks previously reserved for men. By the early 1850s, a new style of clothing based on these ideas had come on the scene. The outfit, consisting of a shortened skirt worn below the knee over loose trousers, found popularity with many women looking to reform society. While notable women's rights leaders and suffragists soon adopted the outfit, it was Amelia Bloomer, an activist and lecturer living in New York State and then Iowa, who brought broader exposure to the garment. Writing in her women's journal, *The Lily*, Bloomer endorsed the outfit and began wearing it herself. Called by a variety of names (including the "reform dress" and "freedom dress") many people began referring to it as the "Bloomer costume," in honor of the activist who spoke so positively about it.

After its adoption by the women's rights movement, the Bloomer costume received mixed reviews. But whether people liked it or not, no one could deny that it was eye-catching. In fact, the outfit had become well-known enough to be referenced in popular songs, and its image appeared on sheet music covers.[5] While some women wore it for comfort alone, others made it a symbol of revolt against all restrictions on women. In fact, this link between the outfit and equal rights became so strong that the public soon began referring to women's rights advocates as "bloomers."[6]

Despite some positive reviews, however, the Bloomer costume soon became a point of ridicule as well. Writers and editors of popular publications made it the punchline of jokes, and women who wore the outfit complained about the constant staring and harassment they received.[7] While backlash in the press was bad enough, many wearers also encountered family, friends, and strangers who saw the outfit as a sign of moral decay for the women who wore it. Others believed it a threat to male power. Suffragist Mary S. Bull described being followed by a crowd of boys while wearing Bloomers on the streets of Seneca Falls. As the young men harassed her with yelling, laughing, and singing, many other people peered on from their windows.[8] In the end, the Bloomer craze of the 1850s did not last long. The reformers who adopted the outfit decided its comfort did not make up for the constant annoyances and harassment that also came with it. For activists working toward the larger cause of women's rights, the outfit had become a hindrance, not a help, and it distracted from bigger issues such as voting rights. Knowing when to pull the plug, leaders of the movement decided to abandon the outfit by the mid-1850s rather than hurt their cause.

While the Bloomer costume had a short life as fashionable dress, it lived on as an athletic outfit for women, becoming more valuable in that form. In the 1860s, the idea that females should exercise for health took off, and women's colleges offering exercise programs instituted outfits similar to the Bloomer costume for physical education. As the century continued, women became increasingly involved in sporting activities, and by the end of the century, they swam, played tennis, and golfed. In the 1890s, bicycling became the craze of the nation. While the Bloomer costume had flopped as a liberating outfit in the 1850s, in the 1890s females again wore something similar when climbing aboard countless bicycles; the two-wheeled mode of transportation that took women out of the home and onto the streets. In 1896, suffragist Susan B. Anthony shared her thoughts on the topic. "Let me tell you what I think of bicycling," she said. "I think it has done more to emancipate women than anything else in the world. It gives women a feeling of freedom and self-reliance." Regarding bloomers she dubbed them "the proper things for wheeling."[9] While bloomers initially failed as both popular fashion and a reform tool for suffragists, with enough time the style found its perfect moment to advance women's freedom. In many ways the success of the Bloomer costume mirrored that of the suffrage movement. While it was ridiculed when it first came on the scene, eventually the passage of time and changing of society brought about the right moment for its advancement.

Part II

ORGANIZATIONS

After the Seneca Falls Convention of 1848, interest in expanding and improving women's rights spread. The issue of suffrage, which had at first been considered outrageous by many people, quickly gained popularity among educated white women, some male reformers, and African Americans. By the late 1860s, the fight for women's voting rights had broken out as its own movement. Although the crusade had gained a core group of supporters, the work to secure suffrage over the next several decades was neither quick nor easy. To achieve such a monumental task, many people from all walks of life had to work together to create the momentum needed. Seeing the necessity of group mobilization, suffragists organized themselves in many ways between 1869 and 1920. At the national level, activists bound themselves together not only based on their goal of securing female suffrage, but also by their racial views and methods. In each state, leadership formed associations to coordinate their efforts while grassroots groups popped up in local cities and towns. While these organizations all worked toward legislation granting women the right to vote, they did not always see eye to eye. Often, they held each other up. Other times they fought and placed blame. In the end, every group played a part in the long process. Without the countless organizations that came together however, suffragists may never have built up the steam needed to win the vote.

Organizing a Nation

Convention Ribbon, 1917, North Carolina Office of Archives and History,
Raleigh, NC, https://www.ncdcr.gov/about/office-archives-and-history
COURTESY OF THE STATE ARCHIVES OF NORTH CAROLINA

In 1917, Gertrude Weil of North Carolina wore the ribbon seen on the previous page while attending the national convention of the National American Woman Suffrage Association in Washington, DC. Joining other suffragists from around the United States, Weil's attendance helped ensure a unified front of suffrage supporters across the country. In many ways, Weil looked like most of the activists at the meeting. She was white and from a family of financial means. Unlike many of the attendees, however, Weil was a southerner and a strong supporter of women's voting rights, no matter race or ethnicity. The daughter of a German, Jewish immigrant, Weil's faith played a central role in her work for women's suffrage.[1] To explain her passion for equality she brought attention to the Jewish teaching that states, "Justice, mercy [and] goodness were not to be held in a vacuum, but practiced in our daily lives."[2] For Weil, the suffrage cause provided a way to create a more just, humane society and possibly even bring about world peace.[3] Needless to say, Weil enthusiastically supported the message that was communicated at the 1917 conference to do all she could for the war effort. Months earlier the nation had entered World War I, and many suffragists saw an opportunity to demonstrate their patriotism. As attendees left the conference, it was clear that leaders of the National American Woman Suffrage Association had rallied their supporters behind their cause. While the scene leaving the conference appeared to be one of harmony, the history of the organization was anything but.

Following the Seneca Falls Convention in 1848, more women began to see the value in obtaining the right to vote. As they struggled to bring about meaningful social and legal change for themselves, it became obvious how much easier the task would be with a voice in politics. How could they guarantee their opinions would be heard if they could not cast their own ballot? While the idea of suffrage grew in popularity in the years after the convention, it was still just one of many reforms to which women's rights activists devoted their time. In the 1860s, however, the passage of three amendments to the US Constitution spurred women's suffrage supporters to begin an organized movement separate from the broader issue of women's rights.

Beginning in 1865, Congress enacted the first of these legislative milestones when they passed the 13th Amendment, abolishing the practice of slavery. Three years later the 14th Amendment granted citizenship to anyone born or naturalized in the United States; this included formerly enslaved peoples. The 14th Amendment also defined voters as "male" for the first time. Because only state laws had barred women from the polls prior to this, the establishment of a federal definition excluding women came as a major setback for suffragists. Despite the federal government's new definition, many southern states found ways to exclude black males from voting. This caused the federal government to adopt an additional amendment to further define the rights of citizenship. The 15th Amendment provided the solution. With its ratification, black men received the explicit right to vote under federal law. While these legislative advances brought victories for blacks and abolitionists, they also set off a fierce debate among white suffragists. Often strong supporters of abolition, many suffragists felt betrayed by former friends. In granting voting rights to black men, but not white women, they believed their cause was being derailed. Some women quickly vocalized their opposition to the 15th Amendment, while others continued to embrace it. Faced with the reality that their hard work had been pushed aside, women's rights activists began focusing their efforts specifically on suffrage rather than on broader reforms.

Amid these heated emotions, previously allied suffragists split into two opposing camps, drawing a line in the sand. On one side stood the National Woman Suffrage Association (NWSA). Led by Elizabeth Cady Stanton and Susan B. Anthony, the organization was formed in 1869 and vowed to oppose the 15th Amendment unless altered to include women. They firmly believed that educated white women should be allowed to vote before illiterate blacks—an attitude of white superiority that persisted in the movement for years to come. With their leadership open exclusively to females and based in New York, the NWSA focused on obtaining the right to vote through a federal amendment alone. They adopted a radical tone and promoted a wide variety of feminist reforms, attacking both Republicans and Democrats who brushed aside the woman suffrage question.[4] They also made no scruples about taking up the torch for distressed women, no matter their life circumstances. This unorthodox manner often placed them on the fringes; making it difficult to gain followers.[5]

The American Woman Suffrage Association (AWSA), headquartered in Boston, stood opposite of NWSA. Also formed in 1869, this group was led by suffragist Lucy Stone and her husband Henry Blackwell. With leadership made up of suffrage supporters of both sexes, the organization fully supported black male voting rights while simultaneously working for women's suffrage for both white and black females as well. AWSA endorsed a federal amendment granting women the right to vote, but unlike NWSA, it concentrated on developing grassroots support at the state and local level to help shoulder the work. To broaden their appeal, the group was also highly selective in its advocacy of causes beyond suffrage. The group had no interest in getting involved with trade unionism and worked to keep the suffrage cause untarnished by concerns such as divorce and other issues they considered unseemly.[6]

By 1890, the two groups had been dividing suffrage efforts for two decades, and it became obvious that combining their work could strengthen their cause. Rather than continue as two separate entities, both associations agreed the time had come to form a unified front. At the urging of younger suffragists, the movement's aging pioneers cautiously put their differences aside, and after lengthy negotiations, the two groups merged to form the National American Woman Suffrage Association (NAWSA). While continuing to demand a federal amendment, the group's leaders concluded that they must first build support within the states. Once enough states granted women the right to vote, they believed the federal government would follow suit. They also looked to shed any old image of radicalism and focused almost exclusively on winning the vote.[7]

As a singular organization defined by their conservative methods, NAWSA spent the next two decades rebuilding the national suffrage movement. Through hard campaigning they increased their membership across the nation and attracted an overwhelmingly white membership that was socially prominent and politically influential. At the same time, they also recruited a new generation of college-educated females, such as Gertrude Weil. These young and energetic members reinvigorated the movement, and by the twentieth century the group's tactics had expanded beyond conventions and petitions to include events like open-air meetings and parades. They also expanded their educational efforts by distributing literature to schools and libraries and sponsoring debates.[8]

In 1915, the organization's leader, Carrie Chapman Catt, put a new strategy into place that guided NAWSA's activities until the passage of the 19th Amendment. Known as the "Winning Plan," Catt's tactical blueprint aimed to harness the power of the massive, but slow-moving, organization. She insisted work at the state level was vital, but at the same time made it clear that the federal amendment was the group's ultimate goal. Working in that vein, states that had not yet granted voting rights to women launched campaigns at once. If defeat appeared likely, Catt insisted suffragists avoid embarrassing the movement and seek only what they knew they could achieve. The "Winning Plan" also urged suffragists in states where women already voted to pressure their national representatives to support a federal amendment. In the meantime, the organization oversaw a massive lobbying effort in Washington, DC, to enlist congressional support.[9]

During War World I, NAWSA continued to push their "Winning Plan" and aligned itself with the war cause, working hard to gain the support of President Woodrow Wilson. They hoped their efforts for the war would enhance the organization's patriotic image and the vote would be given to them as a reward for their service. The extremely pragmatic NAWSA went to great lengths to avoid having their organization labeled radical in any way. They wanted to ensure suffrage and suffragists carried a respectable image, and in turn they distanced themselves from militant activists who Catt believed alienated politicians. With Wilson and the Democratic Party controlling Congress, NAWSA was not willing to risk losing their votes through outrageous actions.[10]

In many ways, Gertrude Weil agreed. As a dedicated member of NAWSA, she encouraged other suffragists in North Carolina to work with relief organizations and charities, sacrifice personal luxuries, and conserve food throughout the war.[11] At the same time, Weil's own interests reflected the fractures that existed within the organization. While many of Weil's fellow suffragists chose to distance themselves from controversial issues, she continued to support issues she truly believed in, such as protective labor legislation for women and children, as well as black rights. In the 1960s, Weil even convened meetings of the North Carolina Interracial Committee in her home.[12] Despite the differences that set her apart from many of her counterparts, Weil believed in the overall strategy of NAWSA and worked to support the organization at every opportunity. By 1920, the tenacity of women like Weil paid off, and members of NAWSA celebrated as women secured the opportunity to vote through the ratification of the 19th Amendment.

What's Old Is New Again

Belmont-Paul Women's Equality National Monument, built in 1800, Washington, DC, https://www.nps.gov/bepa/index.htm

A visitor stepping inside 144 Constitution Avenue instantly knows they are somewhere special.[1] Surrounding them are objects that tell the story of a community of women who dedicated their lives to the fight for women's rights.[2] Items as small as lapel pins or as large as the house itself encircle the site's guests. At the same time, a sense arises that this place is not only steeped in history, but is still making it. As the current headquarters of the National Woman's Party, the historic building not only welcomes guests as a museum, but also serves as the launching pad for the nonprofit to continue working for full women's equality. Through exhibitions, public programs, book talks, and conversations the National Woman's Party educates the public not only about the history of women's rights but also about the continued need for further advocacy. Through a partnership with the National Park Service, visitors can also take a guided tour of the home.

Built around 1800, the elegant brick structure has been a center of political life in the nation's capital since its construction. Early occupants of the house participated in the formation of Congress and watched as the US capital grew around them. During the War of 1812, the home became the site of the only resistance to the British invasion of Washington, DC. In retaliation, British forces set fire to the structure. Not one to be defeated, its owner, Robert Sewall, rebuilt by 1820, and the property continued to serve as a private residence for many years.[3] From its vantage point behind the US Capitol Building, the home has seen the city change around it and witnessed the transformation of America's government and society.

On April 12, 2016, this long-standing structure became the first national monument to women's history in the nation. In his presidential proclamation, President Barrack Obama spoke of the house and its importance as a testament to the country's continued struggle for equality. He also explained how a home built by a man at a time when few women could own property, had become an iconic symbol of women's history. At the root of such a transformation was the 1929 purchase of the structure by the National Woman's Party. Looking for a new headquarters near the country's seat of power, the house was a perfect choice to serve as the staging ground for the group's advocacy work for women's rights. Just two miles to the west is the White House—the site where more than a decade earlier the National Woman's Party had catapulted itself onto the national scene and became an unexpected counterpart to the National American Woman Suffrage Association (NAWSA).

Despite their success in organizing suffrage work across the nation, many people viewed NAWSA's work between 1890 and 1920 as sluggish. Some suffragists at the time even considered the group's methods too safe, while others felt the organization did not represent their views. Alice Paul, a young activist from New Jersey, embodied this mindset. While working and studying in England between 1907 and 1910, Paul became interested in the issue of women's suffrage. Her participation in meetings, demonstrations, and depositions to Britain's Parliament led to multiple arrests, hunger strikes, and forced feedings. When Paul returned to the United States in 1910, she brought her zest for suffrage with her. In her eyes, the nation's fight for female voting rights lacked sufficient focus and support due to its conservative state-by-state approach. She believed that to succeed, the movement needed to focus on the passage of a federal suffrage amendment to the US Constitution. After joining NAWSA and assuming leadership of its Congressional Committee, Paul created a larger NAWSA-affiliated organization to pressure Congress into passing a federal amendment. This group eventually became the National Woman's Party.[4]

By 1913, it seemed what was old was new again. The spirit of radicalism evident in early suffrage groups like the National Woman Suffrage Association had been rekindled in Paul and her followers. The suffrage movement always had activists who advocated direct action, but Paul's call for the use of militant tactics she learned in Britain proved too extreme for NAWSA's leadership. In turn, Paul and like-minded suffragists had no patience for the slow state-by-state approach that consumed much of the national organization's energy. Amid disagreements and verbal sparring, Paul and her followers split with NAWSA, once again creating two competing groups at the national level.[5]

Central to the rift were opposing views of how to treat the party in power. Unlike NAWSA, who vowed to remain nonpartisan, the National Woman's Party believed in leveraging partisan politics to bring attention to the suffrage cause. With Democrats holding the most seats in Congress, the Woman's Party put their theory to work. They encouraged women who already had voting rights in the west to vote against Democratic candidates as a punishment for the party's failure to support women's suffrage. In Washington, DC, members of the organization publicly heckled President Woodrow Wilson and interrupted Democratic legislative speeches by asking pointed questions on the issues of democracy and suffrage.[6] Rather than cultivate the president's support through relationship building, Paul urged her organization to agitate and withhold party support until women gained the right to vote.

The National Woman's Party further set itself apart from NAWSA in the news headlines it created. Where Catt and her followers looked to avoid an image of radicalism, Paul used it to attract and keep the attention of the press as often as possible. After four years of parades, rallies, lobbying, and petitions that failed to gain either the support of Congress or the president, the Woman's Party broke new ground in waging a political battle for suffrage. Through a revolutionary strategy of sustained dramatic, nonviolent protest, they put the home of the president directly in their sights. On January 10, 1917, Paul led a dozen women to the gates of 1600 Pennsylvania Avenue. Carrying banners emblazoned with phrases like, "Mr. President How Long Must Women Wait for Liberty?" they became the first people ever to picket the White House.[7]

Day after day, rain or shine, these women stood at the White House gates holding banners criticizing American democracy and calling out the government's hypocrisy of denying women the vote while calling for global peace and equality. The picketing became even more controversial when the United States entered military action in World War I. While NAWSA encouraged its members to take up the war cause to gain favor with politicians and the public, the Woman's Party continued daily protests. Using the war as fodder to embarrass President Wilson, their banners began comparing him to the German kaiser. They also proclaimed Russia more democratic than the United States because Russian women had the right to vote.[8]

As the National Woman's Party raised the bar of its actions, the responses to them became equally more intense. During their continued picketing over the next three years, hundreds of suffragists were arrested illegally and jailed. Some organized hunger strikes while imprisoned, and many women faced forced feedings by prison officials.[9] Picketers on the streets endured regular verbal and physical abuse. If harsh words from the public were not enough, NAWSA also took its turn lashing out at them. Anna Howard Shaw, the group's former president wrote, "This little branch of Suffragists do not belong to the National Association . . . and I assure you no woman in the country can feel worse than I do over the foolishness of their picketing the White House."[10]

For NAWSA, the National Woman's Party had become a thorn in its side. When they began lobbying hard in Congress for federal action, NAWSA found themselves constantly answering for the actions of Paul and her followers. They expended a lot of energy explaining that they came from a separate organization, and that they believed in a wholly different approach.[11] NAWSA's disdain for the Woman's Party was no skin off the radical organization's back, however. The National Woman's Party worked equally hard to distinguish themselves from suffragists who they believed approached the movement in embarrassingly moderate terms. No matter their view of one another, ultimately, these two very different groups became unintentional counterparts in the fight for suffrage. Combined, their actions brought about the support needed to pass the 19th Amendment. Without the constant national and international attention the National Woman's Party attracted, NAWSA's successful cultivation of the federal government and President Wilson's support may not have happened when it did. Together, these two organizations convinced both the public and lawmakers that all women, whether brash or cautious, deserved a political voice as citizens of the United States.

Scandinavians for Suffrage

Photograph of Scandinavian Woman Suffrage Association, 1914, Minnesota Historical Society, Saint Paul, MN, http://www.mnhs.org/
MINNESOTA HISTORICAL SOCIETY

Often, the stories of women's suffrage focus on the names and events that have become larger than life.[1] Women like Susan B. Anthony became legendary in their own lifetimes, and events like hunger strikes and pickets gained national attention. The players highlighted in these stories are often white, American born, and from elite or middle-class backgrounds. Because of their means, these women held leadership roles at the national and state levels, created the rules, and often chronicled their own narratives. It is no wonder that their tales fill history books. While the work of these women and large organizations is fascinating and important, the stories of other groups also deserve time in the spotlight.

All around the nation local auxiliaries formed to assist state and national associations with suffrage work. While the large majority mirrored the white, native-born membership of the country's largest organizations, some provided the opportunity for immigrants, blacks, and the working class to play an equally important role in the suffrage movement. In Illinois for instance, black citizens banded together to work for women's voting rights, and many urban and metropolitan areas saw large segments of immigrant and working-class populations fighting for the cause as well. In fact, in New York City, some of the strongest and most consistent support came from the Jewish communities living in Harlem and on the Lower East Side.[2] At times, these groups formed into official suffrage clubs such as the National Progressive Women's Suffrage Union of New York City, made up primarily of German Americans and Jewish garment workers. In other instances, organizations such as the Political Equality League established branches around the city to draw in the efforts of the working class and blacks. Its 14th Assembly District Club attracted many young Irish women.[3]

In Minnesota, the state's Scandinavian population leveraged its ethnic identity to encourage lawmakers and citizens to understand the importance of women's suffrage. Although the Minneapolis-Saint Paul metropolitan area had many suffrage clubs in the early twentieth century, only one group based on ethnic background existed.[4] Formed in 1907, the Scandinavian Woman Suffrage Association (SWSA) worked for social and economic advancement and for the right of suffrage for the women of Minnesota and the United States.[5] Membership was open to anyone of Scandinavian descent, and unlike other suffrage organizations, the group successfully attracted members ranging from the well-off to the working class. Working both independently and with other organizations, SWSA embraced their cultural heritage and did not shy away from their ancestry.

In the photo from the Minnesota Historical Society at the beginning of this chapter, members of the organization march proudly wearing national costume and carrying banners. The women visibly carry flags representing three countries—Norway, Sweden, and Denmark. While notable suffragists such as Carrie Chapman Catt (one-time president of NAWSA) claimed ethnic identities harmed the suffrage cause, Scandinavian suffragists in Minnesota knew differently. In their state, Scandinavians made up the largest immigrant population.[6] This fact made SWSA the best candidate to convince fellow Scandinavians of the need to support women's voting rights.

For many Scandinavians, female suffrage made complete sense. In their eyes, the United States lagged behind many of their native countries in the progression of women's rights. For example, in Norway, tax-paying women obtained full suffrage in 1907. This left Minnesota's Scandinavian suffragists with a sense that their cultural heritage provided a unique strength; other organizations did not disagree. In fact, the perceived ties between Scandinavian Americans and effective suffrage movements made SWSA a valuable part of the larger suffrage state network.[7] On the national level, the leadership of the National Woman's Party viewed these Scandinavian suffragists as the key to attracting new members to their organization. While SWSA maintained a relationship with the Woman's Party through financial support, they also provided recruitment advice. If the National Woman's Party became aware of Scandinavian communities anywhere in the country interested in suffrage, they contacted SWSA. Minnesota's Scandinavian organization was more than happy to use their ethnic connection to encourage women in these communities to support the suffrage cause.[8]

During their thirteen years of existence, SWSA worked to persuade their fellow men and women to support women's voting rights. To succeed, they put several strategies into motion, including appealing to national pride. They maintained a strong presence in the Minneapolis cultural scene, organizing Scandinavian American cultural events with a distinct ethnic flair. They also made sure to join forces with other suffrage clubs at rallies and meetings. When the Political Equality Club asked members of SWSA to translate speeches by noted Norwegian suffragists, members gladly agreed. This made the group indispensable to nonethnic associations.[9]

Over time, the association earned a reputation for its outstanding fund-raising skills, and in 1917 they used that know-how to benefit all suffrage organizations in Minnesota. Like other states around the nation, Minnesota's suffragists utilized the state fair as a venue to educate fairgoers about voting rights. Working from booths, SWSA entertained the public with literature, films, and folk dances. Hoping not only to keep their audience enthralled, these women also looked to convert them to the suffrage cause.[10] While these temporary booths served their purposes well enough, they also knew that a permanent building would allow them to provide much better services in educating the public about women's voting rights.

As master fundraisers, SWSA got to work. In late February 1917, the group organized a large event to raise money for the construction of a suffrage building at the state fairgrounds. Appealing to their ethnic base, SWSA planned a grand evening tailored for the audience they knew they would attract. As girls dressed in Swedish and Norwegian costumes guided guests to their seats, the night started out with a performance of the noted Swedish play *The Prime Minister's Daughter*, in its original language. Following up the show-stopping performance, a one-act play based on a Scandinavian folktale took the stage. The crowning feature of the evening, however, came in the form of a festival of folk dances. The high-tempo performances were staged in a whirlwind fashion, and dancers performed Spanish fandango and traditional gypsy steps. To the audience's delight, the close of the event featured a group of elaborately costumed dancers who performed Swedish folk dances.[11]

The event drew more than one thousand attendees, putting SWSA well on its way to funding the building for the fairgrounds. By September, the structure had been erected, thanks to the work and funding of the association. Named the "Woman Citizen Building," SWSA gifted the structure to the state suffrage association as a sign of loyalty to the cause.[12] Staying true to their cultural distinction, SWSA proved that ethnic identity could play a crucial role in the fight for suffrage. In an area where Scandinavian Americans made up a significant portion of the population, suffragists of similar heritage simply had an upper hand.

Votes for Justice

Church Pew, 1891, National Museum of African American History and Culture, Washington, DC, https://nmaahc.si.edu/

COLLECTION OF THE SMITHSONIAN NATIONAL MUSEUM OF AFRICAN AMERICAN HISTORY AND CULTURE, GIFT OF QUINN CHAPEL AFRICAN METHODIST EPISCOPAL CHURCH, CHICAGO, IL

Quinn Chapel, located in the heart of Chicago, holds many distinctions. Along with its stunning architecture, the church is home to the city's oldest black congregation.[1] It is also the site where Chicago's African American women joined together to fight for women's suffrage. With roots stretching back to 1844, the church's early congregants strongly supported the abolition movement. They played an important role in advocating for black rights; and prior to the passage of the Emancipation Proclamation, some served as conductors on the Underground Railroad. After the abolishment of the practice of slavery in 1865, Quinn Chapel continued to serve as a platform for social movements in the city. Since construction of the current building in 1892, the church has welcomed an array of notable speakers and frequently opened its doors as a meeting place for social justice activists. From pews like the one seen on the previous page, congregants and community members felt the passion of Frederick Douglass's words in 1893, and in the mid-twentieth century, Dr. Martin Luther King Jr. captivated Quinn's congregation from the pulpit.[2] To say Quinn Chapel has been a proud cornerstone of Chicago's black community would be an understatement. Throughout its rich history the church has provided spiritual guidance, and the congregation has promoted social change in a variety of ways.

As early as the 1860s, congregants of Quinn Chapel, as well as Chicago's larger black community, showed an interest in women's voting rights. In August 1865, when no other venue would provide the space, Susan B. Anthony spoke to a crowd of hundreds of Chicago's black citizens at the church. The topic of her speech was universal suffrage; the idea that voting rights should extend to all citizens, regardless of sex or race. In describing her manner, the *Chicago Tribune* described the suffragist as clear, logical, earnest, and truthful.[3] Within four years, however, Anthony became embroiled in the racist tension surrounding the suffrage movement's discontent with the 15th Amendment. While many white suffragists turned their backs on African American women, a growing number of blacks continued to actively support universal suffrage. At Quinn Chapel, Reverend Archibald J. Carey Sr. considered the ballot box the black community's best defense against racial injustice. Inspired by both Anthony's earlier words and Carey's leadership, the women of Quinn Chapel became adamant supporters of the women's suffrage movement.[4]

On January 5, 1913, Chicago's "No Vote No Tax" League held a public meeting at the chapel to encourage black women to form an organization to help fight for women's voting rights. At the meeting, Belle Squire, one of the city's prominent white suffragists, stood alongside black Chicago activist Ida Wells-Barnett.[5] Demonstrating the cooperation between black and white suffragists in the state, Squire said, "The time has come when we suffragists must broaden our views and enlist all women to our cause, regardless of race or color, if we are to be successful."[6] With the state legislature preparing to vote on a suffrage bill in a few months, the time was ripe to establish as much public support as possible. While Squire issued the call to action, Wells-Barnett immediately took the reins, establishing the Alpha Suffrage Club—the first black suffrage organization in Illinois and the only one of its kind in Chicago.

With Wells-Barnett assuming leadership of the organization, she made sure the Alpha Suffrage Club kept its focus on advancing Chicago's black community. To ensure black control and decision making, African Americans held all elected offices and the majority of the club's meetings, and work took place in the largest black neighborhood of the city. Although this placed them in the center of their core audience, the group also recognized the role they could play in the larger suffrage movement. Looking to do so, in March 1913 more than sixty of the club's members joined national and state suffrage organizations in a large parade and demonstration in front of the White House.

Almost like providence, within five months of the Alpha Suffrage Club forming, the state of Illinois granted women the right to vote. This not only made Illinois the first state east of the Mississippi River to do so, but it also marked a huge milestone for black women who could now cast ballots in presidential and municipal elections.[7] For the city's African Americans, this placed them in a unique position. While black suffragists in the South could barely imagine their dream being realized, in Chicago, African American women lived the reality of deciding what to do next. Rather than encourage members to see their work as finished, the Alpha Suffrage Club ramped up its activities. On the national level, they lent their support to larger suffrage organizations, but their work at home captured most of the attention.

Having already earned the right to vote, these extraordinary women began mobilizing their fellow black women to exercise that right. To do so they put together an effective strategy. Through their newsletter, the *Alpha Suffrage Record*, they sought to educate the community about candidates and local issues appearing on the ballot.[8] At monthly meetings women learned practical skills, like how to use voting machines. Political candidates visited, eager to discuss their platform with the engaged group of women. Through these meetings, group members learned canvassing techniques, met candidates seeking office, and developed analytical skills. In turn, the candidates gained insight into the issues important to women.[9] The Alpha Suffrage Club further broke the mold by holding suffrage meetings for female prisoners at the Bridewell

Penitentiary. Rather than leave these women stigmatized and ignored in prison, club members took the opportunity to educate them about their new voting rights, like those of any other deserving citizen.[10]

While the Alpha Suffrage Club had great successes, they did not happen without difficulties. Wells-Barnett herself wrote of black men who became suspicious of the suffragists' efforts, verbally insulting the women as they canvassed black neighborhoods to recruit voters. In response to these male fears, clubwomen repeatedly told them their intention as registered voters was to put black men into elected office; a goal they saw to fruition. As the number of black women and men registered to vote in Chicago grew, African Americans were encouraged to run for office.[11] In fact, the support of the Alpha Suffrage Club proved a decisive factor in electing Oscar De Priest as the first black alderman in Chicago's history, in 1915. He would later make history again when he became the first northern black elected to Congress, in 1928.[12] Eighty years later, the city of Chicago sent another of their well-respected black politicians to Washington, DC, when Illinois senator Barrack Obama won the 2008 presidential election.

Just as whites and immigrant communities mobilized in support of women's voting rights, so did dedicated black suffragists. In Chicago, the women of Quinn Chapel and the Alpha Suffrage Club fought for black women's right to vote. When they earned that privilege, the club found even more energy to make sure black women cast their ballots and actively worked to support their community through political action. By 1920, 77 percent of the city's black citizens had registered to vote, making Chicago's African Americans a powerful voting force.[13] Around the nation, other black women took equal interest in the cause. While they did not all form suffrage-specific organizations like the Alpha Suffrage Club, voting rights for women often became one of the primary goals of black clubs and organizations like the National Association of Colored Women.[14] As issues of racism and inequality grew in the United States, black suffragists worked even harder to gain their voting rights. To them it was a crucial tool to protect black communities from violence and injustice and to work toward greater racial reform in the country. By the time ratification of the 19th Amendment occurred in 1920, countless suffrage groups, ranging from the national to the local level, had formed around the country. The diversity of their memberships proved that the work of all organizations and women was needed in order for females around the nation to secure the opportunity to vote.

11

One of Many Cogs

Crazy Quilt, 1880–1935, Kansas Historical Society, Topeka, KS, https://www.kshs.org/
KANSAS STATE HISTORICAL SOCIETY

Scrapbooks, Instagram accounts, shoeboxes full of high school trophies—these are just a few of the many ways people keep reminders of important activities and memories.[1] Long before countless patterns for turning old T-shirts into blankets filled the internet, people had been finding ways to incorporate their mementoes into beautiful items. The Kansas Historical Society collection holds the quilt seen on the previous page. Made of many brightly colored scraps of fabric, this crazy quilt also incorporates numerous organizational ribbons bearing the names of groups like the Bar Association of the State of Kansas, the Kansas Council of Women, and the State Association of Kansas Fairs. Edged in soft velvet, it is easy to imagine someone pulling the blanket over their lap. Looking over the names and events represented in the quilt, the owner could easily travel down memory lane anytime they pulled out the warm covering.

In the late nineteenth and early twentieth centuries, crazy quilts became very popular in the United States. Taking the name "crazy," these beautiful objects were indeed wild in design, but the name also referred to the asymmetrical Japanese art and crazed ceramics that inspired their patterns.[2] Unlike the implication that the blanket might be haphazard, most crazy quilts were carefully thought out, becoming showstopping pieces. While some incorporate fine fabrics such as velvet, silk, and brocade, others utilize more utilitarian swatches of flannel and cotton. No matter the fabric choice, quilts often carry hallmarks of their makers and the people who use them. Whether it is a name embroidered in a corner, the intricate hand stitched patterns, or the inclusion of unique textiles to celebrate an event, every quilt has its own story to tell. As a historic object, the quilt highlighted here serves as a record of the activities and interests of the owners. Belonging to Lucy Browne Johnston and her husband, Chief Justice William Agnew Johnston, of Topeka, Kansas, it is no wonder that the quilt contains eight separate ribbons commemorating events of the Kansas Equal Suffrage Association scattered throughout it. As active supporters of women's voting rights, both Chief Justice and Mrs. Johnston held memberships in their state's suffrage organization. No stranger to civic work, Mrs. Johnston also became active in several women's clubs and spent time lobbying for better libraries around the state. In 1911, she took on the role of president and campaign manager of the Kansas Equal Suffrage Association. As she did, the group ramped up activities and Kansas's legislature prepared to consider granting female citizens the right to vote in their state.[3]

Encouraged by national suffrage organizations like the National American Woman Suffrage Association, every state except Wyoming formed state-level suffrage groups in the years surrounding 1900. In some locations, like South Carolina, these organizations remained relatively small, but in other states, like Massachusetts, thousands of women joined state clubs to fight for women's voting rights. In many cases, organizing these state suffrage associations typically served as one of the first steps in launching a state-wide movement. In fact, in many instances there tended to be little suffrage activity before a state organization got off the ground. After its formation however, suffragists engaged in a variety of acts meant to persuade lawmakers that women should have voting rights.[4]

In Kansas, campaigning for suffrage had a long history. As early as 1854 (the year the territory formed), issues of women's rights bubbled to the surface. When preparations for statehood began in 1859, a small group of men and women worked to convince the state constitutional convention to include voting provisions for women and black citizens in state laws. Despite their efforts, when Kansas became a state in 1861, they only succeeded in securing the female right to vote in local school district elections. By 1867, however, the issues of full suffrage for women and blacks had come into the public eye again. As the first women's suffrage referendum to come before a state, Kansas gained national attention. It was not long before noted national leaders in the women's rights movement arrived in Kansas to campaign on behalf of suffrage. With the state legislature considering voting rights for both African Americans and women however, the ensuing battle grew bitterly divided along racial lines. In the end, after months of tense campaigning, the issues of both black and female suffrage went down in defeat.[5] While the effort ended in failure, the significance was not lost on suffragists. They knew the battle had been an important first step, and in later years national organizations adopted gold, a nod to the Kansas sunflower, as an official color of their movement.

After the defeat, women in Kansas planned their next move. Heeding the advice of national leaders, in 1884 they formed the Kansas Equal Suffrage Association (KESA).[6] Through their organized efforts, women in the state continued to chip away at the suffrage issue, and in 1887 they earned the right to vote in local elections. For KESA this victory was not enough. They wanted full voting rights in their state. Looking to make their demands a reality, suffragists rolled up their sleeves and got back to work. After staging several campaigns to sway the state legislature to grant women full suffrage, they finally got traction in 1910 when Governor Walter Stubs advised lawmakers to begin debating the issue. The following year the state suffrage association appointed Lucy Browne Johnston president. Under her leadership the organization worked tirelessly to lobby every member of the Kansas House of Representatives and Senate. They also entertained the wives of lawmakers, hoping to encourage influence at home.[7]

After months of hard work their efforts paid off, and in February, lawmakers in the state legislature passed a resolution to amend Kansas's constitution, granting women the right to vote. According to state law however, before the resolution could be put into effect, the issue had to be voted upon by the citizens of the state, in 1912. Needing to ensure the state's population would vote in favor of the amendment, KESA created a plan to ramp up membership, get speakers out into the public, and distribute pro-suffrage literature to citizens around the state.[8]

In a creative effort to gain support the group even sponsored an essay contest in local schools. Heavily advertised in newspapers around Kansas, they structured the contest as an elimination competition. Open to any student enrolled in a public school, each participant wrote on the topic, "Why Women Should Vote." To incentivize participation, first-, second-, and third-place winners received monetary rewards. For any pupils needing additional information to form their argument, KESA's travelling library prepared packages of suffrage literature sent to students and teachers upon request.[9] As each district held its own contest, the winning essay was passed on to a county competition. From there, first place winners entered in the final round at the state level. While KESA knew students could not vote in favor of women's suffrage, they hoped the competition would turn participants' parents into supporters.[10] Throughout the year-long essay contest KESA sent suffrage literature to two-thirds of the counties in Kansas. Many rural areas were reached that may not have been otherwise. As each level of the competition held ceremonies where winners read their essays, parents made up captive audiences.

When Election Day arrived in November, hundreds of women worked all day at the polls and sat up well into the night waiting for the results. After many hours of anticipation, the state of Kansas came through, becoming the seventh state in the country to grant women the right to vote. Like other state suffrage organizations that had achieved victory, KESA did not sit on its laurels after its win. As just one of several cogs in a larger suffrage network, it continued to advocate for a federal law, and through its work, the responsibility for advocacy cascaded from the national level, to individual states, and down to county and local groups. As many suffragists would come to realize, each organization had to work for its own citizens' rights while also supporting the larger suffrage effort.

Part III

SYMBOLS

Symbolism is a powerful tool. Ideas, events, and even consumer products can take on deeper meanings through representative imagery and communication. Each day, businesses, politicians, groups, and individuals put many symbols into action to promote their messages and goods. The glimpse of a set of golden arches can turn into a drive-thru visit to tame a craving not noticed minutes before, and an apple with a bite missing signifies first-rate technology. Likewise, a sea of red, white, and blue calls to mind thoughts of patriotism and Americanism. Just as these emblems have taken on unspoken meanings, suffragists deployed a variety of symbols when demanding the right to vote, and at times they were met toe-to-toe by their opponents' own devices. By using representative colors, slogans, and strong imagery, they stitched together a recognizable brand. A brand that stimulated emotions, sold ideas, and compelled individuals to join their fight. Some of the choices directly tied to events at the time, while others appropriated the stories of historic figures. Woven into a complex web of meaning, suffragists used these symbols to inform and convince the American public of the benefits they would gain by allowing women to vote.

"Votes for Women"

Sash, 1910–1920, Atlanta History Center, Atlanta, GA, http://www.atlanta historycenter.com/
ATLANTA HISTORY CENTER

"Votes for Women"—three simple words, but three mighty words. For suffragists this phrase served as a rallying cry for activists; a mantra to help stay focused on their end goal; and one of their most recognized publicity slogans. It appeared in popular songs, on lapel buttons, and even adorned luncheonette plates. Much more than just a catchphrase, it was a battle cry for a movement. Picketers wore their voices thin calling it out, and wherever suffragists gathered, the expression could be seen or heard.

For those familiar with the classic family film *Mary Poppins*, the name Mrs. Winifred Banks recalls a well-dressed woman singing about her sister suffragettes. As part of the song-and-dance routine, the character dons a suffrage sash and she enthusiastically places one around the necks of her household cook and maid. Printed with the bold words, "Votes for Women," there is no mistaking Mrs. Banks's cause. As one of the most common items used by suffragists, sashes provided a unique way to present their number-one slogan to the public. Often worn by supporters during large demonstrations, such as suffrage parades, the sash made a strong visual impact when vast numbers appeared at once. And with the words "Votes for Women" often printed in bold black lettering on the front, it was impossible for onlookers to miss the message. Much like Mrs. Banks's sash directly communicates her convictions, so does the sash pictured on the previous page. Held in the collection of the Atlanta History Center, it fearlessly declares its demand. It also serves as a reminder of how Atlanta's own suffragists harnessed the power of the simple, yet powerful phrase to show their support for women's voting rights when the public least expected it.

If asked to name a place that comes to mind when hearing the word "suffrage," Georgia is probably not high on the list. History books are filled with tales of suffragists, but often these stories focus on the areas connected to national leaders and organizations. With so much activity unfolding in Washington, DC, and with roots in the northeast, it can be hard to remember that the work of the suffrage movement took place in every region of the nation. Not a hotbed of early suffrage activity, the American South is often thought of as a region heavily against women's voting rights. In fact, not many southerners expressed an interest in enfranchising female citizens until the 1890s. Even then, by 1920 most southern states refused to ratify the 19th Amendment extending the opportunity to vote to American women.[1] It was no secret that many white southerners blatantly opposed the idea because it not only meant giving white women the right to vote, but also black women. Many southern states had already worked to limit the voting rights of African American males through biased literacy tests, civics quizzes, poll taxes, and intimidation. Steeped in this discrimination, for many people the idea of giving black women the right to vote was inconceivable. Some southern anti-suffragists, like their counterparts around the country, even formed organized groups to work against the spread of women's voting rights. Believing the issue should be decided on a state-by-state basis, not by the federal government, they made it clear to state legislators that they did not support it.[2]

While these anti-suffrage attitudes could be found across Georgia, segments of the state's women, both white and black, did support the expansion of voting rights to women. Like their northern sisters, their support was not always unified. While some black and white suffragists genuinely worked to secure voting rights for all races and genders, many white suffragists had a more cynical outlook. One persistent view assumed that by enfranchising female citizens, white women could outvote the total number of black male and female voters—ensuring white supremacy and wiping out the African American voice. While some suffragists solely supported this extreme view, others attempted to play both sides of the fence. They advocated suffrage for women of color when it advanced their agenda, and downplayed their support of black voting rights when they thought it could hurt their own chances.[3] Amid this complex web of support, by 1913 several pro-suffrage organizations had formed in Georgia, particularly in the Atlanta area. While the Georgia Woman Suffrage Association and many other groups only allowed white membership, black suffragists found a voice through African American organizations such as the Federation of Negro Women's Clubs of Georgia.[4]

Although dedicated to their work, the efforts of Atlanta's suffragists had not taken on the extravagance of some northern organizations. In fact, no group—white or black—had yet to stage a suffrage-specific public rally or major demonstration.[5] Always eager to stand for their demands, however, southern suffragists found unexpected ways to campaign for the cause, and in 1913, members of the Atlanta Equal Suffrage Association employed the iconic "Votes for Women" slogan to make sure everyone knew what they stood for.

That November, Atlanta held its fourth annual car show. The popular multiday event drew visitors to the city not only from across Georgia but the entire southern region. With the newest models of automobiles on display, dealers as well as the general public could inspect the cars in person and talk to company representatives from around the country. At a time when automobiles were just beginning to become attainable by more than the wealthy, the event created a unique buzz and provided the ability to dream of the future. Another major draw of the show was the motor floral parade held on November 11. With ten thousand people and their cars lining the sidewalks and streets of Atlanta's business district, twenty-five beautifully decorated cars paraded down the city's thoroughfares for countless eyes to see.[6]

Promoted as a contest with awards in categories such as prettiest driver and best decorated automobile, a panel of judges scrutinized each car while onlookers of all races and classes took in the scene. With weeks of promotion ahead of time, those in attendance knew to expect beautiful cars and creative decorations. What they may not have anticipated was that a group of white suffragists planned to use the non-suffrage event to drive their message past an unsuspecting audience of thousands. Knowing a captive audience was a guarantee, suffragists saw their opportunity to grab public attention. As the cars rolled down Atlanta's streets, the white activists filled three automobiles decorated in yellow bunting and chrysanthemums. Draped from the cars' sides, rears, fronts, and anywhere else room could be made, flags and banners emblazed with "Votes for Women" were draped and hung. While none of these cars took home a prize that day, the real reward came with the thousands of people who saw their slogan. For those people who had considered giving their support to the cause, the suffragists' display ensured them that like-minded people did exist in Georgia. And for anyone who may not have given it a second thought in the past, activists hoped their barrage of enthusiasm might encourage others to rethink their decision.[7]

Within a year, Georgia's white suffragists, perhaps spurred on by their demonstration in the automobile parade, held their first public rally in Atlanta. In 1916 they continued their string of bold action and formed a sizeable parade at the end of Atlanta's Harvest Festival, again taking advantage of a non-suffrage event to reach an already gathered audience. Like they had done in 1913, the activists who took to Atlanta's streets for the parade leveraged their succinct and popular slogan. As suffragists would do around the country, they wore sashes and carried banners begging for "Votes for Women."[8] Although the message was short, it got to the heart of the matter and proved, over many years, the ability for those three words to sustain energy and grab attention. In Georgia, the phrase stirred emotions in both white and black supporters and proved an effective rallying cry for the suffragists who proudly spoke, wore, and displayed those meaningful words.

13

Loyalty, Purity, and Life

Banner, 1913–1920, Museum of Connecticut History, Hartford, CT, http://museumofcthistory.org/
MUSEUM OF CONNECTICUT HISTORY

Waiting for election results can be a nail-biting activity.[1] Every four years people across the United States keep track of presidential votes through social media, election maps, and special broadcasts. As tallies roll in, states on the map change from red to blue and back again, until a single color emerges as the winner. Without thinking, it is understood that a red state will cast its electoral votes for the Republican Party, while a blue state grants its favor to the Democratic Party. For many people it seems like red has always stood for conservatism, while blue has represented liberalism. In reality, these symbolic colors have only been the standard since the presidential election of 2000. That year neither candidate earned the required 270 electoral votes to win the presidency. Hinging on the results in Florida, ballots were so close that a recount was ordered. In the end, the US Supreme Court decided the outcome of the election, and they declared Republican George W. Bush the winner over Democrat Al Gore. Throughout it all, the *New York Times* and *USA Today* published the first full-color election maps, with red representing the Republican Party and blue representing the Democratic. As the coverage dragged on for weeks, news outlets in print, television, and the internet continued to use the designations. By the end of the tedious process the symbolic colors had grown so familiar, they became part of everyday political language.[2]

Just as the colors blue and red represent political ideas and factions, in 1920 the purple, white, and gold of the banner shown on the previous page communicated its connection to the suffrage movement. No slogans necessary—the sight of the tricolors let the spectator know that the woman hoisting the banner favored votes for women. Carried proudly by radical suffragists in Connecticut, banners like this became iconic symbols of the movement and the colors became synonymous not only with suffrage but of women's rights in general. While this tricolor flag was an instantly recognizable brand, its adoption by activists had a long evolution, much like the movement itself.

As early as 1867, the colors gold and yellow became linked to the battle for women's voting rights. That year Kansas began its suffrage campaign and activists adopted the sunflower (a native wild bloom growing across the region) as their badge. Decades later, the state itself would designate the striking blossom as its official state flower as well. Believed to always turn to face the sun, suffragists viewed sunflowers as righteous blooms. Seeing this same honorable characteristic in themselves, they hoped linking their movement to the image of the sunflower would be a perfect way to promote their virtue.[3] Looking to make that association, it did not take long for supporters of women's voting rights to begin incorporating sunflower imagery into their literature and suffrage materials. They also started wearing homemade gold and yellow ribbons mimicking the color of sunflower petals. Over the next several decades, the practice became so popular both inside and outside of Kansas that the National American Woman Suffrage Association (NAWSA) adopted yellow as its official color. By 1910, sashes, pins, banners, and a wide array of other yellow and gold items dominated the organization's events around the country. In fact, it became practically impossible to attend any function associated with women's voting rights and not be met with a heavy dose of bright yellow or gold.

Because NAWSA and Kansas's organizations were not the only suffrage groups working for the cause however, other symbolic colors found their way into the suffrage arena as well. With the complex network of national, state, and local groups growing throughout the late nineteenth and early twentieth centuries, organizations looked for ways to distinguish themselves from one another. Just as their opinions about how to fight for the right to vote did not always align, neither did their visual branding. This created a small handful of distinct color schemes used by American suffragists to identify their organizational allegiances as well as their philosophical approaches.[4]

In New York, Connecticut, and New Jersey a small number of suffrage organizations preferred to use the British suffrage colors of purple, white, and green to identify themselves. This color scheme appeared on everything from banners and buttons to pennants and posters. Very distinct from Kansas yellow, this color scheme not only visually separated these groups from NAWSA but also aligned their organizations with British suffragists known for progressive thinking and militant action. Like all things they did, the color scheme was intentional. Green represented hope and new life; purple indicated ambition, loyalty, and dignity; white was for purity and honor. If having two sets of suffrage colors for the public to keep track of did not complicate things enough, another color scheme emerged as well. This one eventually overshadowed the others in its longevity and appeal.

Formed in the 1910s, the National Woman's Party adopted the tricolor flag, an image of which is shown at the beginning of this chapter. More successfully than the organizations before them, these suffragists developed an instantly recognizable brand that set them apart from conservative suffragists in the United States. They also communicated their appreciation of the work of radical British activists. Comprised of purple, white, and gold, their ensign combined the existing color schemes already circulating in the nation. This approach gave a nod to the militant tactics of the British who put their colors of purple, white, and green to use in a tricolor flag of their own. At the same time, it recognized the past work of women in the United States by swapping the British-preferred green for Kansas gold. The National Woman's Party's colors quickly gained recognition and popularity when they took prominent roles in the organization's parades, pageants, and public demonstrations. With a repertoire of bold tactics that included hunger strikes and picketing of the White House, the National Woman's Party became highly visible. The high level of press coverage the group received explains why their flag gained such wide recognition and appeal. Although news coverage in the 1910s was not in color, the purple, white, and gold of the National Woman's Party still provided a striking contrast of shades when printed in black and white, making for attention grabbing photos.[5]

Early on the National Woman's Party made clear the intention of their choices in color. Speaking about their flag, they said, "Purple is the color of loyalty. . . . White, the emblem of purity . . . and gold, the color of light and life . . . the torch that guides our purpose, pure and unswerving." Additionally, the color white also served some very practical purposes. When worn by suffragists, the light hue allowed their colorful sashes, buttons, pins, and banners to stand out. Whether seen by onlookers in person, or picked up in newspaper and magazine photos, a sea of white created a blank canvas to display their carefully selected colors and slogans. Additionally, white provided an unthreatening look, making it difficult for opponents to characterize suffragists as aggressive or masculine. By aligning suffrage support with colors, activists also ensured that women from many social classes, races, and cultures could easily participate in their cause. Even if someone could not afford to purchase a suffrage-specific outfit or accessory, they could easily add purple, yellow, or green trimming over one of the white dresses or blouses they likely had in their wardrobe.[6]

While suffragists reported slightly different meanings of the colors over time, the power of those colors remained steadfast, providing activists and the public with a sense of unity and recognition. No matter what the individual colors may have signified, the National Woman's Party's tricolors, along with the other official colors of suffrage, became universally known and recognized as symbols of women's equality. A message so strong that in the 1970s the National Woman's Party's colors rose again as a sign of solidarity during the campaign for the Equal Rights Amendment.[7] In the years since, suffrage colors have continued to bubble up in use, particularly by women in the political arena. When Shirley Chisolm became the first black woman to throw her hat into the presidential ring, her campaign posters featured a striking photo of the politician in a white suit. Geraldine Ferraro, the first woman to appear as a vice presidential candidate, also sported white when delivering her acceptance speech. And in the twenty-first century, a sea of congresswomen paid a nod to the work of suffragists during President Donald Trump's 2019 State of the Union address by wearing white, many accessorizing with purple, yellow, and green.[8] Whether suffragists thought their branding would last for a century after their work ended, no one can know. No matter their intention, the symbolic colors they chose remain relevant today as women and men continue to work toward expanding rights for women across the nation.

The War of the Roses

Anti-Suffrage Stamps, created by Maine Association Opposed to Woman Suffrage around 1918, Maine Historical Society, Portland, ME, https://www.mainehistory.org/
COLLECTIONS OF MAINE HISTORICAL SOCIETY

Often, deciphering the meaning of a phrase, title, or name can become much more difficult than initially expected. As frequently observed, life does not happen in black and white, but rather in shades of grey. That said, the phrase "war of the roses" can mean different things to different people. For European history buffs, the War of the Roses might recall a series of English civil wars in the fifteenth century. Movie fans may first jump to, "Oh, you mean that Michael Douglas movie from the eighties?" This war of the roses has nothing to do with the throne of England or a divorce battle, however. In 1920, a very different war of the roses took place in Tennessee between suffragists and their opponents.

As suffrage advocates expanded their repertoire of symbols, other yellow blooms besides the sunflower began appearing at their events, often in the form of yellow jonquils or roses—both easier for suffragists to get. Although not sunflowers, the color yellow had become so synonymous with suffrage that these flowers, in various shades of the hue, proved wildly successful as pro-suffrage emblems so much so that anti-suffragists adopted the red rose to counter their opponents.[1] From the beginning of the suffrage movement, for every woman or man supporting female voting rights, at least one person opposed them. By the 1890s, these adversaries began coordinating their efforts in a similar manner to suffragists themselves, and over time anti-suffrage organizations formed in every region of the nation.[2]

While suffragists supported a heavy dose of colorful symbolism and display, anti-suffragists liked to avoid big public splashes. Unlike women's voting advocates, their opponents disapproved of street parades and other sensational tactics they believed unwomanly. Perhaps a bitter pill to swallow—despite their aversion to public displays, they knew it would be necessary to develop a recognizable brand promoting their point of view.[3] Just as suffragists used colors and imagery to give their organizations instant recognition, anti-suffragists adopted their own official symbols. They selected red, black, and white as their official colors, which appeared on a sampling of mass-produced items, such as the stamps seen on the left. White standing for purity, black for steadfastness, and red for the American Beauty rose, this was the anti-suffragists' first formal emblem.[4]

Worn to identify themselves in solidarity, anti-suffragists distributed red roses at suffrage parades and other events to signify that not all women wanted the right to vote. The Woman's Anti-Suffrage Association in Boston even published a song in 1915 titled "The Anti-Suffrage Rose" to bring their message to the masses. That same year a new breed of rose named the Mrs. Arthur M. Dodge debuted in New York City. Its large petals took on a deep shade of pinkish red and the bloom emitted a rich fragrance. But why would a flower be named after a woman? With the bloom having a strikingly similar appearance to the American Beauty rose but with a new distinct shade, its breeder chose the president of the National Association Opposed to Woman Suffrage as the inspiration for the bloom's name. While anti-suffrists had already succeeded in linking the red rose to their cause, Socialists threw a wrench into the works. With Socialists also using a red rose as their symbol, anti-suffrists spent a lot of time explaining that they were not Socialists, when they would rather be articulating why they believed women did not need or want the right to vote. The creation of the Mrs. Arthur M. Dodge rose was intended to minimize the issue. Ultimately, anti-suffrists hoped the distinct, deep pink color would set them apart from the other political and social reform organizations using similar emblems.[5]

By 1920, the symbols of suffrists and anti-suffrists were well seared into popular culture. Red or pink roses represented those who did not believe women needed voting rights, and yellow roses represented those promoting the franchise for females. That August, amid hot and humid weather in Nashville, Tennessee, these two factions saw their own "wars of the roses" play out at the state's legislature. A year earlier Congress had voted in favor of the 19th Amendment to the Constitution, extending the opportunity to vote to women. Before it could be put into action however, the amendment required ratification by thirty-six states. By the time Tennessee's state legislature prepared to vote on the issue in August 1920 the amendment was only one state shy of ratification. With a dramatic debate and vote soon to ensue, suffrists and anti-suffrists from around the nation swarmed the city.

Both camps set up their headquarters at the Heritage Hotel in downtown Nashville. Practically on top of one another, suffrists and anti-suffrists fine-tuned their plans and put them into action. In front of reporters who had also travelled from around the country to cover the events, these women made compelling arguments for both their causes. They wrote letters, made speeches, and canvased lawmakers. As they had often done before, anti-suffrists distributed red and pink roses to those opposing ratification while suffrists distributed yellow roses to those supporting the 19th Amendment.

Practically overnight, it seemed like every place and person in Nashville had sprouted roses. At the state house, legislators even got in on the action and displayed their voting intentions by wearing roses in their lapels. These telltale signs of friend or foe made it easy for each camp to keep track of support for their side of the argument—a tally that had been almost too close to count leading up to the state's congressional debate.

On the day of the final vote, more red roses than yellow walked onto the floor of the Tennessee House of Representatives. If suffragists had been worried before, their fears certainly grew at the sight of so many red petals, while anti-suffragists let out a cautious sigh of relief. As votes began, each side kept a careful count. Surprisingly, when they reached the end of the roll call, the vote was deadlocked, and after a second pass, the number of votes remained tied. After two nerve-wracking votes a third roll call began. In a move that would change the lives of many women in the United States, during the third vote, Representative Harry T. Burn changed his vote from "nay" to "aye." Despite the red rose pinned to his lapel, Burn had cast a vote decidedly favoring yellow. By changing one word, he proved that life does not in fact happen in shades of black and white, or red and yellow, but often in the colors that fall in between.

The Spirit of 1776

Wagon, around 1840, New York State Museum, Albany, NY, http://www.nysm.nysed.gov/

In the late nineteenth and early twentieth centuries, a wave of nostalgia swept across the United States. Following the close of the Civil War, a sense of uneasiness rose in the nation's native white citizens as they coped with dramatic social and cultural changes, as well as economic and political discontent. Overwhelmed by the effects of industrialization and the influx of immigrants, white Americans became disillusioned with the changes overtaking their lives. To cope with their anxieties, residents looked back to an idealized colonial past for security and reassurance. In short order, their self-soothing nostalgia crept into many areas of daily American life. Architecture, home decoration, fashion, and even gardening took on a flare known as Colonial Revival. No longer was the Colonial Revival design movement simply a coping mechanism for white elites, but it had become a fad for the entire nation.[1] Boxes of colonial themed tea could be purchased at the nearest grocery store, and popular fiction carried a distinctly patriotic flair. The October 28, 1915, issue of *Leslie's Illustrated Weekly* even carried an image of a woman wearing the uniform of a revolutionary minuteman with a yellow "Votes for Women" sash draped across her chest. Just two years earlier, local suffragists in New York State took similar advantage of the public's fascination with the nation's idealized past. The wagon seen on the facing page harkens back to the early days of the nation when activists used it to align their demand for suffrage with the rights of citizenship that colonists and patriots fought so hard to secure.[2] Painted with the words, "Spirit of 1776," the old, yet roadworthy vehicle, brought considerable attention to the suffrage cause and stirred feelings of patriotism and history as it drove through the streets of Long Island.[3]

On July 1, 1913, the "Spirit of 1776" wagon departed the New York State Woman Suffrage Association headquarters in Manhattan for Long Island. On board were suffragists Edna Kearns, Irene Davison, and Kearns's eight-year-old daughter, Serena. Despite the sunny, hot weather of the day, the suffragists stayed in high spirits as they passed out literature and delivered speeches along their route.[4] As they did, some passersby waved and cheered while others shook their fists in disapproval. No matter what others thought, suffragists saw their work as the unfinished business of the American Revolution—considered by many to be the ultimate act of patriotism.

To make their point, they did not wear the usual yellow sashes and pins of suffrage. Instead, Kearns and Davison both dressed in costumes of the Revolutionary War. Their heavy blue coats with yellow facings and tricorn hats made them the perfect picture of revolutionary minutemen ready for battle. Serena's outfit of patriotic red, white, and blue provided the perfect compliment. If pedestrians and other drivers on New York City's streets wondered what was afoot, a closer inspection of the wagon itself helped answer their questions. In addition to the hand-painted phrase, "Spirit of 1776," suffrage banners and hand-painted signs covered the wagon. A particularly eye-catching one read, "If taxation without representation is tyranny in 1776, why not in 1913?"[5] Since the suffrage movement's earliest years, activists had frequently drawn on the colonial grievance of "no taxation without representation" to demonstrate why tax-paying women deserved the right to vote.

Through their words, costumes, and transportation, Kearns and Davison directly equated their cause with the nation's founding fathers. They also pointed out that as nonvoting citizens they were under direct oppression from the government. As far back as the Seneca Falls Convention, activists had referenced the words, actions, and decisions of the nation's founders to justify their own work for equality. While suffrage pioneers in 1848 called for expanded women's rights in the Declaration of Sentiments, by 1913 most women still found themselves excluded from the democratic process. In New York, Kearns and Davison planned to do their part to move the needle forward using a heavy dose of patriotic symbolism.[6]

Once arriving on Long Island, the "Spirit of 1776" wagon continued its journey for a month-long organizing campaign. Traveling from town to town, the wagon drew eyes and provided suffragists with a platform from which to speak and grab attention. It became increasingly obvious that if American women wanted to secure the right to vote, a federal amendment would need to be added to the Constitution. This would require not only the support of national organizations and state leagues, but also the hard work of countless local suffragists. Understanding this, Kearns and Davison shepherded the wagon along its journey in the hopes of drawing more attention to women's demand for equal voting rights.[7]

As hoped, by the end of the month the wagon and its drivers had received considerable attention from both supporters and opposition. When the suffragists arrived in the town of Huntington on July 26, however, they may not have anticipated the very public clash awaiting them. As the wagon pulled into the village, hundreds of shoppers and onlookers crowded the town. Obviously, the novelty of their wagon and the revolutionary cause had drawn the attention they hoped, but now it came crashing back on them.[8]

As the wagon made its way through the center of town, with a fife and drum corps following, one of the state's anti-suffragists stepped out directly in front of it. Halting the procession, Mary Jones stood facing the suffragists as a hush fell over the onlookers. "No longer will this old wagon be put to such a base use!" she proclaimed. According to Mrs. Jones the "Spirit of 1776" wagon had been improperly taken from her relatives and sold to I. S. Remson, the Brooklyn company that had donated the wagon to the suffrage movement. Jones then proceeded to inform the suffragists she fully intended to pursue a lawsuit. If Jones had not made enough of a scene, she went on to attack the activists' claims of the link between the wagon and the American Revolution. While suffragists passionately connected the vehicle to patriotism and the noble right for equality, Jones felt just as passionately that doing so insulted her family. Her ancestors had not been good patriots, but instead proud loyalists of the British throne. In the 1770s, Jones's family considered all patriots traitors, and in 1913, she believed suffragists no better.[9]

Although the journey of the "Spirit of 1776" wagon came to an abrupt halt in Huntington, Mary Jones's threats of legal action never came to fruition. In fact, neither the suffragists' nor anti-suffragists' claims of the wagon's ties to the patriot and loyalist causes turned out to be true. Although they may have honestly believed the wagon dated to the eighteenth century, in truth wagons made in its style did not exist before 1820. Distancing it even further, the "Spirit of 1776" wagon likely dates to around 1840—more than fifty years after the end of the Revolutionary War.[10]

The true age and history of the wagon does not change its importance to the suffrage cause. As an object used to propel interest in the movement, the wagon represents the wide variety of ways suffragists used symbolism and spectacle to make news and gain exposure. Not only did the wagon assist suffragists in physically moving through the streets of Long Island, but it also allowed them to carry on the nation's long tradition of pursuing equal citizenship. In creating a new nation, patriots had the right to fight for equality and establish freedoms for themselves and their fellow citizens. In suffragists' eyes, however, they had come up short regarding women. To pick up where founders had left off, early women's rights activists and suffragists first took up the cause of patriotism at the Seneca Falls Convention, crafting their own version of the Declaration of Independence. In 1913, the torch passed to the next generation who continued to work toward equal suffrage from a wagon embodying America's continual push for equality, as well as the spirit of 1776.

Identity Erased

Statue—*Sacajawea and Jean-Baptiste*, created by Alice Cooper, 1905, Washington Park, Portland, OR, http://explorewashingtonpark.org/#

In 1902, a new novel landed on bookshelves across the nation. Chronicling the familiar tale of Lewis and Clark's expedition across the American West, *The Conquest: The True Story of Lewis and Clark* earned instant popularity with readers. While this page-turning work of historic fiction served as a semi-biographical telling of the life of William Clark, author Eva Emery Dye also used the book to introduce readers to a character that would become a new female icon to the American public.

While little historic documentation exists regarding Sacajawea's life, more public statues have been erected of her than of any other woman in the United States.[1] Surprisingly, prior to the centennial of the Lewis and Clark Expedition in 1905, very few people had heard of Sacajawea. Her name appeared on brief occasion in the diaries of Lewis and Clark, but they gave little explanation of her role in the expedition. Journals note that she gave birth to a baby boy during the long trek and continued to care for the child while traveling with the party. She also served as an occasional interpreter and assisted in digging roots and picking berries as food sources. When the expedition needed to decide where to camp for the winter, Sacajawea secured a vote in making the decision.[2] A strong believer in women's abilities and rights, these few threads of evidence appealed to Dye as she sought a heroine for her book. Upon finding these references to Sacajawea, she elevated the native woman to the status of guide for Lewis and Clark's travel party. Not only did this provide *The Conquest* with a strong female character, but Dye, an ardent suffragist, also created a symbol perfectly molded for the suffrage movement.[3]

By 1900, suffragists had been grinding along for several decades with minimal results to show for their hard labors. While they had successfully found ways to promote their ideas through slogans, colors, and physical symbols like sunflowers and roses, the figure of Sacajawea seemed to provide the perfect embodiment of their cause. Because Lewis and Clark's accounts of the native woman were bare bone, a considerable amount of room was left for interpretation and embellishment. White suffragists quickly grabbed onto the story of Sacajawea and reinterpreted it for their own use. In doing so, they whitewashed Sacajawea and molded her to benefit their cause with little regard to facts or the native culture she represented.

Soon after the publication of *The Conquest*, women of Portland, Oregon, organized the Sacajawea Statue Association and named Eva Emery Dye president of the group. Their main goal was to secure a statue of Sacajawea for the Lewis and Clark Exposition scheduled to take place in Portland in the summer of 1905. To fund the sculpture the association looked to women's organizations from across the country to contribute to the cost. In Oregon, women raised part of the funds by selling Sacajawea buttons and souvenir spoons.[4] Ultimately, the group raised the $7,000 necessary to hire noted sculptress Alice Cooper, of Colorado, to design the monument and have it erected.

From its conception, the creation of Portland's Sacajawea monument had strong connections to the suffrage cause, and local planners (many suffragists themselves) looked for ways to link it to the national suffrage organization. In 1904, they took steps toward doing so, sending an invitation to the National American Woman Suffrage Association (NAWSA) asking them to hold their next annual meeting in conjunction with the Lewis and Clark celebration. The symbolism was obvious to NAWSA leadership, who eagerly accepted the invitation and became involved in the fundraising efforts for the statue. When their meeting was called to order in June of 1905 in Portland, Anna Howard Shaw, president of the organization, praised Sacajawea's character and achievements.

On July 6, the thirty-four-foot monument was unveiled in Portland's Washington Park. Suffragists from every state attended the dedication, including Susan B. Anthony. This towering version of Sacajawea reflected Dye's idealized vision. With baby on her back, the figure's features look more European than indigenous. She looks forward into the distance, a model of strength and femininity. In a brilliant marketing strategy for their cause, suffragists wrapped the statue in an American flag, framing the events as pure patriotism.[5] In her remarks to the crowd, Dye spoke of woman's role in the civilization of Oregon and the American West. According to the author, women made it all possible. Women created homes, reared families, and were responsible for creating the backbone of civilization. Directly linking her heroine to westward expansion, she stated, "And Sacajawea led them all, the dark-eyed princess of the native race . . . beckoned the white man on, toward her ancient home in the Orient."[6]

White suffragists embraced this appropriated vision of Sacajawea. They considered her not only the first "American" woman to vote, but also a young woman who could participate in a backbreaking mission, hold her own among men, and still perform her duties as a mother. If the vote did not cause detriment to Sacajawea's health, reduce her fertility, or interfere with her social responsibilities, suffragists argued that their opponents should not fear the same about them. To suffragists this version of Sacajawea presented an ideal prototype who stood for everything they did. She demonstrated that a woman could play an important role in public life without sacrificing her femininity. Not only was she a brave and strong companion, but she was also a nurturing, self-sacrificing, and uncomplaining mother.[7]

Although presented only with Dye's fictionalized account of Sacajawea's life, it was of little importance to suffragists to find out more, or to understand that in truth she was little more than a captive of the expedition. Sacajawea's value to Lewis and Clark was not that of an irreplaceable guide, a beacon of morality, or a necessary voter. Rather her value took the form of a commodity to the explorers' travels. In fact, the mere presence of a native woman and child communicated the group's peacefulness to other native peoples, something highly valuable to Lewis and Clark who did not want to be mistaken for a war party. While Sacajawea's life had already been reduced to a few mere mentions in historic diaries, the publication of Dye's novel and the erection of Portland's Sacajawea monument erased the remainder of Sacajawea's true identity from history. Rather than be remembered for her native culture (one that had existed far longer in the United States than those of white settlers), Sacajawea instead came to represent white American suffragists' idealized attributes of modesty, purity, domesticity, and moral superiority.[8]

Martyr for the Cause

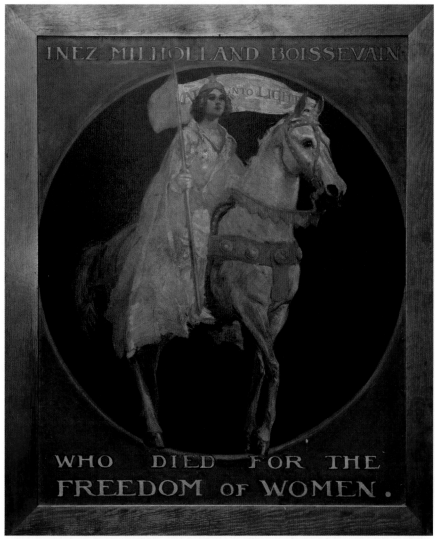

Painting—*Inez Milholland Boissevain*, undated, National Woman's Party at Belmont-Paul Women's Equality National Monument, Washington, DC, http://nationalwomansparty.org/

Since 1886, the Statue of Liberty has stood as a symbol of freedom and democracy on Liberty Island—along with Ellis Island, a gateway to the United States for millions of immigrants between the early 1890s and 1950s. Just as Lady Liberty embodies the ideals of the United States, the figure featured in the painting on the facing page represents the thousands of suffragists who fought tirelessly to secure voting rights for women. In 1913, American suffragists took a cue from their British sisters and introduced yet another historic figure to their playbook of symbolism. While suffragists played a large role in lifting Sacajawea into the realm of mythic legend, their newest icon needed no introduction.

Burned at the stake in the fifteenth century, Joan of Arc was already well on her way to sainthood, something that would coincidentally happen in 1920, the same year of the ratification of the 19th Amendment. For centuries, this teenage warrior of France fascinated the public. Born a French peasant, she claimed to have received a revelation from God at the age of thirteen instructing her to lead the French to victory over the English. After convincing the leaders of her nation of her divine powers, Joan of Arc took up her banner in the name of God and country. Although she had no experience with the military, she rode alongside French royals and soldiers, fearlessly guiding the army in battle against their enemy. At every town and village she was praised as a heroine—a role that Joan embraced, often visiting with them daily to distribute food and supplies, as well as messages of encouragement and inspiration. At the age of nineteen, however, she was captured and turned over to the English who tried her as a heretic and had her executed. In death, Joan of Arc got her justice when a retrial found her innocent. It did not take long for her tragic story to spread, and in the centuries following her death countless artists, writers, composers, and filmmakers have depicted her life. From the time Joan of Arc was declared innocent, she became a martyr of her cause. As the ultimate symbol of female strength, women looked to her as the epitome of heroism.

It is no wonder that in Britain, the militant wing of the suffrage movement claimed her as their patron saint. At many protest parades a suffragist would appear in armor at the head of the march, bringing Joan to life for their cause.[1] While the British movement was pushing full speed ahead in the early 1900s, suffragists on the American side of the Atlantic Ocean had hit a rut. No states had granted women the right to vote since the 1890s. On top of that, new enthusiasm for the cause seemed sluggish at best. By 1910, however, things started to look up for American suffragists. Washington State granted women the right to vote, kicking off a string of state victories. New suffragists also become involved in the movement.[2] Among the young leaders was Inez Milholland, a woman who would soon become America's own Joan of Arc.

On March 3, 1913, nearly eight thousand suffragists gathered in Washington, DC. That afternoon suffragists held a large parade in support of votes for women. Inez Milholland led the throng. Noted for her striking beauty and spunk, Milholland sat atop a white steed. Dressed in flowing white robes and wearing a golden headpiece she looked every bit like a modern-day Joan of Arc.[3] Supposedly, she simply depicted a generic figure called "The Herald," meant to represent the women of the American West who already had the vote. Almost immediately the public dismissed the concept. It seemed clear to everyone that this was instead the American version of Joan of Arc.[4]

For those at the parade, Milholland was a regal site to behold that harkened back to the age of heraldry and martyrdom. People not present at the procession also became familiar with the image as newspapers around the country printed photos of her. Long before the parade took place, Milholland had become a favorite among the press. Coming from a wealthy white household full of opportunity, the young woman led a privileged life. In addition to providing his family with financial stability, Milholland's father was also a noted social activist. He not only supported voting rights for women but also founded the National Association for the Advancement of Colored People. Without a doubt, he passed his social activism and progressive politics on to his daughter.[5]

Well traveled, well dressed, intelligent, and used to getting most of her desires, Milholland attended Vassar College. Active in the school's social and athletic scenes, she appeared in theatrical productions and earned world records in shot-put, basketball throwing, and jumping.[6] In 1908, she also gained a reputation for bucking authority when she organized a pro-suffrage lecture despite the school's rules forbidding it. After leaving Vassar, Milholland did not slow down. She earned a degree at New York University School of Law and secured a job at a law firm where she handled criminal and divorce litigation. She also worked as a journalist, and in addition to her support of suffrage, she advocated for worker's rights. In 1910, she was arrested alongside striking shirtwaist workers in New York City. It is no wonder that Milholland became a darling of the press. Outlandish for her time, she also had charm and beauty, two traits people quickly recognized.

Often described by opponents as old maids and unattractive, suffragists looked for ways to break the stereotype. Milholland provided the perfect platform. With long dark hair, noted beauty, and impeccable taste in clothing, she embodied the vision of femininity the movement desired, and suffrage leaders capitalized on Milholland's popularity. She participated in parades, gave speeches, and made public appearances in the name of women's voting rights. Loving the spotlight and motivated by activities that drew attention and promoted her image, Milholland had no issue with the arrangement.[7]

By 1916, both the suffrage movement and Milholland had gotten a lot of mileage out of her celebrity. In October of that year, she drew enormous crowds during a countrywide speaking tour for the National Woman's Party. Despite her robust appearance, Milholland's health had gone into decline and she suffered from a blood disorder. Pushed on by her prima donna behavior and the urging of suffragist Alice Paul, she ignored her symptoms. On October 23, while speaking before a crowd in Los Angles, she collapsed at the podium. Milholland was rushed to the hospital and treated for anemia and infected tonsils, but her condition only worsened. On November 25 she passed away at the age of thirty.

If Milholland's celebrity had been large in life, it grew even bigger in death. Quickly, the National Woman's Party resurrected the image of her as Joan of Arc. A memorial service in her honor was organized to take place in the US Capitol on Christmas Day of 1916. The brilliantly staged pageant utilized suffrage imagery and capitalized on the sorrow of her loss. In early January, a group of three hundred suffragists headed to the White House. Before her collapse, Milholland spoke these words, "President Wilson, how long must this go on?" Spurred by her call for action, they asked the president to honor Milholland's death by supporting their cause. They met his refusal with determination. Inez Milholland had been transformed from a figurative representation of Joan of Arc into a real-life martyr for suffrage. The National Woman's Party widely circulated the idealized image of her shown in the painting highlighted in this chapter, and adopted it as the organization's logo. In death, Milholland's martyrdom became the rallying cry for militant suffragists at the national, state, and local levels, propelling them into more extreme action.[8] Together with an array of figures, colors, and slogans, suffragists around the nation had built a network of symbols that took on deep meanings and, over time, promoted the idea of women's voting rights to lawmakers and citizens around the country.

Part IV

CONSUMER CULTURE AND PUBLICITY

From photographs documenting marches to quilts pieced from campaign ribbons, the women's suffrage movement has left behind a rich physical record of its story. While some items, such as letters, were private, other objects had always been intended for public consumption and to publicize the suffrage message and cause. By the twentieth century, both the suffrage movement and society had changed drastically since the time of the Seneca Falls Convention. With booms in urbanization, mass production, and communication, Americans had turned into modern consumers. Colorful advertisements dotted towns, large and small, around the country. And department stores catered to both shoppers' needs and wants. As the sheer volume of products, from clothing and household goods to trinkets and postcards, saturated the consumer market, Americans filled their homes with more and more things. At the same time, new entertainment options like motion pictures burst onto the scene, and businesses, companies, and organizations found new ways to publicize their ideas and commodities. This fast-paced, product-driven world of the 1910s bore little resemblance to the early years of the movement, and suffragists saw an opportunity. Hoping to appeal to modern America, they viewed this new consumer culture as a way to publicize their message, share information, and boost support for the movement. Whether the public knew it or not, suffragists hoped to influence its opinion on female voting rights through mediums as bold as cinema and as seemingly mundane as the everyday cookbook.

The Modern Shopper

Macy's Herald Square, National Historic Landmark, opened in 1902, New York City, NY, https://www.nps.gov/subjects/nationalregister/index.htm

JINWOO CHONG FOR UNTAPPED CITIES

What is Thanksgiving Day without the Macy's parade? While the annual tradition began in 1924, and in-person attendance grew steadily from year to year, not until after World War II did the event explode in size. The release of the 1947 film *Miracle on 34th Street* assisted in the parade's appeal. With real-life footage from the previous year's parade incorporated, the motion picture helped permanently link Santa Claus and Macy's in the public mind. Today, the parade draws millions of onlookers to New York City's streets, and countless more watch for Santa's arrival outside Macy's Herald Square from the comfort of their living rooms.[1] Before the parade or Santa's televised appearance, however, the department store at 151 West 34th Street already had a global reputation.[2] In fact, in the 1910s, its name recognition, beautiful window displays, and ability to draw hordes of shoppers became desirable commodities of suffragists looking to capitalize on consumerism.

Founded in 1858 on 14th Street and Sixth Avenue in New York City by Rowland Hussey Macy, Macy's originally functioned as a dry goods store. As the company expanded its wares it also looked for ways to distinguish itself from the competition. In 1861, the store's iconic red star was added to its logo, letterhead, and price tags.[3] By 1877, the company had moved beyond its humble beginnings, developing into a full-fledged department store occupying the ground space of eleven adjacent buildings. After outgrowing its storefront in 1902, the company moved uptown to the location at Herald Square. Its expansion in 1924 made it the largest store in the world, with more than one million square feet of retail space. Outfitted with modern amenities such as escalators, Macy's became an attraction for shoppers from around the world. Upon arriving at the store in the morning, customers could spend the rest of the day shopping for everything on their list. Under one roof shoppers could purchase clothing, housewares, food products, furniture, and more. They could have lunch, send their mail, and visit the salon.[4] Macy's was not just a store, it was a shopping experience and a destination.

While Macy's and other department stores expanded their national appeal in the early twentieth century, the suffrage movement worked to get the vote on a state-by-state basis. After early attempts to secure a federal amendment for women's voting rights flopped, suffragists turned to individual states for a solution. They hoped to build support piecemeal in order to eventually win suffrage on the federal level, but despite decade's worth of work, by 1911 only five states had enfranchised their female citizens.[5] For the new generation of suffragists entering the fight, it was clear that the movement needed to tune into modern society if it wanted to broaden its appeal to more people. And what was more modern than the department store?

Shopping districts had certainly existed in the past, but the emergence of the department store in the late nineteenth century transformed these urban centers into destinations, drawing thousands of individuals daily. At Macy's, Margaret Getchell LaForge, superintendent of the store and the first female executive in the industry, led this vision of grandeur.[6] By the twentieth century, the department store had become the domain of female shoppers. With the number of mass-produced goods constantly increasing, women no longer needed to produce items like clothing in their homes. Instead, middle-class women swarmed department stores around the country to undertake their new role as family consumer. Thanks to these establishments, they quickly realized that shopping for their families' needs could not only be done under one roof, but they were also a source of entertainment and amusement.[7]

The fit was natural. Suffragists needed a way to reach women, and department stores needed to increase their base of female shoppers to boost profits. For the politically-minded woman, a pair of "Womanalls," rather than overalls, could be purchased for tending the garden. While the "suffrage blouse" looked no different than other similar garments, the purchaser could feel as if she advocated for expanded rights whenever she wore it. On top of fashions, many stores also offered a variety of other suffrage-themed wares, such as postcards and jewelry.[8] Completing the link, suffrage publications like the *Woman Voter*, invited department stores to advertise in their pages and often endorsed specific products and businesses. Drawing further inspiration from the advertising strategies used by retailers, the movement embraced the art of publicity. Learning from example, they began producing billboards, posters, calendars, and even films to promote voting rights for women.[9]

At physical retailers, window displays became one of the most visible ways the suffrage cause found promotion. Over many years, department stores had refined the use of such spaces to produce eye-catching displays. When done correctly, they not only drew potential customers to the window but also through the doors. Activists saw this as a huge potential for communication to mass crowds. Using the tactics developed by retailers, activists could catch the eye of the public, transforming commercial spaces into venues for marketing suffrage-themed goods and political speech. By setting up displays filled with suffrage colors and merchandise, storeowners signaled their support of female customers while simultaneously showing off goods shoppers may want to buy. For male customers, the sight of a suffrage window proved that if successful businessmen considered women's enfranchisement a worthwhile cause, they might want to consider supporting it as well.

Following this trend, in 1912, Macy's and New York suffragists found the perfect way to blend their two interests. After suffrage victories in Michigan, Arizona, Oregon, and Kansas, New York's activists planned to celebrate with a nighttime torch parade. In addition to the numerous newspaper articles leading up to the event, Macy's department store created an elaborate window display to herald the upcoming march. Decorated in shades of yellow and orange, the display included a large portrait of Julia Ward Howe (an early suffrage advocate) and an American flag. On view were official suffrage hats, pennants, buttons, and other items that women could purchase inside. The trade journal *Merchants Record* described it as a "golden window, down to the gilt buttons, and even the fixtures." A leather saddle sat in the center of the display in honor of the many women who would appear on horseback during the march. In turn, suffragists named Macy's the headquarters for suffrage supplies and encouraged supporters to head to the store to stock up on the proper regalia for the event. For only $1.69, shoppers could purchase a complete marching outfit—including war bonnet, hatpins, lanterns, wide sash, chrysanthemum, stole, two buttons, and a pennant.[10] Upon entering the store, shoppers looking for such items were directed to the special suffrage section set up for the week of the parade.[11] If the newspaper reports were any indication, the window display, endorsement, and advertisements likely worked. The event drew thousands of participants with lanterns, hats, and other regalia. Even if only a portion of the marchers purchased their items directly through Macy's, the department store certainly profited from suffrage, and suffragists reaped the benefits of the department store's crowds.

As the suffrage movement embraced America's emerging consumer culture, department stores around the country proved themselves useful partners in the push toward women's voting rights. In San Francisco, the downtown shopping district not only boasted many shop windows, but most of the offices for the city's suffrage organizations. Through both proximity and deliberate partnerships, the area became a center for suffrage activity and advertisement.[12] In Chicago, activists received a boost in exposure when the department store Carson Pirie Scott installed a wax figure of a suffragist in one of its windows to announce the upcoming convention of the Woman's Party in 1916. Wanamaker's department store in Philadelphia took an even bolder step in aligning itself with women's voting rights when it began permitting all female employees to march in suffrage parades during working hours.[13] In Muncie, Indiana, a small industrial city, local suffragists partnered with McNaughton's Department Store in 1915 to place their "melting pot" for financial collections in the front window.[14]

For modern suffragists, this mingling of commercial and political space was celebrated and encouraged. Not only did it bring their movement into the daily lives of countless shoppers, in some ways it made commercial and political desires equal. If women now held the crucial role of household shopper, why not the responsibility of voter as well? By tapping into consumer society, suffragists capitalized on the customer base and name recognition of department stores. In return, department stores increased their own sales by appealing to the most modern of American women and shoppers, the suffragists. The unique relationship between department stores and suffragists has left the nation dotted with many historic buildings and sites with ties to women's voting rights that remain under the radar. While the historic beauty of Macy's Herald Square is undeniable, most of the shoppers who enter the store today have no idea they are walking into a place that was so meaningful to activists fighting for women's right to vote. As they pause at the front windows to consider what they may like to purchase, it goes to show suffragists were right more than one hundred years ago. Consumerism is a strong force, and by harnessing the power of commercial spaces, activists promoted women's voting rights by meeting the modern customer where she was.

19
Posters as Publicity

Poster, designed by Bertha M. Boye, 1911, The Bancroft Library, University of California–Berkeley, Berkeley, CA, http://www.lib.berkeley.edu/libraries/bancroft-library

Posters can be found in a variety of places, at movie theaters, on light posts, and in store windows just to name a few. Through words and pictures, they communicate many messages and publicize many things. With exciting photos, they may inform the viewer about an upcoming concert. A catchy slogan might promote a politician. And large bold lettering could notify shoppers about an upcoming sale. In other instances, a poster may be a mass-produced work of art meant for consumers to buy and hang on the walls of a home. In 1911, California suffragists turned to the poster as a major part of their campaign. Through eye-catching imagery, they looked to increase awareness of their cause, communicate their modernity, and draw support in advance of a vote to enfranchise women in their state. These goals resulted in a visual crusade that saturated the state with the official campaign poster seen on the facing page and put publicity front and center in the movement.

As early as the 1850s, the first posters used by suffragists and women's rights activists appeared in the United States. Meant to promote conventions or advertise upcoming rallies and speakers, these posters contained no illustrations, just words. Referred to as broadsides, they were cheap and quick to produce, proving themselves a tried-and-true standard of advertising. By the last quarter of the nineteenth century however, a new kind of poster burst onto the scene. Known as the art poster, this variety was often printed in color and relied far more on illustrations than words to convey a message or sentiment. While no replacement for the announcements or well articulated arguments broadsides provided, the visual appeal of the posters made them a compelling way to saturate the public with messages and images. By the twentieth century, suffragists began adopting the art poster for their own cause and even used design competitions to engage the public in pro-suffrage campaigns and publicity. As inexpensive, eye-catching propaganda, they were produced in huge quantities and displayed wherever possible, becoming some of the most produced objects of the suffrage movement.[1]

In California, activists in 1911 fully embraced the visual oomph art posters provided. That spring they embarked on the largest women's suffrage campaign yet tackled in the country. The year before, Washington State had run the first successful campaign in sixteen years. Riding the wave of momentum this victory created, California brought together a broad coalition of supporters ranging from waitresses and working women to upper-class society.[2] Even with this frenzy, suffragists anticipated a difficult fight. For far too long their movement had been stalled by the state's powerful liquor industry that feared women's suffrage would lead to Prohibition. Activists knew that to succeed, they needed to run the boldest, most dramatic campaign yet seen in the nation.[3] Fueled by this excitement, activists were willing to try almost anything to bring attention to their cause and reach as many people as possible. The result was a modern campaign that harnessed the latest features of America's booming consumer culture. Activists used and sold suffrage items such as stationery, lapel buttons, baggage stickers, and playing cards. Electric signs, billboards, and lantern slides were put into use for advertising, and literature was distributed across the state.[4] In this sea of products, the color yellow and the state's official suffrage poster always appeared as unifying symbols. Using vibrant colors and evocative imagery, the poster not only displayed suffragists' singular demand—"Votes for Women"—but also served to engage the public in the activities of the movement.[5]

Rather than hire someone to design the poster, on May 13, 1911, the *Oakland Tribune* published a short article announcing a statewide poster competition for a design to be used in the campaign for women's voting rights. Supported by the state's equal suffrage movement and sponsored by the San Francisco College Equal Suffrage League, the contest was open to any man, woman, or child and offered a tempting grand prize of $50 cash. The rules were straightforward: any designs submitted needed to be twenty-two by fourteen inches; yellow had to predominate; and all submissions had to be turned in with a false name written on the back to ensure unbiased judging. A sealed envelope containing the real identity and address of the artist also needed to accompany the design, not to be opened until after the judges made the winning selection.[6] Over the next month newspapers in the San Francisco metro area, looking to create as much interest in the competition as possible, carried similar announcements. At the same time, an additional essay contest as well as a song competition was announced, but neither created quite the buzz the poster contest seemed to generate.[7]

When the deadline for submissions arrived on June 15, more than thirty designs had been received. Careful consideration by the judges resulted in the announcement of Miss Bertha M. Boye as the winner. A local artist practicing both sculpture and painting, Boye had studied at the San Francisco Institute of Art, and with her design, she captured the spirit of California's suffrage movement. Within just a few days of the announcement, Boye's design was on exhibit in San Francisco alongside other works of handicraft created by male and female supporters of the suffrage proposition. At the same time, the artist herself worked to complete a final drawing so the poster could be reproduced by the campaign and distributed across the state.[8] Although already receiving a lot of exposure, an announcement in August that several department stores planned to include the poster in their window displays meant that even more eyes would see Boye's design. Accompanied by festive yellow decorations, flags, and cards with suffrage messages, the elegant poster became a sight to behold by shoppers.[9] In addition to full-size posters, the image was also produced by California's suffragists on postcards, placards, fliers, and publicity stamps, items distributed and sold by the campaign.[10]

In its varying forms, Boye's poster became the primary image used in California's 1911 suffrage campaign.[11] Her image of a chic, young western suffragist communicated that the old-fashion movement had seen its day and the modern woman had taken the lead. At the same time, the residents of California could recognize their culture and traditions in the figure standing in front of the iconic Golden Gate strait, with sun haloing her head. For anyone wondering what she stood for, the scroll in her hands declare "Votes for Women," in a very straightforward manner. With such an evocative image scattered across the state, California's suffragists hoped to appeal to their fellow citizens. The modern elements of the design reassured them that suffragists wanted to advance society, but like the traditional aspects of the artwork, they also respected the state's past.

When the campaign ended, California's suffragists had succeeded and, with a small electoral margin, the state's lawmakers gave their female citizens the right to vote. Recognizing the feat accomplished, suffragists across the nation sought copies of California's suffrage posters, literature, buttons, pennants, and paraphernalia. Mary Ware Dennett, an officer of the National American Woman Suffrage Association, even requested one sample of everything issued by the campaign be sent to her. Convinced many other suffragists could learn from California's modern, visual publicity, she organized a display of its promotional material at the upcoming national convention in Louisville, Kentucky. Without a doubt, several of the items in Dennett's display contained Boye's design, and it was not long before what had been the most popular image in California soon became one of the most recognizable images of the entire national movement.[12] Following the California campaign, states like New York, Iowa, and Pennsylvania drew inspiration from the western state and mounted their own poster competitions. While their winning designs did not reach the level of popularity of Boye's poster, their actions proved that California's bold embrace of publicity had caused a change in the national movement. From that point forward, women around the nation began to argue that publicity and consumer culture were not only crucial for communicating with the public, but also proved the suffrage movement's virtue, modernism, and seriousness.[13]

All Buttoned Up

Button, circa 1912, Arizona History Museum–Arizona Historical Society, Tucson, AZ, https://arizonahistoricalsociety.org/

Whether referred to as buttons or pins, most people have either received or purchased one as a souvenir at some point. For more than a century, the button has been a popular item in the world of memorabilia. Cheap to produce, and easy to distribute, these small items carry a big punch in terms of advertising and promotion. They can also allow individuals to make a statement by pinning a message or image proudly to their lapel. It is no wonder that these unassuming items are everywhere. From local festivals and gift shops to universities and theme parks, buttons provide many individuals, groups, and places a way to reach countless people. When the celluloid button exploded in popularity in the 1890s the political arena quickly grabbed onto it to endorse individuals running for office. While candidates and their campaigns swiftly embraced the item, it was suffragists who saw a greater political potential in the small novelty. They broadened the button's use from promoting a specific candidate into a way to advocate for a larger political cause or idea. As millions of pro-suffrage buttons were made, activists distributed them around the nation. In Arizona, pins like the one seen on the previous page played an important role in the state's final push for female voting rights; a campaign strongly linked with the territory's own fight for statehood.

Although the struggle from women's suffrage lasted for decades, much of the movement's colorful memorabilia was produced during the years between 1908 and 1917.[1] As it would turn out, the small, unassuming button proved to be one of the headliners for suffragists. Some form of lapel decoration had always been available for American presidential campaigns. There were clothing buttons with specialized designs worn to George Washington's inauguration; William Henry Harrison's presidential campaign saw several brooches created to promote his candidacy; and stickpins were a favorite of politicians for many years. In 1896, however, the campaign button became extensively used for the first time. Embraced by presidential candidates William McKinley and William Jennings Bryan, the newly invented, colorful, and inexpensive celluloid button became a major part of their campaigns, and from that point on, it was a mainstay of political elections. The use of the item soon extended into advertising when many manufacturers and companies realized the value of the button as a free giveaway to help hawk their wares.[2]

Seeing the successful use of pins in these various forms, suffragists recognized the graphic appeal of the item and reinvented its political use to meet their needs. If politicians could utilize buttons to promote individual candidates, why couldn't suffragists use them to advocate for a political cause? In the end, suffrage activists distributed countless buttons promoting voting rights for women. While they did not have the capability to produce them on their own, by the early twentieth century many firms were equipped to take suffragists' orders and churn them out at a rapid rate. With buttons in hand, activists sold the pins at their offices for as low as a penny each, while also distributing them at meetings, fairs, marches, and demonstrations. In New Jersey, suffrage leaders advised their followers never to conduct a meeting with speakers alone. Just as important as the special guest was the presence of buttons and other eye-catching items that attendees could purchase at a low price and take home. As a wearable item, buttons allowed the purchaser to boldly declare their own support of the cause and become a walking advertisement for the movement. While hard to tell exactly how many buttons suffragists spread across the nation, in 1918 the National American Woman Suffrage Association supplied campaigns in Michigan, South Dakota, and Oklahoma with fifty thousand pins. And in 1917, the New York campaign alone gave out one million.[3] While there were hundreds of button designs created, the most basic proved most popular. This meant pins in gold or yellow bearing the phrase "Votes for Women" became highly demanded around the nation. Not only did these simple designs appeal to suffragists because they were the cheapest and quickest to produce, but their simplicity also made them easily recognizable.

In the American West, suffragists embraced the new culture of consumerism and products in varying ways. California's 1911 campaign went all in, utilizing posters, billboards, buttons, and any other eye-catching products they could. To the south, Arizona chose to be more selective about the items used in its campaign the following year. In the 1880s, Arizona women saw several unsuccessful bills introduced to their territorial legislature that would extend to them the right to vote. The topic once again came up for debate in the 1890s when the territory looked to apply for statehood, but when President Benjamin Harrison denied the request, dreams of suffrage died along with the appeal.[4]

Over the next several years Arizona's fights for both suffrage and statehood grew increasingly difficult. At the national level, many members of Congress did not look favorably on granting state status to the territory. They viewed it as too sparsely populated; the desert environment insufficiently hospitable;

the economy unable to support steady economic growth; and the residents (many immigrants) too un-American and uneducated. To combat these perceptions, Arizona's territorial politicians waged a public relations campaign to improve their image. Suffragists quickly joined in, arguing that granting women the right to vote would help change the perception of the territory as a cultural backwater.[5] Not all politicians agreed with this assessment, however, and the governor denied female suffrage in 1903. When a second Constitutional Convention convened in 1910, politicians refused to include suffrage in their proposed constitution fearing it would cause the denial of their application once again. Frustration abounded among suffragists who had put in years of work promoting their cause and speaking in favor of statehood. When Arizona finally celebrated becoming a state in February 1912, women were noticeably absent from the festivities.

Not ones to be kept down, Arizona's suffragists quickly reacted. While the new state constitution did not provide women with the ability to vote, it did supply a provision to amend the document through an initiative process. If suffragists could collect enough petitions from male voters in the territory, an amendment granting female suffrage would be put forth to the general voting population; with no legislative action needed. Right away, Arizona's suffragists got to work. Between February and July, they collected the 3,342 signatures required by law, guaranteeing a women's suffrage initiative on the November ballot.[6] Once they had crossed that hurdle, activists began the nonstop work of promotion for the next four months. Now that voters had agreed to consider the issue of women's suffrage, they needed to be convinced that voting in favor of it was the only reasonable option. Arizona's suffragists approached this in a very careful manner, however. Because the state's politicians recently argued against granting women the right to vote, suffragists wanted to tread lightly and make sure voters knew women were not a liability, but rather, intelligent citizens with the best interests of the young state in mind. To do so, they ran a nonpartisan campaign, lobbying political parties, union leaders, and newspapers for their support.[7] These advocates would then use their own means of communication to spread support for women's suffrage.

Primarily using voice and pen, Arizona's activists ran a quiet campaign. Nonetheless, they still understood the need to harness the visual elements California had so effectively employed. In order to do so they went straight to the source, bringing California suffragist Alice Parks to Arizona to run the publicity work at the 1912 state fair. Deliberately chosen as the only sensational feature of the entire campaign, Parks led the distribution of buttons, literature, and flags at the event, an attraction sure to draw residents from every corner of the new state.[8] Taking place in October, the sights and sounds of the fairgrounds would still be fresh in voters' minds as they headed to the polls the next month. With this in mind, Parks wanted to ceaselessly arouse interest in the cause by using eye-catching yellow buttons, banners, and pennants liberally. Besides a dedicated suffrage booth, activists even arranged for the grandstand to be draped in yellow bunting, and for suffragists to distribute "Votes for Women" pins to the crowd between races.[9] A firm believer in the power of the button in particular, Parks once said, "Every badge, pin, or button is a help, arousing curiosity among strangers, stimulating conversation among acquaintances and discussion among friends and antis."[10]

On November 5, 1912, the citizens of Arizona passed their state's women's suffrage amendment with 68 percent of the popular vote. It was only nine months since the territory had become a state, but through a brief, yet carefully crafted campaign, suffragists proved they, too, deserved the right to vote. By deliberately employing the use of visual products during the state fair, they had shown, yet again, that suffragists understood the importance of utilizing the nation's taste for consumerism to meet their own needs. While novelties such as buttons may seem trivial today, they held an important meaning to the suffragists who oversaw their creation and witnessed the enthusiastic response the voting public had for the items.[11] Not only did buttons allow suffragists to produce income through sales, but each time one was pinned to a lapel it also served as a personal statement. Unlike sashes typically worn only during special events, buttons could be put on every day in support of the suffrage cause. Taking it a step further, the wearer also became a walking advertisement for the movement, and through the donning of "Votes for Women" pins, the public helped suffragists button up the issue of female voting rights.

A Recipe for Success

Cookbook—*Washington Women's Cook Book*, 1909, Washington State Historical
Society, Tacoma, WA, http://www.washingtonhistory.org/

In the United States, many citizens looking to satisfy their sweet tooth antici-pate the sale of cookies by the Girl Scouts each year. Whether a fan of the popular Thin Mints or another of the tasty treats, it is easy to snatch up a box or two without much thought. In fact, with the sweet treats motivating sales, many people forget their purchases help fund experiences for local troops, while the program itself teaches entrepreneurial skills such as teamwork and planning to girls across the nation. If the Girl Scouts' purpose and work has slipped the customer's mind at the time of purchase, they will certainly be reminded once the product reaches their home. Every time they grab the box for a quick treat, the organization's logo and information about their mission is visible right on the packaging. In a similar manner, suffragists produced their own products that not only served as fundraisers, but also appealed to the average consumer. In Washington State, suffragists looked to consumer culture for ways to support and advance their agenda, leading to the creation and sale of a cookbook for the everyday woman. Through the publication, ac-tivists made sure each time the owner consulted the pages they not only found tasty recipes and helpful tips, but also a pro-suffrage message.

From their earliest years, suffragists funded their own campaigns and work through donations, membership dues, and fundraisers. Always look-ing for new ways to bring in money, in 1886 the Massachusetts Woman Suffrage Association turned to an idea flourishing in the years following the Civil War. Needing to raise funds for war victims and church-related is-sues, women in the late 1860s and 1870s often produced charity cookbooks. Given the success these projects achieved, Massachusetts' suffragists pub-lished the first in a string of cookbooks infused with a pro-suffrage agenda. In fact, between the late 1880s and 1920, at least a half-dozen cookbooks published by various pro-suffrage associations popped up around the na-tion, from Massachusetts to Washington. While these books did not come off the presses in the same quantities as other suffrage goods, their smaller numbers did not make them less important. Products like posters and but-tons served as vehicles for publicity and blatant personal advocacy. The cookbooks served a different purpose altogether.[1]

Typically conceived as fundraisers, suffragists hoped the sale of their cookbooks would bring in additional funds to help support their activities. While the monetary incentive appealed to activists, it was not the only benefit reaped from the creation of such products. Through selling the books women networked and gained new skills in the fields of publishing, advertising, and sales.[2] More importantly, as items many women consulted daily, cookbooks held a unique ability to promote suffrage while making it accessible to the average housewife. As the home cook picked up the book to reference a favorite recipe, she was reassured that a desire to vote did not mean abandoning her traditional role and female image, the two could easily go hand in hand. The inclusion of pro-suffrage imagery and quotations alongside recipes, household tips, and advice for childrearing further underscored this concept. The cookbooks made it clear that suffragists supported the role of women as housekeepers and protectors of the family. In fact, they believed their culinary duties made them responsible citizens worthy of preserving the health, safety, and morality of the home at the voting booth. [3]

Suffragists also used cookbooks to directly push back against the stereotypes painting them as neglectful mothers and kitchen-hating shrews.[4] With the recipes coming from the tried and true kitchens of suffragists themselves, they knew it would be hard for anyone to claim they did not know their way around a stove. And if that did not do the trick, they could always fall back on wit. A 1915 publication put together by the Equal Franchise Federation of Western Pennsylvania included in its pages a recipe for "Anti's Favorite Hash." Detailing the necessary ingredients for a typical anti-suffragist, the recipe explains that antis ruin the virtue of truth and justice, which women must uphold. Therefore, suffragists surely make better mothers, wives, and homemakers.[5]

In Washington State, the cookbook appealed to activists as a way to quietly slide the suffrage message into the homes of many citizens without making a stir. In its years as a territory, Washington had a volatile suffrage history, including the passage of multiple suffrage bills, all doomed to be overturned. By the twentieth century, Washington had been granted statehood. In 1909, suffragists poised themselves to launch a campaign demanding the legislature pass a measure allowing a vote to amend the state constitution. Rather than make a public splash with large events and public rallies, suffragists in the state instituted what was known as the still-hunt strategy. They focused quietly on the personal, intensive work of wives, mothers, and sisters to influence the men who could vote at the polls. In doing so they distributed one million pieces of literature around the state. They also secured support from influential groups like the Washington State Grange, Labor Unions, and the Farmer's Union.[6] In avoiding big demonstrations like parades and large meetings, suffragists hoped to keep anti-suffragists and a potential countercampaign at bay.[7]

Holding tight to their plan to focus on influencing male voters through everyday women, in 1909 and 1910 the Washington Equal Suffrage Association sold their recently published *Washington Women's Cook Book*. Comprised of recipes submitted by suffragists from around the state, the publication looked to sooth men who worried that voting women would abandon their domestic duties. At the same time, it gave suffragists a way to launch a surprise attack from within private kitchens. In order to sell the books, Washington's suffragists pulled out all the punches. They not only advertised in local newspapers, but also sent workers out on foot with packages of books under their arms. Additionally, they set up booths at state and county fairs, selling the cookbooks alongside traditional consumer goods like "Votes for Women" buttons and pennants. At the same time, various suffrage clubs around the state gave programs on pure food, and discussed and exhibited examples of healthy menus.[8] As an added publicity boost, in September of 1910 suffragists and the *Tacoma News* teamed up. They launched a contest calling for essays to convince men that pro-suffrage women were just as familiar as any other with the problems of the kitchen.[9] Thirty-five miles north, the *Seattle Star* used its regular "Mary's Cook Book" column to highlight dishes from the cookbook. The newspaper also gave a glowing review of the publication, heaping praise not only on the recipes and various household hints for beauty and hygiene, but also on the design. "It is gotten up in very attractive style, with a white oil cover which can be washed, and the yellow suffrage banner with the slogan, "Votes for Women," decorates the front cover."[10]

On November 8, 1910, the cookbook proved its worth to state suffragists when the amendment to the state constitution easily passed. Every county voted in favor of the measure, although it only enfranchised a restricted portion of the state's women. Written to only allow those who could read and speak English to vote, the law excluded many women from the polls. Additional segments of the population, such as Asian immigrants and American Indians, were also kept from voting by restrictive citizenship laws. Despite these shortcomings, by becoming the first state in the twentieth century to pass suffrage for women, Washington's campaign renewed an interest in suffragists around the country to fight for a national amendment.[11] Their cookbook had gained national attention as well, and when numbers were to-taled, about three thousand copies of the *Washington Women's Cook Book* had been sold. Even though the publication failed to turn a profit, it had drawn attention through advertisements placed in the National American Woman Suffrage Association's *Woman's Journal*. In 1913, recipes from the book even made their way from the West Coast to the East Coast, when the cookbook became a special feature of a "Votes for Women" grocery opened in New York City.[12] Washington's suffragists may have never imagined their message and cookbook would reach audiences outside the borders of their own state. When the *Washington Women's Cook Book* appeared on shelves in New York City, it proved the women of Washington had put together a winning product. As the tempting recipes for puddings and cakes convinced customers to purchase a copy, they may not have realized that the volume was much more than a household reference. With each volume sold, the new owners took home a daily reminder that votes for women and the kitchen went hand in hand.

Suffrage on the Silver Screen

Movie Advertisement—"*Your Girl and Mine*," *The Daily Ardmoreite*, April 15, 1915, Oklahoma Historical Society, Oklahoma City, OK, https://www.okhistory.org/
OKLAHOMA HISTORICAL SOCIETY

In the age of technology, video is everywhere and no one can deny the major role it plays in consumer culture. It is imbedded in social media feeds and pops up on screens when pumping gas at the filling station. No longer does an individual have to seek out videos; instead they are served to them without warning and often the content comes preselected based on the viewer's interests and previous online activity. In many ways this constant stream of images has taken away some of the magic moving pictures once held. Rather than being a novelty, videos are commonplace, and without enough action or special effects, may seem mundane. While this comes as no surprise in the twenty-first century, in 1915 almost every movie could shock and amaze. Televisions, smart phones, and streaming devices did not overwhelm the public and vie for its attention. And with cinema still young and fresh, viewing a movie weekly, let alone on a daily basis, was not the norm. Rather than head to a large cineplex of modern standards, the American public took in movies at many small theaters showing only one or two films on specified days and times. Even then, movies could mean big bucks, and cinema had already become a player in the nation's consumer culture.

Needless to say, when the ad seen on the previous page for the film *Your Girl and Mine* hit newspapers in the southern Oklahoma community of Ardmore, the proprietors of the Majestic Theatre knew they would get customers through the door.[1] While the first films to mesmerize audiences in the 1890s lasted less than a minute in length, by the 1910s cinema had blossomed into a full-fledged industry with numerous companies looking to make profits on their big-budget, full-length productions. Still new, however, the novelty of movies had not yet worn off. The demand remained high, and almost any film, no matter its subject or production quality, drew a crowd. This led theaters to show whatever they could get their hands on.[2] With this perfect balance of novelty and demand, suffragists saw an opportunity to sell their message.

Recognizing the growing popularity of this new entertainment form, pro-suffrage activists realized that unlike a speech drawing hundreds of listeners, or a pamphlet influencing thousands, movies had the potential to reach millions of viewers across the nation from a variety of social classes and backgrounds.[3] Additionally, movies had the unique ability to touch people's hearts. Through the staging of pageants and plays, suffragists had already learned that narratives and drama were a sure hook. With the novelty of a movie added to the mix, the results were breathtaking. As the audience watched the story on the screen play out, they unknowingly experienced the same emotions and feelings of the characters on screen. If the protagonist panicked, so did the audience. When star-crossed lovers fell into melancholy, paying customers sympathized with their plight, and cheers erupted when heroines and heroes triumphed. Knowing firsthand that films touched viewers' hearts in such a direct way, suffragists wondered what would happen if those storylines carried messages about women's need and desire to vote. If an audience shared the emotions of suffragists on-screen, would they take a step toward converting to the cause?[4]

To test this theory, suffrage proponents produced four popular films between 1912 and 1914. This was not the first time activists or their ideas reached the silver screen, however. In 1898, they made their on-screen debut when the short British comedy *The Lady Barber* portrayed a suffragist taking over a barbershop and frantically cutting the hair of the bewildered male customers. From then on, suffragists often served as comic parodies in films; women to be laughed at and mocked.[5] This was something activists planned to change.

Of all four films, 1914's *Your Girl and Mine* was envisioned as the "Uncle Tom's Cabin" of suffrage films. Just as the literary work had spurred interest in the abolishment of slavery, suffragists hoped *Your Girl and Mine* would ignite the spark to secure voting rights for all women.[6] Initiated by the National American Woman Suffrage Association (NAWSA), the group pulled out all the stops to make the film as appealing to general audiences as possible. With a long list of professional credentials attached to the film, NAWSA also communicated their own desire to be taken seriously. To bring their vision to life, William N. Selig (a well-known filmmaker and women's rights supporter) and the World Film Company (an important player in the early film industry) joined the group in producing and distributing the motion picture. Selig then brought on Gilson Willettes, an acclaimed writer of other popular silent films, to write the scenario while well-known and respected actors received handsome salaries of "four figures per week" to play the lead roles.[7] Throughout the summer of 1914, the crew worked in a mad rush at the Selig studio in Chicago so the film could hit theaters before the November elections. With suffrage on the ballot in seven states, having the film done in time proved crucial. Nationally recognized suffragists and activists such as Anna Howard Shaw and Jane Addams even worked it into their schedules to make brief appearances onscreen.[8]

Telling the tale of the average woman, *Your Girl and Mine* reveals the myriad of problems any daughter, sister, wife, or friend might suffer in states without women's suffrage. By taking such an approach, activists hoped to show the need for expanded roles and rights for women in a way the everyday moviegoer could relate to.[9] As the action unfolds on the screen, the message becomes clear—women need voting rights in order to amend unfair laws. Looking to keep the interest of varied audiences, however, this message was delivered with a good helping of spice. The story focuses on the plight of a woman forced to pay the debts of an alcoholic husband whose mistress and illegitimate child perish in a tenement fire after he has deserted them. When the main character's husband dies, her father-in-law takes custody of her children according to the terms of the will, even though she is a fit parent. She later abducts her daughters, only to face arrest. Not to worry, however, a female lawyer saves the day when she argues, "If this mother's act was a crime, then all mothers are potential criminals."[10]

When *Your Girl and Mine* finally hit theaters, World Film made sure advertisements for it saturated the media and public. Besides print ads in newspapers, posters, lobby cards, and ads on streetcars abounded. In many instances, suffrage groups also worked to promote the movie and arranged for showings at their local movie houses. Attracting national personalities of the suffrage movement, the Chicago and New York premiers created quite the spectacle, and initial reviews from *Billboard* and the *New York Clipper* raved about the production.[11] Over the next year, the film screened in various states around the country, including Oklahoma, Illinois, Indiana, New York, Pennsylvania, Minnesota, and Texas. Despite the press coverage and favorable reviews, the film failed to attract a substantial audience and ended up a financial flop.[12] Perhaps suffragists had overestimated the crowds they would draw by wrapping suffrage up in the packaging of fun and fanciful melodrama. Although driven by the desire to convert viewers into supporters, time and again promotions of the film emphasized the focus on entertainment instead of suffrage. This focus on attracting paying customers had pushed politics to the back seat. Despite this, the public knew the true intentions of the film, and in the end, people not interested in women's voting rights stayed away while supporters bought up tickets.[13]

By accounts of local newspapers, the Majestic Theatre in Ardmore, Oklahoma, ran two viewings of *Your Girl and Mine* in 1915, and other theaters around the state did the same. Just three years later, Oklahoma's women won the right to vote within the state borders. Whether the film had any direct bearing on the decision cannot be known. Either way, suffragists clearly viewed their foray into motion pictures with utmost seriousness, and with shrewd know-how they used dramatic narrative to connect emotionally with people outside their movement.[14] In the end, turning a profit did not pan out. But, the number of tickets sold had never been their main concern. Instead, activists hoped cinema would inspire new people to support suffrage, even if the venture took a toll on their bank account. By utilizing motion pictures as a communication and publicity tool, suffragists proved once again that they understood modern society and continued to take risks for a cause they believed in wholeheartedly. Throughout the 1910s, they turned to and adapted consumer culture in multiple ways to help meet their own needs. These actions gained the interest of a public eager for the latest and greatest product or form of entertainment, making consumerism and suffrage a winning combination.

Part V

ALLIES

For decades, suffragists toiled to gain voting rights for women. As the struggle dragged on, activists embraced successes when and where they could. It is a rare case, however, for a single person or group to bring about monumental change without outside help. Without fail, allies provide the crucial support and momentum needed to succeed with such huge tasks. For suffragists, this backing came in various shapes and forms at different times. Even before a separate suffrage movement had formed, supporters of antislavery and women's rights became intertwined, making many abolitionists early supporters of those agitating for women's voting rights. Just as many of suffrage's first leaders identified with the abolition cause, many also aligned themselves with the temperance movement—support that was returned by temperance workers around the nation. In the nineteenth century, many suffragists had also spent years trying to distance themselves from the working classes for fear they would discredit their work. In the twentieth century, however, activists woke up to the reality that the labor movement could be a potent ally. If suffragists scratched the backs of laborers, they would return the favor. In the end, each group came closer to achieving their own goals. While the suffrage movement worked to expand the rights of women, support did not come only from the female sex. Men in the private sector got alongside the movement as well, demonstrating to lawmakers that the desire for suffrage went well beyond the wishes of just a few women.

23

Catching Fire

Print—*Destruction by Fire of Pennsylvania Hall, On the night of the 17th May, 1838*, by John Casper Wild, 1838, The Library Company of Philadelphia, Philadelphia, PA, https://librarycompany.org/

Just as a match ignites a fire, at times one action can spark another and one cause may influence others. In the first part of the nineteenth century, the strength of the antislavery movement grew in the United States. While the work of abolitionists focused on ending the practice of slavery, their organizations, methods, and memberships had impacts beyond their own movement. Alongside them, women's rights activists were stirred to action, and in the years before a separate suffrage movement, they began contemplating their own roles in society. It is in pulling back the layers that the complexities and offshoots can be seen. Very rarely is a picture as simple as it first appears on the surface. For instance, the print seen on the previous page tells a much bigger story than what first meets the eye. Executed in 1838 by John Casper Wild, this lithograph documents a destructive event in Philadelphia's history. Meant for mass production, Wild ensured that his artwork documented and commemorated an act of hatred that would resonate into the future. While on the surface it looks to only depict an incident of heartbreak for abolitionists, a deeper look reveals how circumstances and allied support caused fire to catch from one movement to another.

Soon after the end of the American Revolution, Philadelphia gained a reputation as the birthplace of abolitionism—the movement to end slavery. With the newly independent United States forming its own identity, some Christians questioned how the practice of slavery aligned with the ideals of freedom and justice enshrined in the Declaration of Independence. Seeing this hypocrisy, antislavery advocates began to call for the gradual emancipation of enslaved people. By the 1830s, the sentiment had gained momentum in the north, and many advocates began demanding the immediate end of the practice. Looking to capture Christian sympathy, abolitionist leaders like former slave Frederick Douglass and white religious radical William Lloyd Garrison sought to convert churches to an understanding that slavery was a sin. Once this became an accepted teaching, they believed they could enlist church members in the antislavery cause, growing support for their movement.

As progress was made, a hiccup occurred when women looking for ways to become involved in social reform, began joining many of the new abolition organizations. Finding themselves excluded from leadership roles in these antislavery societies, women began speaking out for themselves and their right to play a more active role in the movement.[1] Discussions about women's rights and women's place in society soon followed. It quickly became apparent that many people believed women should not hold any position higher than a man. Even the idea of members of the female sex addressing fellow male abolitionists pushed the envelope too far for some. William Lloyd Garrison and other abolitionists, on the other hand, supported female activists and argued that women had an important role to play in the movement. Amid this mixed bag of support, some women began forming their own separate female antislavery societies in the 1830s. These groups allowed women to work for the antislavery cause and brought women's rights advocates together to discuss other issues important to them, such as women's voting rights. In 1837, several of these female-run organizations held a joint national meeting in New York City.[2] The following year the group met in Philadelphia at Pennsylvania Hall, a newly constructed venue for the free discussion of abolition and other reforms.[3]

Prior to the building of Pennsylvania Hall, abolitionists in the area called for the immediate release of enslaved people from their bondage, but these demands did not sit well with all white citizens of the country. Some believed firmly in white superiority and saw nothing wrong with the institution of slavery. Others resented the mere presence of free blacks who caused competition for employment. As this animosity grew, tensions reached a boiling point. As a result, many churches and meetinghouses refused to rent facilities for antislavery gatherings. To overcome this obstacle, abolitionists in Pennsylvania joined forces to raise money for the construction of a large meetinghouse that could accommodate their needs and be shared with other reforms, such as women's rights advocates. The resulting structure promoted equal rights and free discussion among all people.[4]

To celebrate the grand opening of Pennsylvania Hall on May 14, 1838, abolitionists from around the country attended a multiday ceremony featuring speeches and meetings, including the second annual Antislavery Convention of American Women. For three days, groups met, held discussions, and noted abolitionists addressed crowds made up of men and women, black and white. Among those who spoke at the dedication ceremonies was Lucretia Mott; one of the most famous white female abolitionists in the nation, who also spoke out for women's rights, and later became a supporter of the National Woman Suffrage Association.[5] The triumph did not last long. Almost immediately, resistance to the hall and what it symbolized emerged. Rumors that abolitionists promoted inappropriate behavior between the races swirled and protestors on the streets threw bricks at windows. By the evening of May 17, rioting had escalated. A group of dock workers broke down the doors of the building and upon entering began setting fire to the hall. Fueled by the gas piped to the building for lighting, it did not take long for flames to consume the structure.[6]

In the aftermath of the destruction, two key factors were identified as the primary reasons for the rioters' extreme action: the intermingling of whites and blacks and the presence of women as attendees and speakers. Already, the presence of women in abolitionist circles had caused some people to limit women's roles in their organizations. Now mob action attempted to silence women as well. For some female abolitionists it became clear that their participation in antislavery activities was not just about the plight of slaves, but equally about their own inequality.[7] As disagreement over women's roles in abolition groups continued, female activists turned more time over to the discussion of women's rights. After female delegates, including Lucretia Mott, were barred from speaking at the 1840 World Anti-Slavery Conference, the topic of women's rights became even more enhanced. Eight years later, things came to a head when Mott and a group of abolition supporters convened at the Seneca Falls Convention to discuss issues of gender equality.[8]

Over time, a powerful connection had formed between antislavery and women's rights advocates. In fact, many of the people who came to identify themselves first and foremost as women's rights workers began as abolitionists. Between the time of the Seneca Falls Convention and the Civil War, virtually all women's rights advocates supported antislavery work. In fact, many of these women's first introductions to reform efforts occurred through the abolition movement. For the women who now spent more time focusing on female rights, abolitionists remained a strong ally. Just as women's rights advocates promoted antislavery efforts, many abolitionists promoted female equality. As the issue of suffrage became the focus of the women's rights movement, influential abolitionists like Frederick Douglass, William Lloyd Garrison, and Lucretia Mott lent their support.[9] Working alongside one another, both groups advocated universal suffrage for all citizens, and women's suffrage broke out as a movement on its own.

In the aftermath of the Civil War, however, the two groups began to drift apart. When Republican politicians introduced the 14th and 15th Amendments extending voting rights to black male citizens, not all abolitionists and suffragists saw eye to eye. As Elizabeth Cady Stanton and Susan B. Anthony led one group campaigning against any amendment denying voting rights to women, another group, with support of notable abolitionists like Frederick Douglass, supported the ballot for black males before securing it for women. As a result, the women's suffrage movement broke into two competing organizations: the National Woman Suffrage Association and the American Woman Suffrage Association.

Even with this significant fracture, suffragists owed a substantial debt to the antislavery movement. The work of abolition had served as a training ground for women's suffrage supporters, and the obstacles they faced spawned the women's rights work that formed their early years.[10] When the suffrage movement split in two, antislavery and women's rights advocate Lucretia Mott tried to mend the broken relationship. For her, the sight of old allies quarreling cut deep. As a speaker at the opening ceremonies at Pennsylvania Hall, Mott witnessed the destruction anger could create. Two years later, she joined forces with fellow abolitionists, after being barred from the World Anti-Slavery Convention, and in 1848 she worked with fellow women's rights advocates to make the Seneca Falls Convention a reality. Although her mediation attempts failed, Mott and fellow abolitionists brought years of wisdom to the emerging suffrage movement. As loyal allies, they watched the push for women's rights catch fire, and as the suffrage movement took off as its own cause, echoes of the past could still be heard.

Converting to the Cause

Stained Glass Window, 1898–1913, Whitley County Historical Museum, Columbia City, IN, http://www.whitleymuseum.com/

PHOTOGRAPH OF AUTHOR

Walking into history museums both local and national, visitors encounter objects from the past. These historic artifacts can range from as small as Mrs. Tom Thumb's wedding ring to as large as Charles Lindbergh's airplane. While some have instantly recognizable stories, others can be a bit more mysterious. The same can be said for the institutions that care for the nation's historic treasures. Where nearly everyone has heard of the Smithsonian, there are countless other museums ranging from the very large to the very small that many people have never heard of. No matter the size of their budget, staff, or building, however, each one plays a vital role in telling the collective story of suffrage. In Columbia City, Indiana, a rural midwestern farming community, the Whitley County Historical Museum cares for and displays the stained glass window seen on the facing page.[1] Saved from a former Methodist church in the community, this beautiful window tells the story of the congregation's past. It also bears the image of Frances Willard, one-time president of the Woman's Christian Temperance Union. Considered one of the most recognizable women in the world when she died in 1898, it would be easy to see this window only as a memorial to Willard and her work to promote abstinence from alcohol. Like many historic objects and museums, however, this window has many stories to tell. One even reveals how under Willard's guidance, the women's temperance movement became one of the suffragists' staunchest allies, even when some activists may have wished they were not.

Since the 1840s, female reformers had been concerned with the question of temperance, abstinence from alcohol. Living in a society with widespread alcohol consumption, the issue appealed to black and white women for moral reasons as well as practical ones. Lacking many legal rights, married women often found themselves at the mercy of their husbands' actions. When drunkenness came into play, women had no recourse when their partners squandered money, or in some cases abused them and their children. Recognizing they had no legal redress in such circumstances, many early women's rights activists became temperance advocates, as well as abolitionists and suffragists.[2] In 1874, a temperance crusade with strong evangelical overtones erupted in Ohio and spread across the country. Temperance workers formed vocal groups that held meetings in churches, on street corners, and inside saloons. In the face of their constant singing, praying, and vocal opposition to liquor, many thousands of drinking establishments shuttered their doors. The drama was short-lived, however, and in no time many of the saloons reopened.[3]

Growing out of this crusade, the Woman's Christian Temperance Union (WCTU) formed in Cleveland, Ohio, later that year. The national organization had a succinct goal—protect the home. Through education and example, the group hoped to obtain pledges of total abstinence from alcohol and tobacco. If things went as planned, this would provide women and children with homes better suited for their safety and morality.[4] After the group's founding, Frances Willard, a well respected and ambitious white female educator in northern Illinois, served as the WCTU's first corresponding secretary.[5] Never shy to share her viewpoints, Willard made it clear she believed political influence as well as moral persuasion would be needed if the organization hoped to outlaw all drinking in the nation. In 1876, she spoke in favor of women's voting rights as a tool to achieve legal prohibition at the group's national convention. Although she faced opposition to the idea from the union's conservative president, Willard went on to unseat her within three years, and it was not long before the WCTU transformed into a political force working for the suffrage cause.[6]

In the 1880s, the suffrage movement had already started looking for allies. They knew that in order to win suffrage, large numbers of women and men needed to support their cause. Under Willard's leadership the WCTU grew at an unprecedented rate and was much larger and more powerful than the national suffrage organizations.[7] This made them an appealing target for suffragists. At the same time, Willard promoted a policy of "do everything" and encouraged WCTU members to support any cause that would help restrict and reduce the use of alcohol.[8] This made suffrage a desirable asset for temperance workers. While suffragists tended to claim the vote primarily as a matter of justice, the WCTU asked for the ballot as a tool to achieve their organizational goals. In 1881, the national arm of the organization formed a Franchise Department, and it was not long before members implemented lobbying techniques. Across the country WCTU members collected signatures on petitions, circulated literature, hosted nationally renowned speakers, wrote and produced suffrage plays, and sponsored debates.[9]

So how exactly did Willard convince an organization made up largely of conservative evangelical women to support a cause that seemed blatantly radical to many? First, it helped that she and other leaders genuinely believed in the suffrage cause. To spread support further among WCTU membership,

Willard found common ground between the two groups with the "Home Protection Ballot" campaign. This made it clear to temperance supporters that women were the morally superior sex and therefore needed the vote to protect the sanctity of the home.[10] If any worry remained that supporting suffrage was unwomanly or unchristian, she shared her personal story of conversion. According to Willard, during a time of prayer in the 1870s, God communicated that she should "speak for woman's ballot as a weapon of protection to her home and tempted loved ones from the tyranny of drink."[11] For those worried that suffrage did not align with their Christian beliefs, Willard's assurance that it was God's will soothed their anxieties.

While Willard's personal call to action appealed to the national organization's largely white membership, black temperance workers had their own motivating forces. For decades, many people in black communities blamed political corruption and family breakdown on substance-abuse problems. Knowing that one solution was legislation to control public drinking, black temperance supporters quickly recognized women's suffrage as a direct way for them to legislate against alcohol abuse, and they advocated openly on the issue. In the late 1880s, black activist Frances Watkins Harper took on the role of the Pennsylvania State Superintendent of Work among the Colored People for the WCTU. From her place of influence, Harper persuaded white leadership of the need to include African American women in the organization's work and became the first black woman to serve on the executive board. When it became clear that many WCTU organizations would not open their ranks to integrated membership, however, black women, with encouragement from Harper, formed their own segregated unions to argue for both temperance and women's suffrage. By the twentieth century, numerous black temperance groups had formed around the nation in states such as Washington, South Carolina, Tennessee, and Rhode Island. While these segregated unions allowed African American women independence and leadership roles not available to them in mainstream clubs, the exclusionary actions of the WCTU perpetuated the stereotype of blacks as second-class citizens.[12]

Although suffragists eagerly accepted temperance workers' support at first, over time they began trying to distance themselves from the WCTU. In fact, in many cases white suffrage leadership went to a lot of trouble to publicly deny the existence of an official alliance between their organization and the temperance movement.[13] Not surprisingly, liquor interests had always been in direct opposition of temperance workers. If the WCTU succeeded in their goals it would mean declining liquor sales. When the WCTU began lobbying full force for the vote, the suffrage movement also became a target of opposition from brewers, distillers, and their kind.[14] Fear that liquor interests and their money controlled many politicians' choices led mainstream suffragists to walk a fine line. On one hand, they needed the support that the WCTU could provide. On the other, they feared isolating their political backers.

Always focused on their own goal first, however, the WCTU and black temperance workers continued to work to secure votes for woman to secure prohibition of liquor. Following Willard's death in 1898, the WCTU continued to campaign for suffrage on a municipal and state level. By 1908, thirty-seven of its forty-six state branches had their own Franchise Departments. When the push for a prohibition amendment to the US Constitution geared up between 1914 and 1917, it occupied much of the WCTU's time. They did not lose sight of the ballot however, and when the vote was won the organization began providing civic education to its members so they could become informed voters who would base their political choices on God's teachings.[15] Just as Frances Willard had modeled decades earlier, the WCTU saw voting and Christian beliefs as intertwined components of their work. Although their approach caused problems for the suffrage movement at times, it cannot be denied that their support of voting rights proved crucial to suffrage organizations in the late nineteenth and early twentieth centuries. As the largest and most powerful social reform group at the time, the WCTU's allegiance brought many new supporters to the suffrage cause. Without these allies, suffrage organizations needing to reinvigorate their ranks and attract new members, would have had a much harder fight on their hands.

25

Men for Suffrage

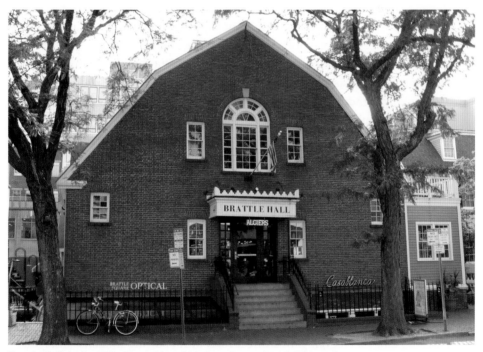

Brattle Hall, built 1889, Cambridge, MA, http://www.brattlefilm.org/

Walking into the Brattle Theatre, not far from Harvard University's campus, patrons find themselves stepping into an intimate theater with a nostalgic feel. Known for its offerings of art house films as well as classics, Brattle Theatre has been screening cinematic treasures since the 1950s. Before its turn as a movie house however, the building was home to the Brattle Theatre Company and other dramatic organizations. From its initial opening in 1890 until its shift to cinema, notable personalities of the theater, including T. S. Eliot, Jessica Tandy, and Zero Mostel graced the Brattle's stage.[1] Above the front door of the building a sign reads, "Brattle Hall," a nod to the structure's early years when it served not only as the home of theatrical productions, but also hosted meetings and lectures. In 1911, one such event caused quite a stir when a noted suffragist took the stage. Her appearance was not at the request of fellow women however, but rather from a group of young men who did not shy away from ruffling feathers at Harvard University to support what they believed a noble cause.

Often, outside appearances can be deceiving. With a strong reputation as a cinema, it is easy enough to assume the Brattle Theatre has a history beginning and ending with movies. A closer look, however, reveals layers of complexity. Similarly, all too often people expect that women supported suffrage and men did not. This could not be farther from the truth. Many men supported voting rights for women, and countless numbers of male citizens around the country found ways to be proud and dedicated allies. Individually, American men had publicly supported the rights of women as far back as the eighteenth century. In 1775, Thomas Paine, the political activist who became famous for his pamphlet *Common Sense*, wrote an essay titled "An Occasional Letter on the Female Sex." In this work he made clear his disgust with the treatment of women and used his voice for their defense.[2]

As time passed, men began writing specifically in support of women's voting rights, and after the Seneca Falls Convention in 1848, Frederick Douglass and Ralph Waldo Emerson both put pen to paper in support of suffrage.[3] When possible, men even played direct roles in supporting women's suffrage organizations. In 1869, when the Connecticut Woman Suffrage Organization formed, George Hickox, a local newspaper editor, served as a vice president of the group and added his signature to the league's founding documents.[4] In Muncie, Indiana, men could not become full members of the local suffrage group, but by paying dues they could hold honorary memberships. When Dr. Lucius L. Ball joined in this capacity he could not vote, make decisions, or hold office, but his membership allowed him to support the group financially and publicly declare his support for women's voting rights.[5]

While some men individually advocated for female voting rights, countless male supporters around the nation organized themselves into their own leagues. First formed in 1909 with chapters in New York City and Chicago, the Men's League for Woman Suffrage grew at an unprecedented rate during the suffrage movement's last decade. It did not take long for branches to pop up across thirty-five different states, including California, Colorado, Florida, Nebraska, Texas, and Virginia.[6] Soon, membership had grown into the thousands, and the National American Woman Suffrage Association (NAWSA) embraced the support it offered. Working alongside mainstream suffrage groups, these men (often husbands or sons of suffragists) marched, spoke, published, hosted banquets, raised money, and lobbied legislatures in the name of women's voting rights.[7] Because they typically held positions of wealth, power, or social standing, the men who joined these groups knew their support could improve the suffrage movement's profile and excite public interest. They did not believe that extending the vote to women would attack their manhood. Instead, they saw it as a way to boost future support for their own anticorruption efforts.[8]

During this explosion of allied organizations, seven students at Harvard University founded the Harvard Men's League for Woman Suffrage in 1911. Their membership eventually grew to fifty-eight members, and the group sought to facilitate open lectures by suffragists throughout the year. Despite their own enthusiasm for female voting rights and a desire to educate others, the Harvard Men's League ran up against resistance at the college. When they petitioned Harvard to grant them use of a lecture hall to host suffragist Emmeline Pankhurst (the founder of the Women's Social and Political Union of England) they were quickly denied.[9] As opposition from members of the student body appeared in the college newspaper, Allen S. Olmsted, the league's president, penned his response. In a letter to the newspaper, he argued that the Men's League for Woman Suffrage and their speakers had as much right at Harvard as any other organization.[10] Olmsted also took his grievances to the top of Harvard's hierarchy, writing a series of inflammatory letters to then–school-president Abbott Lawrence Lowell. In his debate with the president, he pressed the fact that the largely male campus deserved the opportunity to hear women's voices. Olmsted also argued that access to a wide variety of lecture topics was essential to a Harvard education.

Despite Olmsted's heavy correspondence with President Lowell, Harvard would not budge. Officially, the college stated that it was a matter of regulation to keep political matters as far away from their campus as possible.[11] Privately, however, Lowell admitted in letters to faculty that his refusal to provide a lecture hall for Pankhurst was because "we do not think that the subject of women's suffrage comes under the category of our subjects."[12] Not to be defeated, the Harvard Men's League for Woman Suffrage found another way to make sure the student body had an opportunity to hear Pankhurst speak.

On December 6, 1911, Harvard's newspaper, the *Crimson*, announced that Pankhurst would give a talk on "Woman Suffrage" that afternoon at Brattle Hall.[13] Located just outside Harvard's campus and unaffiliated with the school, the college's administration had no authority over the venue. When local newspapers reported on the event the next day, accounts described the hall as bursting at the seams with attendees, many of whom were Harvard students. Whether it was Pankhurst's notability, Olmsted's public tiff with university administration, or simply an interest in examining the issue of suffrage, no one could deny that men were interested in the topic. When the *Cambridge Chronicle* reported on the lecture, they noted that at least two-thirds of the attendees were men, and that many donated to the monetary collection taken at the end of the event to benefit the suffrage cause.[14]

Like the resistance the Harvard Men's League faced, male suffrage allies during the twentieth century often received criticism from the press and public. They were mocked as unmanly, and frequently they served as the butt of jokes. Cartoonists and satirists often portrayed them wearing aprons and tending babies while their wives took to the streets. Over time, however, the sight of male supporters became commonplace—although later forgotten in the public memory. These male counterparts to the mainstream suffrage movement proved crucial in turning the tide toward the passage of the 19th Amendment. The role they played in harnessing support, creating exposure, and lending credibility cannot be understated. As leaders of NAWSA began to cultivate relationships with these well-connected allies, they showed an understanding that they could not achieve their goal alone. Through strategic partnerships, they boosted their support and moved closer to securing the right to vote. While suffragists assumed male allies would take a passive role in advocating for female enfranchisement, to their surprise, these men embraced their role and gave far more than expected. They proved themselves dedicated fundraisers, cultivators of public support, and influencers of politicians.[15] When compiling the official history of NAWSA, the association's press agent, Ida Husted Harper, wrote, "Behind many a woman who worked there was a man aiding and sustaining her with money and personal sacrifice."[16] In many instances this was certainly true. And more often than not, those men gave their support willingly to help promote a cause they fully believed would improve society for all citizens.

If You Scratch My Back, I'll Scratch Yours

Banner, 1914, Museum of Connecticut History, Hartford, CT, https://museumof cthistory.org/

MUSEUM OF CONNECTICUT HISTORY

On May 2, 1914, women, men, and children across the country celebrated National Suffrage Day. To show the breadth of support for women's voting rights, suffragists organized demonstrations, speeches, and events in every state and territory in the country. While some of the gatherings were quite small, others reached monumental scales. In Hartford, Connecticut, one thousand participants joined together in the first suffrage parade the state had seen. Along the streets, thousands more people crowded together to watch in awe.[1] As the sea of marchers passed by, they wore suffrage colors and carried banners like the one seen on the facing page. Unlike the flags and pennants carrying the iconic slogan "Votes for Women," this banner boldly displays two words "Factory Workers." Carried by allied supporters, Hartford's parade not only included suffrage leaders from middle- and upper-class families, but also many working women, including dressmakers, milliners, bookkeepers, and factory workers.[2]

During the suffrage movement's first decades, a complex relationship existed between well-to-do suffrage leaders and the working classes. While Susan B. Anthony and Elizabeth Cady Stanton had occasionally dipped their toes into issues such as trade unionism, they also argued that educated white women deserved the vote in advance of blacks and "uneducated" citizens. Most other suffragists simply attempted to avoid topics like labor issues because they perceived them as unseemly. Combined, these elitist attitudes isolated working-class citizens who already had less time and funds to devote to the suffrage movement. As the twentieth century crept closer, however, working women began supporting suffrage in greater numbers. As they joined labor unions, held strikes for higher pay, and protested for better working conditions, they began to see the vote as a way to gain more political power to achieve their demands. In turn, suffrage leaders began to see the benefits they could reap from aligning themselves with women already politically active in the labor movement.[3] As the old saying goes, "If you scratch my back, I'll scratch yours"—something that suffragists and their allies both learned could be important to their goals.

In Connecticut, the appearance of factory workers in the 1914 parade was only one example of how suffragists and laborers joined forces to promote both of their causes. As the second decade of the twentieth century played out, it became obvious that both the voting booth and the shop floor were two important platforms in the fight for women's equality. As suffragists looked to change the US Constitution, female trade unionists demanded better regulations in factories and trade shops. When these two movements intersected, both groups came closer to their common goal of women's equality.[4] Helping to make this allied effort so effective in the state was a new generation of suffrage leaders eager to incorporate a wide range of issues, such as child labor, prostitution, political corruption, and fair work regulations, into the traditional suffrage platform.[5] Josephine Bennett, founder of the Hartford Equal Franchise League, not only worked for equal voting rights, but she and her husband donated the land to start the country's first residential workers' school in New York. Likewise, Emily Pierson, an active member of the Connecticut Woman Suffrage Association and an organizer of the state's branch of the National Woman's Party, could often be seen speaking to laborers at factories and even marching alongside them at protests.[6]

When possible, Connecticut's suffragists worked to educate members of their organizations on the harsh realities faced by young factory and mill workers. They also agitated for a federal ban on child labor, pensions for mothers, and education reform. While a sense of benevolence spurred them to take on much of this work, it also carried a heavy dose of practicality. Local suffragists, largely middle and upper class, knew they needed to gain the favor of working-class women to increase support for their cause. With that in mind, they invited local shop girls, telephone operators, and other women who would benefit from voting rights to join their movement. They addressed crowds at factories and promoted the idea that what injured one person could injure everyone. This created a feeling of solidarity among female laborers who found themselves victims of trade unions only interested in protecting the rights of white, skilled, male laborers. By throwing support toward the suffrage cause, they hoped to gain the power to change their own situation for the better.[7]

By 1917, suffragists aligned with the National Woman's Party began taking more radical steps to draw attention to their demands. They instituted an intense program of public protests in Washington, DC, resulting in the arrests of countless women. Among these radical agitators were representatives from Connecticut who had keenly observed the protest and picketing tactics utilized by laborers. The next year, Katharine Houghton Hepburn, a progressive suffrage leader in the state (and mother of famous actress Katharine

Hepburn), approached a nineteen-year-old file clerk at Traveler's Insurance with an offer. Young Edna Purtell had recently begun attending suffrage meetings and helped pass out posters around town. Reflecting on the conversation between herself and Hepburn, Purtell said the seasoned suffragist asked if she would be willing to travel to Washington, DC, and demonstrate for suffrage in her place. The file clerk responded, "I've got a week's vacation coming, but I can't afford to go."[8]

After Hepburn offered to pay her way, Purtell quickly accepted. As the daughter of working-class parents, the trip to the nation's capital likely seemed like a dream. When she arrived, however, there was no time for sightseeing and relaxation. Purtell headed straight for Lafayette Park with other protestors. Although the youngest activist present, she quickly climbed a statue, announcing, "Lafayette, we are here!" During the trip, police arrested Purtell four times. When she refused to hand over her banner, an officer ripped it from her hands, breaking two fingers in the process.[9] Purtell's participation in the demonstrations shows just how interwoven suffragists and laborers could become. When she returned to work the following week the president of Traveler's Insurance asked to speak to her. "You know, Miss Purtell, you're liked very well here, but we don't want you to be talking about suffrage and so forth," he said. In a sharp response, Purtell quipped, "Mr. Batterson, during work hours I'll take care of my job. But once I get in that elevator, what I talk about is my business, not yours. And on our coffee break, that's our coffee break, and I'll talk about anything I want."[10]

While the alliance of Connecticut's suffragists and laborers was not the norm in every state, it was not unheard of. In Washington State, the labor movement and women's rights became intertwined in the 1880s and continued to work alongside one another for many years. After Washington women won the vote in 1910, progressive legislators enacted an eight-hour day for women workers, workmen's compensation, mothers' pensions, and child labor laws.[11] In this instance, both groups came out on top. In Illinois, a delegation of suffragists traveling to the state's capitol asked Agnes Nestor, a glove worker from an Irish immigrant family, to join them. Along the journey, Nestor served as the main speaker when the group stopped in the industrial town of Joliet to rally support among the community's working-class citizens. While older suffragists in the state preferred not to entangle alliances, younger activists saw an opportunity. In order to make a stronger case for female voting rights, they needed more public support. And they knew a fellow worker would make the best appeal to laborers, not middle- and upper-class suffragists.[12]

Neither suffragists nor laborers believed the support of the other would be the single solution to their problems. At the same time, they understood the benefits that could be achieved from forming an alliance. Although class bias deeply infected the suffrage movement, laborers still enthusiastically gave their support. For years, their efforts to secure better working conditions had been hampered. With the vote they hoped to turn that around. Suffragists also recognized that they had excluded many people from their movement for years. Their efforts to bring workers into the fold in the final years of their work stemmed from their desire to reap the benefits of the relationship.[13] Although it had taken many years, the suffrage movement began to understand that in order to secure voting rights for themselves they would need to scratch the backs of allies and ask for the favor to be returned.

Part VI

ROADBLOCKS
AND SETBACKS

Roadblocks and setbacks come in many shapes and forms. In the most literal sense of the words, roadblocks stop traffic from moving down thoroughfares, while setbacks reverse progress already made. Sometimes these obstructions may be purposeful, and at other times the hindrance results from something as unexpected as a flat tire. Like cars encountering these interferences, suffragist also stumbled across many obstacles. Theirs were not physical barricades, but rather actions, conditions, individuals, outlooks, or even entire regions of the nation slowing their progress toward securing the right to vote. Sometimes these hindrances took the form of opponents, and other times they were the policies and attitudes of suffragists themselves. Occasionally, suffrage leaders embraced someone bringing new enthusiasm to the cause, only to realize later the person was more of a liability than a boon. Suffragists also found out over time that some setbacks simply were out of their control. Although activists devoted untold energy early in their movement to get their issue before the Supreme Court, when they did, a court system willing to uphold the patriarchal tradition quickly derailed their efforts.

Unrequited Love

Victoria Woodhull Clock Tower, carved by Larry Nadwodney, 1976, Robbins Hunter Museum, Granville, OH, http://www.robbinshunter.org/
PHOTOGRAPH COURTESY OF ROBBINS HUNTER MUSEUM, GRANVILLE, OH

B uilt in the 1840s, the Avery-Downer House graces Granville, Ohio, with its beautiful Greek Revival architecture. Today, it houses the Robbins Hunter Museum, a historic home highlighting architecture, decorative arts, and the stories of the people who lived there. In addition to these main interpretive themes inside the house, outside, visitors find an interesting tribute to one of Ohio's noted daughters—Victoria Woodhull. Situated above one of the structure's doorways is a large clock tower and bell. Each hour, when the bell tolls, a wooden figure of Woodhull appears to greet visitors. Erected in 1976 by Robbins Hunter (the owner of the home at the time), this clock is no ordinary cuckoo; it is one of only two monuments in the nation honoring the first woman to run for president of the United States. While no one can deny she was ahead of her time, in addition to diving headfirst into politics, Woodhull's modern social attitudes and beliefs also got her into hot water. In the 1870s, suffragists who admired her tenacity quickly embraced her, but it was not long before they realized scandal and rumor trailed her. What they believed would be a boost to their movement turned into a liability and a major bump in the road.

Born in Homer, Ohio, in 1838, Victoria Woodhull grew up in a home steeped in spiritualism and her father's moneymaking schemes. By the age of fifteen, Woodhull had not only worked as a child preacher, fortune-teller, and clairvoyant, but she had also married. After having two children with her much older husband, Dr. Canning Woodhull, the marriage could no longer stand his alcoholism and abuse, so she filed for divorce.[1] Left destitute and with two children to support, Woodhull's experience shaped her later views on women's rights, love, and sexual relationships. In 1866, she married Colonel James Blood, a spiritualist and Civil War hero. Bucking traditions of the time, after the wedding Woodhull did not take Blood's last name but instead continued to use the name of her first husband.[2]

Two years later, Blood encouraged Woodhull, along with her younger sister Tennessee Claflin, to move with him to New York City. Once there, the two sisters, who had been traveling as spiritualists and healers, met railroad magnate Cornelius Vanderbilt. It did not take long for the two persuasive women to establish a close relationship with him and gain his trust. The connection between the three had become so close that in 1870 the railroad giant provided money for the two women to start their own stock brokerage firm. When Woodhull, Claflin, and Company opened on Broad Street in Manhattan, it was the first female-run firm of its kind in the nation. Public attention and media quickly followed. Some lent praise for the women's accomplishment, while others criticized them harshly for getting involved in the male world of business and commerce.[3] Not one to have thin skin however, the criticism did not bother Woodhull. With the reported $700,000 the sisters made in their first six weeks of business, they did not doubt their success. They then heightened their position in the limelight by using the profits to start their own newspaper, *Woodhull and Claflin Weekly*. In its pages, they took up a variety of social causes considered radical by many people at the time. Their articles advocated for eight-hour workdays, gender and racial equality, and sex education for teenagers.[4]

With a growing interest in social reform, in 1869 Woodhull attended her first suffrage meeting. Based on the ideas she learned there, she developed her passionate arguments for women's rights. Preaching these views, as well as a broad range of other social causes in her newspaper, Woodhull found herself naturally aligned with leaders of the radical National Woman Suffrage Association (NWSA). While conservative suffragists put forth great effort to distance themselves from ideas and individuals that might put them on the fringes, NWSA had other ideas. While NWSA believed suffrage of primary importance, its members also viewed it as just one of many women's rights causes.[5] In her own radical newspaper, *The Revolution*, Susan B. Anthony remarked, "These two ladies (for they are ladies) are determined to use their brains, energy, and their knowledge of business to earn them a livelihood. . . . The advent of this woman's firm in Wall Street marks a new era."[6]

Anthony's ardor with Woodhull also marked the beginning of an episode in suffrage history many activists came to regret. By 1870, members of NWSA became frustrated with Congress's resistance to the idea of a federal suffrage amendment. Even with this frustration, they still did not support the state-by-state approach the American Woman Suffrage Association (AWSA) advocated; they instead preferred direct federal action. Looking to succeed where NWSA had not yet, Woodhull made it her mission to lobby for a 16th Amendment to the Constitution, granting women the right to vote. Her plans soon changed, however, when she teamed up with Massachusetts senator Benjamin Butler. With Butler's support, Woodhull instead promoted the idea that the 15th Amendment already gave women the right to vote because its wording did not explicitly deny the ballot to females. In

January 1871, as Woodhull continued to push the argument, she became the first woman to appear in front of the Judiciary Committee of the US House of Representatives.[7] Having made her case to Congress, Woodhull was invited by Anthony to speak to the NWSA membership at their national convention.

Appealing to the crowd with her natural charm and persuasive speaking, Woodhull won them over. Not only did the argument that women already had the vote appeal to them, but Woodhull also pledged to donate $10,000 to the group. The love affair between Woodhull and suffragists was short-lived, however. By 1872, leaders of NWSA had severed all ties. After her initial fame in suffrage circles, Woodhull went one step too far when she tried to take over leadership of the organization.[8] She then announced her intent to run for president of the United States in 1872 as a candidate of the Equal Rights Party, which she founded with her sister. Woodhull proceeded to sell out venues like New York's Steinway Hall and drew crowds interested to see the woman bold enough to make a bid for the presidential role. In a pivotal move at one of these speeches she declared herself a "free lover." Without holding back, she articulated her approval of complete sexual freedom. She also pointed out that American society unfairly criticized women for indiscretions that men could repeat time and again with no recourse.[9]

As Woodhull's support of free love continued both in her speeches and in her newspaper, her likeness became a mainstay of ridicule in political cartoons of the time. Despite suffrage leaders' previous attempts to cool the relationship, Woodhull's ties to the movement began to undermine the work of NWSA. That spring, Woodhull even tried to extort several of the group's leaders by threatening to publish stories of supposed sexual indiscretions if they did not pay her $500 each to keep quiet.[10] In October, things blew up when she accused prominent minister Henry Ward Beecher of a torrid affair with Elizabeth Tilton, his parishioner and friend's wife. Splashed across the front page of her newspaper, the article contained titillating details about the prolonged relationship. This bombshell implied that suffragists and their supporters (Beecher was the first president of AWSA) had lax morals and condoned extramarital affairs. Not playing out as she expected however, Woodhull found herself arrested and jailed for printing and distributing obscenities.[11]

The trial that followed dragged on for months, smearing Woodhull's reputation. Although she had never appeared to believe she would win the 1872 presidential election, the negative publicity of the trial certainly did not help, and she spent election night in jail. After the ordeal finally ended, Woodhull found herself without friend or ally and almost completely broke. Within a short time, her hunger for the spotlight had caused her fall from a pedestal of notoriety to a place of ridicule.[12] For suffragists, damage control was in order. With opponents already working to link lax morals and suffrage, Woodhull's actions only added fuel to the fire. Caught in a net of scandal, NWSA membership dropped severely, and for decades to come an occasional shout of "Free Love!" could be heard at suffrage gatherings. In Boston, an Anti-Suffrage Committee formed and quickly offered Woodhull as proof of the serious threat suffragists posed to the sanctity of the family. Countering this attack, AWSA paid three lecture agents to set up twenty to thirty suffrage meetings a week in cities and towns throughout New England. Their hope was to convince the public that Woodhull did not speak for them.

Despite their attempts to avoid blowback from the very public ordeal, support for women's suffrage at the state and local level dropped. Lawmakers also advised activists to table national women's suffrage legislation for the time. Over the next several years, AWSA continued with a state-by-state approach, while NWSA struggled to counter their tarnished image. While the memory of the scandal faded, it did not happen without taking its toll. In future years, suffragists became highly sensitive to their image and went out of their way to cut off groups of people they believed would sully their name. Never again did they want to make the mistake of aligning themselves with someone they believed to be a savior of suffrage, but in reality, a major liability.

Rampant Racism

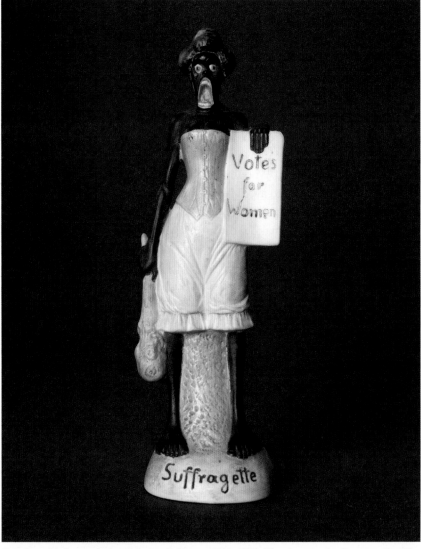

Figurine, likely made by Schafer & Vater, 1900–1920, The Anacostia Community Museum, Washington, DC, http://anacostia.si.edu/
ANACOSTIA COMMUNITY MUSEUM, SMITHSONIAN INSTITUTION

Trinkets and knick-knacks: these decorative ornaments and objects tend to be inexpensive and are often seen as trivial and valueless. Likely produced by German ceramics company Schafer & Vater, the figurine seen on the facing page could easily run the risk of falling into this category, but it is much more. Founded in 1896, the company produced several ceramic items, such as planters and hair receivers, but it was their series of caricature figurines that proved top sellers. Typically sold in England, the company's suffrage themed figurines proved highly popular and made their way to the United States. Today, surviving examples are not inconsequential baubles; they are strong reminders that suffrage and its white leadership should be commemorated, but not always celebrated.

The figurine pictured here only stands a bit more than six inches tall. While its size may be small, the diminutive package carries a guttural punch. The stereotype depicted is uncomfortable and painful to modern eyes. Unlike real-life black suffragists who were intelligent, charismatic, and strong beacons of hope, this figural version was meant to solidify the untrue depiction of African Americans as unintelligent, animal-like brutes—a portrayal often used by whites for amusement. Sadly, in many instances, these representations did delight the masses, and white consumers snatched up the statues for their entertainment value. Beyond its misguided use for amusement, the figurine also serves as a reminder that racial rhetoric and blatant discriminatory action ran deep in the leadership of the suffrage movement. From within its own ranks, white suffragists placed obstacles in the path of many black women who played vital roles in the fight for women's right to vote. This rampant racism meant that in many cases white suffragists were willing to win the vote for themselves at the expense of leaving their black sisters behind, all too often making suffrage leadership their own worst enemy.[1]

From its earliest years, the women's rights movement and the movement for African American rights had a close, yet erratic relationship, attracting both white and black activists.[2] While whites such as Elizabeth Cady Stanton have been immortalized in the popular pages of history, black women like Frances Watkins Harper, have largely been forgotten. Noted widely around the country during her lifetime for her oratorical skills, Harper was a powerful abolitionist, author, lecturer, and women's suffrage advocate. In 1866, when speaking at the eleventh National Woman's Rights Convention in New York, she addressed the issue of racism head-on. Harper, a well-educated woman, firmly believed that shared interests existed between blacks and whites. To her, the sooner they realized it, the better it would be for both races. Speaking to a mixed crowd she boldly stated:

> We are all bound up together in one great bundle of humanity, and society cannot trample on the weakest and feeblest of its members without receiving the curse in its own soul. You tried that in the case of the negro. You pressed him down for two centuries; and in so doing you crippled the moral strength and paralyzed the spiritual energies of the white men of the country.[3]

Having advocated for joint efforts and support across the races, it appeared a tide may have been changing when at the same conference the American Equal Rights Association (AERA) formed to work toward securing equal rights for all American citizens, regardless of race, color, or sex. With a membership comprised of men and women, black and white, AERA focused on securing the right to vote for all citizens and worked to refine its idea of the United States as an interracial democracy.[4] Their unified fight for universal suffrage—voting rights regardless of race or sex—was short-lived, however, and soon white women's support of the black ballot began to splinter.[5]

With the writing of the 14th Amendment, the word "male" was added to the description of voters in the Constitution. Inside AERA a debate ensued over who should vote and under what terms. As disagreements heated up, factions emerged over how a goal of universal suffrage could be achieved. Then Congress proposed the 15th Amendment, prohibiting laws limiting voting based on "race, color, or previous condition of servitude."[6] While this was a remarkable step for black men, the action meant states could still easily keep women from voting. For AERA, the new legislation forced members to decide if the organization should support constitutional protection for black men when a similar provision for women looked unattainable. Noted black leaders like Frederick Douglass argued that the lives of black men depended upon their ability to protect themselves with the vote. To him, and many other black activists, the answer was simple—all support had to be put behind the cause of securing black male voting rights. The path forward had to be accomplished in steps. For many white suffragists, a sense of betrayal set in. After years of working for black freedom alongside their own cause, they felt as if black activists had stuck a knife in their backs. Trying to soothe the hurt feelings of white allies, Douglass remained adamant that they still had the support of African Americans but insisted voting rights for black men needed to be accomplished first.[7]

Douglass's words did little to alleviate the anger of many white suffragists however, and in an about-face, leaders like Susan B. Anthony and Elizabeth Cady Stanton abandoned their support of African Americans. Revealing an ugly side of the suffrage movement, they threw their support behind blatantly racist politicians like George Train, a white Democrat advocating women's voting rights while denouncing them for black men. When speaking on the issue he belittled blacks by telling the Kansas electorate that they had to choose either "Beauty, Virtue, and Intelligence" or "Muscle, Color, and Ignorance."[8]

While Douglass's advocacy for fellow black men may not have come as a huge surprise, Frances Harper's words at the 1869 AERA convention likely struck an entirely different nerve among her fellow women. Although Harper supported voting rights for all men and women, she sided with Douglass saying, "If the nation could only handle one question, she would not have the black women put a single straw in the way, if only the men of the race could obtain what they wanted." Then she pointed her words directly at the white suffrage leaders who had so blatantly taken on antiblack actions and rhetoric. "I do not believe that giving women the ballot is immediately going to cure all the ills of life. I do not believe that white women are dewdrops just exhaled from the skies. I think that like men they may be divided into three classes, the good, the bad, and the indifferent." Harper went on to state that racism kept white women from working with their black counterparts. She also called for delegates to stop pitting the privileged classes against the unprivileged. Instead, she demanded that black women be included as part of "one great privileged nation."[9]

Harper's bold words did little good, however, and after the conference AERA effectively broke into two separate suffrage organizations. While members of the American Woman Suffrage Association (AWSA) called for the enfranchisement of black men and all women (in that order), the National Woman Suffrage Association (NWSA) shared Stanton and Anthony's belief that if black men gained the vote, the hope of women's voting rights would die away.[10] In the pages of their newspaper, *The Revolution*, they even unleashed a flagrant barrage of racist sentiment against African Americans. Not only did they make unfounded claims that black men were their enemies, "more hostile to woman than any class of men in the country," they also instilled fear in their white readership. By using venomous words, they painted a monstrous picture of the black man as a rapist. According to Stanton, if black men earned the vote it would encourage "fearful outrages on womanhood." She further warned that woman's "degradation" would be complete, and "persecutions, insults, horrors" would descend upon her.[11]

Over the next twenty years, suffragists remained split into two factions. By and large, black suffragists affiliated themselves with AWSA, working for universal suffrage at the local and state levels. At the time of its establishment, Harper even became a founding member alongside other white activists, despite her disillusionment with many of them. Like Harper, even with NWSA's blatantly racial rhetoric, a small number of blacks also linked themselves with the more radical organization because they supported the group's push for a federal amendment. In fact, when white leaders of the organization began urging members to attempt voting in the 1870s to test the legal system, black suffragists were among those who participated.[12] Despite this continued black activism and support, by the 1890s white suffragists still showed little appreciation for their black counterparts when AWSA and NWSA merged to form the National American Woman Suffrage Association (NAWSA).[13]

Under white leadership NAWSA attempted to walk both sides of the line. While they did not ban black women from membership, they certainly did not encourage it. In response, African American suffragists formed their own local groups to work for voting rights, or incorporated suffrage advocacy into the agendas of their other clubs and organizations. Magnifying their own racist agenda, white leadership also took advantage of black activists to draw support for the larger suffrage cause. For instance, after the demise of AERA, leaders of the suffrage movement mended their relationship with Douglass and he once again became an honored guest at their conventions. They exploited his star power when needed, but as NAWSA planned its 1895 convention in Atlanta, Anthony personally asked him to stay away. She explained that his presence might antagonize white suffragists that the movement desperately needed.[14]

Heading into the twentieth century, the relationship did not improve. NAWSA leadership attempted to court southern suffragists by instituting their "Southern Strategy." No less than a racist and exclusionary agenda, the plan took steps to convince southern lawmakers that they could ensure white supremacy by granting women the right to vote. As NAWSA argued, when enfranchised, white female voters would outnumber black men and women combined, in the South. Whites would then have an easy voting bloc able to pass discriminatory laws based on race, ensuring white power.[15] Throughout the remainder of the suffrage movement's years, white racism remained intact in the movement's leadership. When black women's organizations tried to affiliate with the national movement, they were discouraged from doing so. When NAWSA wrote its own history, dedicated black activists were left out of the narrative. In 1913, white organizers told black suffragists to march in a segregated, blacks-only section at the end of their monumental parade in Washington, DC. Black activists even participated in picketing the White House in the late 1910s alongside members of the National Woman's Party, but the pages of the group's publication only featured photographs of white suffragists—again pushing black women into the shadows. In many of these instances, white leadership gave the excuse that it did not want to upset the southern contingent. It is clear however, that racism was ingrained in white northern suffragists well before they became concerned with wooing white southerners and continually used them as a scapegoat for their own actions and words.

Like the obvious racism displayed in the figurine highlighted here, the discrimination black suffragists faced from white activists was clear to them when it occurred. Despite the constant barrage of racist actions and words, black women remained persistent in their work toward women's suffrage. Just as abolitionists argued after the Civil War, they knew the vote was essential for their own protection and for the progress of African American society.[16] Even as white suffragists painted them as a lesser class, they knew they needed a political voice to bring about change for the black race—even if it meant putting aside their own fears of the blatant racism they regularly faced.

Despite the continued efforts of black suffragists and their successes in building support in black communities, white leadership remained its own enemy, denying the vast majority of support African Americans offered the suffrage movement. It came as no surprise then when white leadership yet again abandoned black women following the ratification of the 19th Amendment. Decades earlier Frances Harper stated, "I do not think the mere extension of the ballot a panacea for all the ills of our national life. What we need to-day is not simply more voters, but better voters."[17] Indeed, providing women with the opportunity to vote did not mean all women used their political voice for the betterment of all society. Years earlier, white suffrage leadership encouraged black women to prod male African American voters to support woman suffrage legislation, only to reverse the policy when they feared it would isolate southern lawmakers. Likewise, after the celebrations died away in 1920, white suffragists left black activists to form their own voter education groups, alone. For many black women the passage of the 19th Amendment was no reason to celebrate. Taking their own lives into their hands however, black women embraced the limited voting opportunities the 19th Amendment provided and drew on their experiences to look toward the future and set their sights on their own political goals.[18]

A Formidable Opponent

Anti-Suffrage Pennant, 1900–1920, Lorenzo State Historic Site, Cazenovia, NY, https://parks.ny.gov/historic-sites/15/details.aspx

Comic book and action film fans know that when the name Batman is mentioned the character of the Joker quickly comes to mind. Since the Joker's creation in 1940, the two comic book characters have existed together; each with their own view on life and constantly in a battle as archenemies. However, not all adversaries have a struggle as deadly as this hero and supervillain duo. While gaining the vote was seen as a matter of life or death by some suffragists, no one unleashed lethal joy buzzers, razor-edged playing cards, or acid-spraying lapel flowers. Instead, suffragists and their counterpart unleashed a war of carefully crafted words. In many ways, anti-suffragists resembled their opponent while disagreeing on the fundamental issue of voting rights. They organized into leagues, published their own newspapers, made their case to the public, and even produced items like the pennant seen on the previous page. When displayed or held aloft at public events, it allowed the owner, Charles S. Fairchild, to communicate his support of the anti-suffrage cause. Proudly working against women gaining the right to vote, Fairchild was not alone in Cazenovia, New York. Many of the community's prominent residents considered themselves avid supporters of the anti-suffrage cause and the Cazenovia Anti-Suffrage Society became very active in the town.[1] Like other organizations working against suffrage around the nation, Cazenovia's anti-suffrage activities represented the formidable opponent suffragists faced from their earliest years until 1920.[2]

In the twenty-first century, it might be hard to imagine anti-suffragists as anyone but men. All women must have wanted to vote, right? Not necessarily. While plenty of men like Fairchild worked against women's voting rights, women by-and-large led the anti-suffrage movement. Even at the time, suffragists often stated that men in powerful industries such as railroad and liquor led the opposition against them. In some instances, they may have believed it.[3] In others, they knew it would directly undercut their own arguments to admit that not all women wanted the right to vote, so they knowingly placed the blame on men. Despite what suffragists wanted lawmakers to believe, a conservative countermovement existed alongside them, with a mostly female membership.[4]

From the beginnings of the suffrage movement women protesting female enfranchisement had always existed, even if only sporadically at first. As suffrage victories began to mount in the western states, however, women who did not believe their sex needed the right to vote began to organize at the local level for thoughtful, direct opposition. This defensive manner continued, and as the suffrage campaign intensified or slowed down, the anti-suffrage movement followed the same ebb and flow.[5] When suffragists succeeded in securing state referenda, anti-suffragists quickly expanded their local societies to statewide organizations. Because the suffrage movement's success was limited to state and local levels for so long, not until 1911 (when the suffrage movement began to intensify at the national level), did the National Association Opposed to Woman Suffrage form to coordinate the activities of state leagues. Like their counterparts, anti-suffrage leaders were often wealthy, socially prominent white women with considerable experience in philanthropic work. And while they made periodic attempts to recruit working-class women, the bulk of anti-suffrage participants came from middle-class communities.[6] In many ways, the stories of suffragists and anti-suffragists dovetail. One major difference, however, is how their movements grew. When suffragists first began their work to secure the vote, it was only one of many rights they demanded for women. Over time this broad platform narrowed as they focused in on voting rights. Anti-suffragists on the other hand grew from a very narrow goal, focused solely on stopping suffrage, to a broader one including many conservative reforms.[7]

When these two movements interacted with one another it often occurred through hotly debated words. Looking to uphold the virtues of womanhood, anti-suffragists refused to spar with their opponent by picketing or mounting large spectacles such as parades. They believed such activities inappropriate for women and therefore beneath them. Rather, they looked to refute suffragists' arguments through printed materials and occasional in-person debates. An examination of both sides reveals that in many ways suffragists did not organize their reasonings as well as their opponents.

Throughout its history, the women's suffrage movement had no single recognized ideology. Instead, its members used every conceivable view and position to argue their case. Although they all agreed women should have the right to vote, they did not necessarily agree on why. Early on, many activists argued that women should have the vote as a natural right. If all men were created equal, inherently representing themselves in government by voting, then women should too. They believed the female sex was created equal to men, and therefore, should have the same natural rights. As time passed however, suffragists also argued that as the more moral of the sexes, women needed the vote so they could protect the home. Another common argument of pro-suffrage activists expanded on their belief that the electorate would be made more intelligent by the inclusion of well-educated women.[8] After decades of making their case, in the twentieth century their reasoning shifted. While the natural right argument never disappeared, suffragists now argued more often that women needed the right to vote because of the good it could accomplish. If women had the franchise, the interests and intellect of all females would be enlarged; women would be better mothers due to their ability to more thoroughly teach their children the meaning of citizenship; and women would be better wives when they became their husband's equal. On top of the benefits for women themselves, suffragists also argued that female voters would improve society by voting in favor of prohibition, child labor legislation, pure food laws, and countless other reforms society needed.[9] In many ways, suffragists desperate to secure the vote looked to appeal to anyone they could, even if it meant creating a chaotic argument for why they needed suffrage.

For those in the anti-suffrage camp, this mixed bag of rationales proved beneficial. By throwing in everything and the kitchen sink, suffragists had not created a foolproof argument. Instead, they had left room in their position for considerable debate with anti-suffragists.[10] When suffragists went left, anti-suffragists went right. They did not make their arguments just to be contrary, however. Anti-suffragists truly believed women should not have access to the ballot and put forth a thoughtful, tight argument against it. While suffragists believed women should be granted the vote, anti-suffragists encouraged lawmakers not to impose it upon them. If the law forced the ballot upon women, they argued, it would diminish woman's purity and higher morality. It would also threaten the stability of the family.[11] At the time, society functioned on a model of separate spheres. One sphere encompassed the world of business, commerce, and industry; a world where men were considered naturally equipped to work and encounter humanity's underbelly. The other sphere was the territory of women and domesticity. As the natural caretakers of the family, females ruled the home, providing moral guidance and protection from the outside world.

This link of women to the home underpinned the entire anti-suffrage argument. Logically, if women were moral beings, then the rough-and-tumble battlefield of politics would soil and injure them. Anti-suffragists also argued that women were politically incompetent and unprepared to vote. But unlike suffragists, they did not see the need for women to become better educated on the topics of politics—their husbands' votes already represented and protected them. They believed adding an additional layer of female voting would be unnecessary and add nothing beneficial to the existing system. Anti-suffragists also feared that in cases where a wife may disagree with her husband, destruction of family morals would ensue.[12] Additionally, the time needed to become an informed voter would take mothers and wives away from their natural duties. Rather than become more equipped to raise their children, their time would simply be taken away from them. Referencing biblical teachings, they argued that over time this would weaken the entire familial institution of the country.[13] Their arguments were not to say that women should not play active roles in public affairs, however. On the contrary, they believed women had a crucial role in reform work, but they could best do so as nonpartisan participants. The ballot, anti-suffragists believed, would destroy any way for women to remain unattached to party politics. In their minds this would make them less impactful in achieving societal reforms, an argument in direct opposition to suffragists.[14]

By keeping tight and focused talking points, anti-suffragists positioned themselves as one of the suffrage movement's strongest roadblocks. At a time when society's views of gender roles varied greatly from today's, anti-suffrage arguments made a lot of sense. Most people saw life as two distinct halves, with men ideally suited by nature to rule public life while women reigned in the home. Their introduction into the political ring would mean chaos in both spheres, an eventual doom to all of society.[15] As 1920 drew nearer, however, it became clear that society's views started to shift. With more women entering the workforce, attending college, and participating in activities outside the home, even anti-suffragists realized the inevitability of suffrage. With the fear of major societal shifts coming, anti-suffragists transformed from a movement laser-focused on stopping votes for women to one broadly fighting against all radical reform. As they tried to maintain the status quo, they pushed back against not only suffragism, but also feminism and socialism.[16] Once again, anti-suffragists crafted their arguments around what they believed best for society. It was through this intentional framework that they posed the problem that suffragists had to solve and asked the questions suffragists had to answer.[17] The national debate that carried on for many years kept both groups on their toes and shaped the arguments of one another.[18] If suffragists truly believed men of big business led the opposition, they did not pay enough attention to their own arguments. Again and again pro-suffrage activists spoke about the intelligence and abilities of all women. In turn, anti-suffragists proved them right. Through their own effective and organized work, the groups fighting against women's voting rights proved that all women were in fact capable of more than ironing and making dinner. But, that did not mean they all wanted to put those abilities to use at the polls.

Courting the System

National Susan B. Anthony Museum and House, built 1859–1864, Rochester, NY,
http://susanbanthonyhouse.org/index.php

On November 14, 1872, a federal warrant for Susan B. Anthony's arrest was issued. When authorities picked her up at her Rochester, New York, home, pictured on the facing page, she did not resist. She did revolt against paying the streetcar fare to the police station, however. As Anthony explained, she was "traveling under protest at the government's expense," and therefore would not shell out one penny of her own.[1] But what had caused the apprehension of one of the nation's most high-profile suffragists? Nine days earlier, Anthony and fourteen other women appeared at the polls in Rochester in an attempt to cast ballots. Like these activists, between 1868 and 1873, hundreds of black and white women attempted to register to vote in local, state, and federal elections around the country.[2] Not just simple acts of protest, these actions were intentional attempts by suffragists to test the Constitution of the United States and the nation's court system. According to their understanding of the law, their mere citizenship already enfranchised them. Therefore, by voting, or attempting to cast ballots, they publicly demanded the federal government protect their rights of citizenship against states denying them suffrage. Knowing full well this meant breaking state and local laws that could result in arrest, countless brave women set out to the polls hoping to force test cases into the federal court system.[3] Ultimately, this widespread tactic went awry. Instead of solidifying their right to vote, the court system defined women as second-class citizens—a setback that would plague suffragists for years to come.

At the time Anthony appeared at the polls, a poll watcher challenged her claims to suffrage. This forced the inspectors of elections to consult state guidelines to determine if she met voting qualifications. During the process, they asked Anthony under oath if she was a citizen, a resident of the district, and if she had accepted a bribe for her vote. When she answered the questions to their satisfaction, the inspectors registered her ballot.[4] Because of her notoriety, the press widely publicized news about Anthony's successful vote—an issue authorities did not intend on letting go unaddressed.[5]

According to the indictment against her, Anthony had "knowingly, wrongfully and unlawfully voted for a representative to the Congress of the United States."[6] After being released on bail, Anthony got straight to work. She spent the weeks leading up to her trial giving public speeches and making the case that she had indeed voted legally. She also let it be known that she had done so in good faith and believed she could not be held guilty of criminal action or intent. Anthony's argument was so compelling and drew so much attention, the prosecuting attorney obtained a change of venue to another county for fear potential jurors might be prejudiced in her favor.[7]

Ironically, when the day of Anthony's trial arrived in 1873, the jury's opinions and findings did not matter much. Judge Ward Hunt, an associate justice of the Supreme Court of the United States and member of the Republican Party, presided over the case in New York's federal circuit court. What unfolded at the trial was not only unorthodox, but also indicated Hunt may have been eager to please fellow Republicans and the president who did not support voting rights for women.[8] As the case unfolded, Anthony's lawyer argued her case to the best of his abilities, but clearly, Justice Hunt had already made up his mind. When Anthony's lawyer attempted to call her as a witness, Hunt barred her from testifying on her own behalf. In an unconventional and historic move Hunt then ordered the jury to return a guilty verdict, refused to poll them, and read an opinion he had written before the trial even began. He stated unequivocally that Anthony had intended to commit a criminal act because New York law expressly forbid women to vote. On top of the guilty verdict, Hunt also issued her a $100 fine. When Anthony refused to pay, he purposefully chose not to imprison her. Ultimately, Anthony hoped for imprisonment because it would provide the opportunity to file an appeal and force a hearing of her case before the US Supreme Court. By taking the actions he did Hunt made sure Anthony's case never reached the nation's highest bench. The judicial system had exploited Anthony's celebrity, sending a warning message to all women.[9]

While Justice Hunt was focused on using Anthony's notoriety to set an example for the nation, another case in Missouri made waves and gained momentum that Anthony's never could. One month before the New York activist's arrest, a Missouri suffragist named Virginia Minor attempted to register to vote in the upcoming election. When she did, St. Louis' sixth district registrar, Reese Happersett, refused based on Minor's gender. In response, Minor and her husband, lawyer Francis Minor, brought a civil suit against Happersett. According to the Minors, women were established as US citizens under the 14th Amendment to the Constitution and were therefore entitled to all the benefits and immunities of citizenship, including the right to vote. While they leveraged this argument in their civil suit in 1872, it was not new to the couple. Three years earlier, they had published and distributed around the country a pamphlet clearly outlining the theory. Indeed, it was the Minors who spurred a wave of testing the court systems in 1872. And it was their clearly articulated position that Anthony, Victoria Woodhull, and other suffragists around the nation relied upon to argue that women already had the right to vote.[10]

For the Minors, their civil suit quickly moved beyond the city courts. Unlike Anthony's trial, the Minors submitted their arguments to the court as written statements and no jury ever entered the courtroom. Despite an all-star legal team including attorney Francis Minor and Senator John B. Henderson (author of the 13th Amendment and supporter of the 15th Amendment), the Minors quickly lost their case in the lower court. Undeterred, they appealed to the Missouri Supreme Court. The court ruled that the purpose of the 14th Amendment was meant to extend voting rights to newly freed slaves, giving African Americans "the right to vote and thus protect themselves against oppression."[11] Although the state supreme court had not ruled in their favor, the Minors remained steadfast in their hopes of success and appealed to the Supreme Court of the United States.

Before the highest judicial body in the nation, Francis Minor made his argument in *Minor v. Happersett*. He explained that the denial of woman suffrage in the states was not a matter of law, but rather one of practice. As an example, he pointed out that women in New Jersey voted between 1787 and 1807, when the state constitution was not always clear-cut in its language regarding female suffrage. And he again laid out his argument that similarly, while the 14th Amendment to the US Constitution did not explicitly call out woman suffrage, it already enfranchised them. According to Minor, individual states could not deny the vote to women.[12]

Having carefully listened to Minor's argument, in October of 1874 the US Supreme Court handed down a unanimous opinion upholding the lower court's decision. While Virginia Minor had achieved something no other suffragist had, by getting her case before the highest court in the nation, the result had not been what she'd hoped for. According to the justices, the Constitution did not confer the right to vote on those who were citizens at the time it was adopted. Nor were citizenship and suffrage automatically equated. Therefore, in their judgment, the 14th Amendment did not extend suffrage to women, because unlike black men, it did not explicitly give them that right.[13]

As a whole, the trials of suffragists in the early 1870s played a critical role in forcing the courts to consider the definitions of national citizenship. They also prompted the legal system to contemplate the federal government's role in protecting citizens from states' laws, and most importantly, it forced the courts to determine if voting was an inherent right of all citizens.[14] When the US Supreme Court handed down its opinion on *Minor v. Happersett*, it defined women as second-class citizens, not worthy of equal rights with men. Like they had previously done when denying married women the right to hold professional positions, the courts upheld the patriarchal tradition. Suffragists had attempted to harness the male dominated court system for their purposes but ultimately failed. As verdicts were handed down in cases such as Anthony's and Minor's, it became obvious to suffragists in cities and states around the nation what their strategy needed to be going forward. If they wanted to cast ballots, the suffrage movement could not rely on existing legislation. They needed to work toward establishing new state laws, as well as a separate constitutional amendment guaranteeing women's right to vote.[15] The roadblock that the Supreme Court placed in front of them most certainly shaped the work of activists throughout the next four decades. And Virginia Minor proved to local and state suffragists that celebrity power was not needed to court the judicial system.

The South

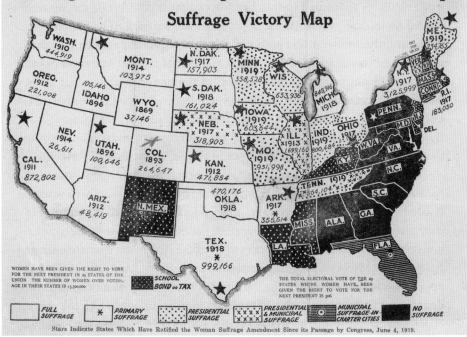

Suffrage Victory Map, 1920, Equal Suffrage League of Virginia Papers, Library of Virginia, Richmond, VA, http://www.lva.virginia.gov/

M aps communicate lots of information. Typically the most familiar, geographic maps provide a flat depiction of the world, a nation, or state. When examined, the viewer can glean information about boundaries, bodies of water, the locations of cities, and a host of other facts. Specialized maps may even provide in-depth information about elevations and topo-graphical features. Others might depict interior layers of the earth's core or show railroad routes crisscrossing the country at a specific point in time. In the early twentieth century, suffragists in states across the nation began using suffrage maps to illustrate the spread of suffrage rights on posters, pamphlets, and broadsides.[1] By visually representing the progress of suffrage on a map, activists hoped to garner more support by proving that women's voting rights were favored across the majority of the nation. Printed in 1920, the suffrage map on the previous page lays out what voting rights had been made available to women in the then forty-eight states.[2] While the western United States had overwhelmingly provided full suffrage to its female resi-dents, and the Midwest was on board with providing women the opportu-nity to vote in presidential and municipal elections, the American South visibly sticks out from the other regions of the nation. Unlike other areas, even in 1920 southern states still overwhelmingly provided few opportuni-ties for women to exercise the ballot. This lack of support for women's suf-frage in the American South plagued the movement for decades, proving that an entire region could be an obstacle almost impossible to overcome.

From its earliest years, the suffrage movement struggled to gain ground in the southern United States. While a sprinkling of individual southern women favored voting rights in the years leading up to the Civil War, no widespread collective of like-minded women emerged. Following the close of the conflict, however, a small number of branches of both the American Woman Suffrage Association (AWSA) and the National Woman Suffrage Association (NWSA) popped up in the South. Despite the efforts of individual members, their in-fluence and visibility never gained much traction or influence with the public or lawmakers. After the merger of AWSA and NWSA to form the National American Woman Suffrage Association (NAWSA), organizational activity saw a slight increase. The newly formed group put an emphasis on the forma-tion of local suffrage clubs around the country, including in the South. While this focus resulted in the creation of some suffrage groups across the southern states, it was only mildly effective. Often, the southern clubs relied heavily upon the work of a single woman who had lived part of her life in the North-east. All too often, when this leader left the organization, or had to reduce her involvement, the clubs went into decline or folded completely.[3]

While anti-suffrage attitudes existed in all areas of the country, its prevalence in the South reached levels not seen elsewhere. At the root of the sentiment lay a variety of cultural and historic factors. Following the Civil War, economic recovery for the South had been painfully slow. With much of the warfare occurring in the southern states, the region suffered unthinkable levels of devastation to their infrastructure and landscape—this did not leave a lot of time or desire for lawmakers to consider expanding rights for southern women. Prior to the outbreak of the conflict, far fewer women had worked for their own living in the South than in other regions of the nation. And in the years after its end, education for most southern women still ended at the secondary level. In terms of broader women's rights, the South was a mixed bag in the years after the Civil War. In Louisiana, the "Code Napoléon" was so restrictive that women did not even have legal title to the clothes on their backs. In Georgia, a woman could work, but her earnings legally belonged to her husband. Meanwhile, in Mississippi, some safeguards had been placed on female property rights, and in Florida, a working woman could control her own earnings.[4] With a fairly erratic and limited spectrum of women's rights, southern lawmakers and many influential women saw no need for female enfranchisement. In their eyes, the vote and entrance into the political world would unsex women and bring about the destruction of genteel southern society. Why should women vote when they could fulfill their southern duty of caring for the home and family without entering the world of politics? For many southerners, the idea of suffrage simply did not align with their cultural ideal of retired, refined ladyhood protected by chivalrous manhood.[5]

Also playing into the equation was the southern fear of the black vote. After the close of the Civil War, Reconstruction policies looked to stamp out remnants of the American Confederacy, bring the United States into unity, and rebuild the devastated southern landscape. As the federal government handed down pre-prescribed policies to southern states that firmly believed in states' rights to make their own laws, the 14th and 15th Amendments expanded civil rights for blacks around the nation. While this undoubtedly created tensions in all areas of the country, they were especially high in the South—a region whose economy, social order, and way of life had been underpinned by a strict racial order for generations. Fearing the disappearance of their culture and values, hate groups such as the Ku Klux Klan emerged to terrorize African Americans. The South also began establishing local and state laws enforcing racial segregation. Known as Jim Crow laws, these legal actions kept the races separate in public facilities across the South. To combat the large number of newly minted black male voters, southern states and communities instituted measures to keep black men from the polls. By the turn of the twentieth century, southern states had created elaborate disenfranchisement measures, such as poll taxes and literacy tests, and the federal Supreme Court had upheld them as constitutional.[6] When these tactics did not prove effective, physical intimidation or force was used. In almost every instance, black men found these barriers impossible to overcome given their limited access to education and employment opportunities. For white southerners, the idea of enfranchising all women, both black and white, made no sense. Most lawmakers saw no need for white female votes that would replicate their own. And many feared that black female voters may be harder to control than black men. Across the South, black women were viewed as more educated and more responsible with finances. This led many white Southerners to fear that poll taxes and literacy tests might prove fruitless in keeping black women from the ballot box.

In an attempt to play into southern concerns, northern leadership of NAWSA instituted their Southern Strategy in the 1890s. Hoping to churn up interest in their cause and gain new support from the public and southern lawmakers, the group's leaders promoted women's voting rights to the South as a way to solve the "negro problem." According to NAWSA, woman suffrage would help ensure southern white supremacy. With more white women than black in the South, white female votes would not only cancel out those of African American women but also help enforce southern laws and values.[7] Despite this morally flawed effort, NAWSA had little success in wooing southern support through this argument. With wounds from the Civil War still raw decades later, many southerners equated the suffrage movement with the abolitionist origins of their pioneering leaders.[8]

While the Southern Strategy had failed to cultivate new support for the larger suffrage cause, in the 1910s, the South's emerging urban middle class proved more fruitful. The women in this newly forming southern population had links to national markets and urban centers. Through the industrial work of their fathers, husbands, and even themselves, they created connections to small business, education, the law, and local banking. This set them apart from the traditional southern elite that was tied to the plantation economy and the textile manufacturing, railroads, and mining industries that served it. Through their work experiences and educational opportunities, many became involved in reform work as settlement workers and clubwomen, avenues often exposing them to pro-suffrage ideas.[9] Slowly, suffragists began to see progress in the South, and during the 1910s pro-suffrage sentiment grew in states like Texas, Tennessee, Georgia, Virginia, and Arkansas.[10]

Despite these successes, the American South remained a hard obstacle to overcome, and the journey to the ratification of the 19th Amendment remained tough. While pro-suffrage support had begun to grow, so had organized anti-suffrage clubs. For those southerners supporting women's voting rights, their energies were often split between organizations varying widely in their political objectives and strategies. Some women joined local groups associated with NAWSA, such as the Equal Suffrage League of Virginia. A few even aligned themselves with the radical National Woman's Party. Still others supported the uniquely southern states' rights suffrage movement. Headed by Kate Gordon of Louisiana, the states' rights suffragists opposed a federal amendment while pressuring state legislatures to enfranchise only white women. As early as 1896, Gordon used the states' rights strategy as the basis for her Equal Rights for All Club in New Orleans. The club not only understood states' rights as a truly southern way of political thinking, but also saw state-level woman suffrage as a way to maintain white supremacy. While her success earned her the position as corresponding secretary for NAWSA in 1903, by the 1910s she had alienated herself from the national movement, which had begun pushing the need for a federal amendment. When she created the Southern States Woman Suffrage Conference in 1913, the group became a direct adversary of NAWSA—working outright against a federal woman's suffrage amendment. [11]

By the time enough support built among federal lawmakers to pass the 19th Amendment, most southern politicians still withheld their endorsement, and only a few voted in its favor. Solidly standing behind the traditional ideals of the South, they had no intention of pushing for ratification within their state boundaries even though the federal congress had approved the measure. Knowing that thirty-six states would have to ratify the amendment to put it into effect, many southerners believed they would ultimately be able to kill the legislation. Demonstrating how opposed to the federal amendment many southerners were, suffragists Kate Gordon of Louisiana and Laura Clay of Kentucky even traveled to Nashville, Tennessee, to lend their support to anti-suffragists working to stop ratification of the amendment.[12] In the end, Tennessee's vote would end the ordeal, but not without a fight. As lawmakers convened, they were met with activists boldly denouncing the federal amendment as an infringement on southern values, state sovereignty, traditional womanhood, and even white supremacy.[13] Countering the arguments were suffragists from around the nation speaking for the countless Americans who supported the amendment. When the lawmakers' final tally was marked, ratification passed by the slim margin of two votes. Tennessee joined the southern states of Kentucky, Louisiana, Texas, and Arkansas in pushing the 19th Amendment into enactment. The remainder would not ratify the amendment for years to come. In fact, Mississippi held out until 1984.[14] As suffragists around the nation learned, provincial values could not be taken for granted. In the case of the American South, their regional identity created a unified front across the southern states. A force so strong, it nearly brought failure to the suffrage cause.

Part VII

TACTICS AND PUBLIC DEMONSTRATIONS

From its earliest years, participants in the women's suffrage movement knew their end goal—secure the right to vote for women across the United States. To make this dream a reality, suffragists created a menu of tactics from which to draw. Each strategy served a role in courting supporters and potential converts to the movement. While some tactics, such as distributing pro-suffrage literature took on a subtle tone, suffragists also employed large scale public demonstrations when necessary. In the nineteenth century, suffrage supporters mastered the art of orchestrating conventions and social events. These gatherings brought together members and sympathizers to rally support for women's voting rights and ensure a unified message. While more assertive actions were few and far between in these early years, suffragists did work to discretely lobby state legislators. By the twentieth century it became apparent that if activists wanted to move the needle forward, they needed to expand their methods of gaining support. Responding to this revelation, suffragists employed new and bold actions. They injected a new level of drama and pageantry into parades and other public gatherings, modern transportation promoted the cause, and bowls of soup brought together the wealthy and working class. Together these varied strategies formed a tactical blueprint meant to rally suffragists' base, bring the curious into the fold, expand the public's knowledge, and attract media coverage to draw attention to the suffrage cause.

Read All about It!

Literature Bag, made by Calhoun Show Print, Hartford, CT, 1910–1920, Cornell University Library, Ithaca, NY, https://www.library.cornell.edu/

"Extra! Extra! Read all about it!" This iconic call of newsboys conjures up images of days gone by, a time when the big events of the day appeared in newsprint rather than on digital platforms. While movies and Broadway musicals have romanticized the lives of newsies, the often underpaid, homeless youth who hawked newspapers on city streets proved vital to publishers looking for ways to edge out their competition. In the late nineteenth century, more newsboys on the streets meant more dailies made their way into the paying hands of customers.[1] This on-the-ground method of advertising and sales proved extraordinarily strong in the time before radio, television, and the internet. Always quick to observe and adapt strategies for their own use, suffragists took note, and in the twentieth century, they began employing similar methods to circulate their own literature. Not only did grown women stand out in contrast to the youth who peddled mainstream newspapers, but they also left little doubt about what they stood for by carrying publications in bags like the one featured on the previous page that proudly bears the words, "Votes for Women."[2]

For most of their seventy-two-year fight for enfranchisement, printed literature remained a mainstay of suffragists' tactical repertoire. Pamphlets, flyers, and newsletters provided ways for activists to spread the word and elaborate on why they believed women should have the right to vote. In the years following the Seneca Falls Convention, suffragists and their allies also began promoting the women's suffrage cause in newspapers. While Amelia Bloomer marketed her newspaper, *The Lily*, to women, which occasionally carried suffrage news, temperance remained its foremost focus in the early 1850s. Likewise, abolitionist William Lloyd Garrison's publication, *The Liberator*, also carried occasional women's suffrage news during its multidecade run from the late 1830s through the mid-1860s. For many African American suffragists, black newspapers regularly provided a direct pipeline to African American communities. In 1890s Kansas, black suffragist Carrie Langston (mother of Harlem Renaissance poet Langston Hughes) wrote about the suffrage cause in the *Atchison Blade*. The *National Presbyterian*, a temperance newspaper published in Georgia, gave African American activist Mary McCurdy a venue for expressing her support for women's voting rights. And Ida B. Wells, using the pen name "Iola," advocated for suffrage in the pages of several black newspapers, such as *The New York Age* and Chicago's *Conservator*.[3]

When Susan B. Anthony and Elizabeth Cady Stanton began publishing *The Revolution* in 1868, however, they tried out a new model. Looking to appeal to readers hungry for a heavy dose of feminism, they put together a publication focusing specifically on suffrage and related topics they believed would be of interest to suffrage advocates. Carrying the bold motto, "Men, their rights and nothing more; Women, their rights and nothing less," the newspaper circulated for just four years. Even with such a short lifespan, the newspaper filled a crucial need. As the official publication of the National Woman Suffrage Association, information that members wanted to know filled its pages. Much like its parent organization, *The Revolution* also earned a reputation for radicalism. Alongside news pertaining to suffrage, the publication carried items confronting issues such as sex education, rape, domestic violence, divorce, prostitution, and reproductive rights.[4]

Although *The Revolution*'s circulation never exceeded three thousand, it had a much larger influence on the suffrage movement. The publication brought news to American women often unavailable to them in the mainstream press. It also spurred the establishment of the most successful suffrage publication, one that ran for sixty-one years in various formats and names. First published in 1870, the *Woman's Journal*, was promoted as a conservative response to *The Revolution*. Started by Lucy Stone and Henry Blackwell, founders of the moderate American Woman Suffrage Association, it comes as no surprise that the newspaper took a more traditional tone. Over the next several decades the publication benefitted greatly from its unofficial connection to major organizations.[5]

As a weekly-newspaper-turned-monthly magazine, the *Woman's Journal* waged an unceasing battle on behalf of women's voting rights and citizenship. It provided suffragists around the country with campaign information, propaganda, camaraderie, and hope. The publication also supplied women with one of the first forums for serious political thought and discussion. While its importance as a voice for political equality grew, that alone could not keep the *Woman's Journal* in business. Along with publishers' concerns for high-quality content, they also worried about paying the bills—an anxiety that stuck with the publication for its entire existence. In fact, in its sixty-one-year history, the *Woman's Journal* never once broke even.[6]

After years of the *Woman's Journal* draining the resources of owners and benefactors, it became obvious the publication would need to increase revenue and consumption to keep pace with mainstream publications. They adopted commercial marketing strategies, running advertisements for products they believed reputable. The owners also solicited direct donations, but resources still did not meet publication costs. In 1910, a solution appeared to arise. The National American Woman Suffrage Association (NAWSA) proposed adopting the *Woman's Journal* as its official publication. With the new partnership in place, circulation expanded rapidly, and by 1912, almost twenty thousand people regularly received the paper.[7] While most of the subscribers were white, the newspaper did reach across racial lines. In Alabama, black suffragist Adella Hunt Logan regularly read the publication. In addition to her dedication to the group's newspaper, Logan was a lifetime member of NAWSA. With her fair complexion, it is not known if most white suffragists at the club's meetings realized they sat next to an African American. Either way, Logan listened intently, carrying the information she learned back to black suffragists in the Tuskegee Woman's Club at Alabama's Tuskegee Institute.[8]

Under NAWSA's guidance, a new business manager, Agnes E. Ryan, had been put in charge of growing the publication's readership.[9] A talented and creative individual, Ryan looked for ways to give the *Woman's Journal* a more public and personal face. Who better to sell a newspaper about suffrage then suffragists themselves. As early as 1909, several American activists emulated their British comrades by selling the *Woman's Journal* on the streets of Boston.[10] Ryan took the practice one step further by systemizing the work of newsies for the cause. Articles and letters encouraged women around the country to order canvas news bags and take to the streets. Ryan even put together a short pamphlet titled *Selling the Woman's Journal* to alleviate any concerns and answer any questions a woman might have about peddling the newspaper. With practical guidance, suffrage newsies were reminded to find out if sellers needed permits, to always carry ample change, and to dress warmly in winter. It encouraged them to use clever sales techniques, and if business was slow it suggested they arrange for suffrage supporters to surround them, creating a scene and setting an example for other potential buyers.[11]

With Ryan's goal to increase readership and sales, she looked to get more papers in the hands of newsies by paying them on a commission basis. Half of the proceeds of each sale went directly into the newsies' pockets, meaning the more they sold, the more they made. This arrangement particularly appealed to suffrage clubs. By selling copies of the *Woman's Journal*, and devoting the profits to their organizations, they could raise funds and increase visibility at the same time.[12] It was not long before other suffrage publications took note of the *Woman's Journal*'s success and began sending suffrage newsies onto the streets. Cities around the country began reporting their presence selling a wide variety of suffrage publications. In Detroit, the local press noted that college alumnae carried bags of the *Woman's Journal*, in 1912.[13] In Helena, Montana, reports in 1914 indicated that copies of the *Suffrage Daily News* could be purchased from newsies around town.[14] By the following year, the appearance of suffrage newsies was no longer unexpected, but they had not yet lost their ability to grab attention. In Rochester, New York, a local newspaper reported, "women wearing 'votes-for-women' sashes and carrying newsboys' outfits will be a common sight in this city today."[15] Despite Ryan's progressive marketing campaign and success through the use of newsies, the increased circulation of the *Woman's Journal* simply meant more expenses, and the publication still failed to turn a profit. However, the value suffragists placed on the *Woman's Journal* was unmeasurable, and despite its shortcomings in revenue, it continued to operate until 1931.[16]

The suffrage newsies who hit the streets to sell the *Woman's Journal* and other suffrage publications were a new breed of activists. While pioneering reform had dabbled in the use of publications, it was the younger generation that increased the spectacle and made the tactic more impactful. By loading literature into brightly colored and boldly lettered bags, suffrage newsies drew attention to their publications and disseminated information about women's voting rights to the masses. As their voices carried the names of newspapers over streets and alleyways, the women's suffrage movement firmly stood in a public arena dominated almost exclusively by men.

Suffrage with a Side of Soup

Plate, made by John Maddock & Sons, Ltd., around 1910, New-York Historical Society, New York, NY, http://www.nyhistory.org/
NEW-YORK HISTORICAL SOCIETY

After a busy morning, sometimes the best thing to do for a recharge is to head out for lunch. Somewhere quick with good, affordable food, and an atmosphere completely different from the workplace. This daily ritual of many people is nothing new. In the 1910s, workers longed to get out of offices and off the sales floor for a midday nosh just as much as today. To meet the demand, corner drugstores offered lunchtime menus, and lunchrooms and cafeterias popped up across the urban landscape. At some of these establishments an order of roast beef and mashed potatoes might be served up on a plate similar to the one seen on the facing page. Printed with the iconic slogan "Votes for Women," the John Maddock Company of England made this plate for wealthy New York and Rhode Island socialite Alva Belmont.[1] Around 1908, Belmont became interested in suffrage and was soon wholeheartedly committed to the cause. Believing America's suffrage movement needed a good dose of publicity, Belmont took it upon herself to open her pocketbook and fund initiatives she thought would draw attention from both the wealthy and the working class.[2]

As a woman at the top of the social ladder, Alva Belmont knew that in addition to her own finances, she could help deliver the support of other wealthy Americans to the suffrage movement. What better way to capture the support of her peers than to host suffrage meetings at her home in Newport, Rhode Island? Known as the playground of the country's most well-to-do, summer mansions dripping in opulence lined Newport's oceanside avenues. In the summers of 1909 and 1914, Belmont held two highly successful suffrage meetings, drawing crowds to her Newport home and garnering loads of attention in the press. At the first meeting, an admission fee of $5 gained an individual entrance to tour the home and grounds as well as access to suffrage lectures. The conference in 1914 again spurred interest for voting rights among the wealthy when eight speakers tackled the topic of suffrage. The occasion also marked the opening of Belmont's new Chinese teahouse on her property and may have included the use of Belmont's specially ordered "Votes for Women" dishware.[3]

Despite Belmont's own abundance of riches, she made efforts to reach out to the working classes of American society. She understood that the message of suffrage could not be considered by the upper class alone. To reach her own social sect and beyond, in 1909, she set up a campaigning group called the Political Equality Association (PEA) under the umbrella of the National

American Woman Suffrage Association (NAWSA). Around the same time, Belmont urged NAWSA to move its headquarters from Ohio to New York City, where it would be more visible on the national stage. With Belmont offering to pay for a new office in Manhattan, the cash-strapped organization could not refuse. The relationship became strained however, when the often-bossy Belmont began pushing for NAWSA campaigners to get out of their offices and connect more with masses on the streets. When met with resistance, Belmont decided that if others would not do it, she would, and she began establishing PEA settlements all over the city.[4]

Drawing on the example of the British suffrage movement, Belmont's eleven settlements took the form of street-front suffrage clubs. These eye level spaces hosted meetings and public speaking classes, arranged for musical entertainment, and housed shops for the public to purchase items such as suffrage themed literature and merchandise. Additionally, Belmont opened a lunchroom. Run by suffrage supporters, the establishment offered working-class women a place to purchase a nutritious meal for as little as five cents. If anyone doubted the lunchroom would succeed, those worries soon faded away because wherever Belmont went, the press followed. Newspapers practically glowed about the bustling lunch establishment. Not only did it teem with working girls needing a quick meal, but it also attracted middle-class shoppers and men escaping their work offices.[5] For those hoping to catch a glimpse of the proprietress herself, customers were in luck. The lunchroom became a pet project of Belmont's, and she could sometimes be spotted standing at the door "like a head waiter."[6]

In fact, Belmont's lunchroom quickly became so popular, others followed her lead. Elsewhere in New York City, Sophia Kramer opened a similar establishment.[7] In San Francisco, the Votes for Women Club set up a restaurant near a high-end department store, not to attract wealthy shoppers, but rather the shop girls and office workers needing a midday meal. Lunchrooms run by suffragists were not isolated to the coasts, however. Newspapers also described similar businesses in Chicago and other cities around the nation.[8]

To draw in customers, the restaurants offered home cooking at an affordable price. The menus featured popular items like chicken soup, lamb stew, salad, roast beef with mashed potatoes, codfish, and cakes.[9] Once there, young working women who may have never attended a suffrage meeting found themselves exposed to suffrage ideas.[10] Banners, posters, and pictures decorated walls, and diners might be engaged in a conversation about the need and benefits of the vote. At many establishments, the food itself even came served on dishes bearing the iconic phrase, "Votes for Women." In many ways, patrons were served up suffrage with a side of soup, and in the case of Belmont's lunchroom, the rock-bottom prices even tempted skeptics. Men not yet supportive of women's suffrage could not ignore the lure of affordable prices. When they arrived, a hostess ushered them to tables reserved specifically for male guests. Always prepared, once doubters showed even a glimmer of support, the lunchroom pointed prospective converts to additional pro-suffrage pamphlets at the attached PEA settlement.[11]

Through her suffrage lunchroom, Belmont proved the American suffrage movement could not only attract middle- and upper-class support, but also be made accessible to working-class women. The broad spectrum of people gathering together over lunch demonstrated that women's suffrage was truly a universal concern shared by all walks of life. Whether she used the plate seen at the beginning of this chapter in her New York City lunchroom or at her home in Newport is unknown. Either way, it represents one woman's attempt to combine politics, business, and publicity. Through her example, suffragists across the country came to realize the tactics needed to secure voting rights had to be wide, varied, and, occasionally, appealing to something as common as the hungry stomach.

On the Road to Victory

Hood Ornament, made by The Henry Bruml Company, New York, NY, 1910–1920, The Henry Ford, Dearborn, MI, https://www.thehenryford.org/

Cars are everywhere. They jam highways, cruise down rural lanes, and sit in the parking lots of businesses. Whether driving alone or hopping in the nearest rideshare, it is safe to say most Americans rely on automobiles during their daily lives. Because cars, trucks, and SUVs dominate American roadways today, it is hard to imagine that just over a hundred years ago automobiles were not a common sight. A car did not have to be a Bugatti to turn heads, but a little bit of bling never hurt. Outfitted with hood ornaments like the one seen on the facing page or decorated in even bolder manners, automobiles played a crucial role in suffragists' promotion of equal voting rights. By hopping behind the wheel, women took to the road to recruit support and in doing so, proved their independence and modern know-how.

By the end of the nineteenth century, the United States successfully moved large numbers of people around the country on an elaborate system of railways. Seeing the benefits and popularity of quick and easy travel, many individuals began looking for additional ways to replace the horse-drawn wagons and carriages people had long relied on. In the 1890s, roadworthy vehicles began dotting thoroughfares, but these early autos proved expensive and clunky, as inventors continued to identify the best form of power. By the 1910s, affordable vehicles, such as Ford's Model T, made cars more widely accessible.[1] Although not the rarity they had once been, the sight of a well-crafted Mercedes or a visually-stunning Studebaker could still turn heads.

Always looking for fresh ways to spread the word about voting rights and recruit new supporters, suffragists seized the opportunity automobiles provided. If a flashy car could turn heads, how about one also driven by a woman? In many areas, women were not the typical drivers, so when suffragists exercised their independence and got behind the wheel, they drew a captive audience.[2] From 1910 until 1920 the automobile played a significant role in how suffragists promoted the need for equal voting rights. They delivered speeches from parked vehicles, decorated them for use in parades, and at times even organized processions comprised only of cars.[3]

In the summer of 1912, suffragists in Iowa set out in an automobile to travel throughout the state. As they approached the edge of a town a woman on board would begin playing her cornet to signal they were drawing near. After finding a central location to park, the group would speak to anyone who gathered around and pass out colorful flyers filled with arguments in favor of suffrage.[4] In Connecticut, activists set out on a similar tour in the summer of 1914. Unlike the women in Iowa who relied on spontaneous speeches, the suffragists in Connecticut scheduled sixty meetings in advance. Driving three vehicles named "The Conservative," "The Radical," and "Votes," they headed to various factories and mills serving as the sites for the gatherings.[5] Their cars grabbed the attention of both the press and public, proving that cars were not only functional in moving suffragists from place to place, but also had the ability to liberate women and open new opportunities for them in public.

In 1916, the National American Woman Suffrage Association (NAWSA) looked to expand the concept even further. Capitalizing on the popularity and practicality of the automobile, in April the organization sent two women out on the road. In a media splash, Alice Burke of Illinois, Nell Richardson of Virginia, and their kitten piled into a yellow, gas-powered car donated by the Saxon Motor Company. Proving automobiles were as much for the modern woman as for men, Burke and Richardson drove and serviced the vehicle themselves.[6] Christened "The Golden Flyer" by NAWSA, Carrie Chapman Catt broke a bottle of gasoline over the hood as the group headed out on their six-month trip.[7] Departing from New York, the two suffragists traversed the nation: Louisiana, Texas, New Mexico, Arizona, California, Oregon, Washington, across the Midwest and back to New York. Throughout the trip, they rallied support and carried news of NAWSA's plans to promote women's suffrage at the Democratic and Republican national conventions in St. Louis and Chicago later that year.[8]

At a time when roads were either dirt or gravel, motor travel could be difficult and dangerous. Cars of the era often broke down, putting Burke and Richardson's knowledge of mechanics to the test. These obstacles did not prove too large for the women, however, and they stopped frequently to give speeches from their car and recruit supporters.[9] During the 10,700 miles on the road, the automobile served as their stage, and a sign reading "Votes for Women" dangled from the back. In addition to the suffrage-yellow paint, the body of the car also became inscribed with personal testimonials as women across the country covered it with their signatures in support of equal voting rights.[10] With the press tracking their journey along the way, "The Golden Flyer" became a symbol of the suffrage movement. For those not impressed by cars, the group's third passenger, the kitten, appropriately named Saxon, drew his own attention, while for six months people around the country followed his growth from town to town.[11]

NAWSA was certainly not the first or the last group to utilize the automobile for the promotion of suffrage. The group's use of new technology proved so successful, however, that the Saxon Motor Company itself became linked with the movement. While they never signed on as the official car of suffrage, the 1916 auto tour became a great promotional tool for the company. Ads reading "Two Noted Suffragists Travel 10,000 miles in Saxon Roadster" not only proved the quality of their product, but also gave extra exposure to the suffrage cause.[12] In the last ten years of the suffrage movement, automobiles driven by women became a standard part of their efforts to expand support and educate the public. Women had found a means to free themselves from social and geographic limitations, and suffragists identified a tool that was both efficient and eye-catching. In grabbing the wheel, women proved they could cover more ground while bringing themselves a little closer to the full citizenship they desired.

Lifting as We Climb

Banner with motto of the National Association of Colored Women's Clubs, 1920s, National Museum of African American History & Culture, Washington, DC, https://nmaahc.si.edu/

The word "convention" can bring many images to mind. Some people will automatically have thoughts of costumed Comic-Con attendees enter their heads. Others envision rooms of professionals in suits, listening in earnest to the latest trends in their field. For women's suffrage supporters, conventions played an important role in the strategic playbook of many activists. These formal assemblies provided organizations with the chance to gather their membership together, discuss current issues, and rally their base. Used by the Oklahoma Federation of Colored Women's Clubs, the banner seen on the facing page carries the official motto of the National Association of Colored Women's Clubs (NACWC). Although not a suffrage-specific organization, NACWC was one of the largest and most influential African American organizations in the nation. They put suffrage at the forefront of their work and made it clear that the vote for black women was integral to the uplift of all black society. Through national conventions, they coordinated work, bringing what they believed to be the most important issues of the black community to the forefront of state and local efforts.

For affiliate organizations all around the country, "Lifting as We Climb" was not just a memorable phrase. Reducing the motto to such trivialness would downplay the importance of African American clubwomen in the fight for black rights. "Lifting as We Climb" was adopted with the intention of showing "an ignorant and suspicious world that our aims and interest are identical with those of all good, aspiring women."[1] Furthermore, the motto reflected the belief that as each black woman gained, they lifted the status not just of themselves but of the entire black race. Living out this belief to the fullest, NACWC toiled to bring a unified sense of work and communication to the numerous African American women's clubs around the country. To do so, they utilized a tactic that had proved successful for suffragists and activists for decades.

From its earliest years, the suffrage movement understood the power of gathering like-minded individuals. When white reformers looked to do just that in 1848, they settled on the idea of holding a convention in Seneca Falls, New York. The effect of this local gathering proved so impactful that within two years, activists in Massachusetts hosted the first women's rights convention targeting a national audience.[2] From then on, conventions remained a mainstay of the broader women's rights movement, drawing attention from both black and white activists. When suffragists broke out on their own and formed national organizations, white leadership looked to previous work for inspiration in rallying supporters around a unified message. As a tried and true method, conventions rose to the top of the list. Although suffragists found the need to expand their tactics over time, the convention remained an important tool for collective buy-in until the passage of the 19th Amendment.

As racial divisions persisted in the national suffrage movement, however, many black suffragists found it difficult to participate in the activities of the white-led national organizations, including their conventions, which were often racially segregated in the south.[3] In response, black women around the country formed a variety of local- and state-level organizations to tackle not only the issue of suffrage, but also a host of broader social concerns. Women's clubs looking to improve life for African Americans could be found in such varying locations as Oklahoma, Colorado, Rhode Island, Illinois, and Alabama, just to name a few. As this network expanded, many began communicating with each other by word of mouth or letters. At the state level, organizers formed themselves into units, holding statewide conventions where clubs could come together for support and to discuss common issues. As this continued, it became apparent that the work of black club women would benefit from a national umbrella organization to serve as a central connector, promote self-help among black women, and advocate for the causes most important to black communities.[4]

In July of 1896, this hope for an overarching group came to fruition when the National Association of Colored Women's Clubs formed. Serving as the first president was Mary Church Terrell, a lecturer and author born in Memphis, Tennessee. The daughter of former slaves, Terrell had extraordinary opportunities presented to her in her formative years. After gaining his freedom, Terrell's father excelled as a businessman and eventually became one of the first black millionaires in the American South. Taking advantage of his success, he made sure his daughter had the best education possible. Traveling to Ohio, Mary Terrell attended Oberlin College, earning a bachelor of arts in 1883 and a master of arts in 1885. After completing two degrees, Terrell began a teaching career, first at Wilberforce University and then at M Street Colored High School in Washington, DC. After her marriage in 1891, Terrell was forced to give up her teaching position, according to school policy. Although no longer teaching, Terrell remained highly active in education, becoming one of the first two women appointed to the board of education for public schools in the District of Columbia.[5] She also had a drive for social activism, working for women's suffrage, anti-lynching campaigns, and the uplift of African Americans. Her words—"Lifting as We Climb"—became the motto of NACWC.[6]

From the time of its formation, women's suffrage was a notable component of NACWC's work. A department dedicated specifically to the franchise was established and a national representative assigned to head up the efforts. This created a hierarchy for disseminating information to educate state and local club members about the benefits of supporting voting rights for women.[7] Always taken up alongside issues such as lynching, education, and citizenship, it became obvious that for black women the vote was not just about improving their own lives, but those of all black women, men, and children.

In addition to the regular circulation of educational information, conventions proved crucial in the work of NACWC. Held biennially in different locations around the country, the organization's national meetings provided an opportunity for delegates from affiliate clubs to come together. Attracting representatives from all over the nation, a larger sense of community was created, and diverse voices heard. The conventions regularly continued the discussion of the national umbrella of issues concerning clubs at the local and state levels. In this way, the national association not only led local and state club work by setting a national agenda, but also listened to, took pride in, and supported their work. By coming together in this way, delegates from around the nation built a working relationship with national leadership; and a common philosophy and mission from which to gain civil rights, privileges, and first-class citizenship for all African Americans was developed.[8]

By July of 1920, NACWC had been in existence for more than two decades. In that time, they had grown into the largest association representing black women in the country, and references to their support of women's suffrage had steadily increased.[9] The issue had become a regular point of discussion at their conventions, and 1920 was no different. With the ratification of the 19th Amendment looming, the issue of voting rights was unquestionably top of mind for leadership and delegates. Over five days in Alabama, hundreds of black clubwomen from around the nation met on the campus of the Tuskegee Institute, a prominent center of education for African Americans. Arriving by the trainload in fashionable pullman cars, delegates marveled at the beautiful campus. They were greeted by the institute's president, and it was reported that no expense was spared in making the women comfortable. According to *The New York Age,* "The dormitory space and private homes were taxed to capacity" with the arrival of the activists.[10] Helping to host NACWC was the Tuskegee Women's Club, a local organization focused on uplifting black society and also interested in securing the vote for African American women.

Throughout the course of the convention, delegates heard speeches and engaged in discussion regarding current issues and affairs around the nation. They also took time to reflect upon the past. In a ceremony involving hundreds of women, a wreath of roses was placed upon the grave of Booker T. Washington, founder of the institute and one of the most revered leaders of the African American community.[11] When the convention ended, NACWC issued a set of resolutions outlining the recommendations of the organization and its delegates. Boldly stated first, the association declared, "Since it is evident that the women of the nation are soon to be invested with the right of full franchise, We recommend that the colored women give their close attention to the study of civics, to the laws of parliamentary usage, and to the current political questions, both local and national, in order to fit themselves for the exercise of the franchise."[12]Having made it clear that black women should ready themselves as voters, the resolutions further stated, "We also urge our National Congress to enforce the Fourteenth and Fifteenth Amendments to the Federal Constitution."[13]

For decades, black suffragists had been working from the ranks of many women's clubs to advocate for universal suffrage. Theirs was not simply a desire to secure the vote for themselves, but to also ensure that black men had the opportunity to exercise the ballot as well. While the right had existed on paper for many years, all too often African American men had their vote stripped away through the use of poll taxes, literacy tests, and other discriminatory actions. For African American suffragists, the 19th Amendment did not stand alone, but was part of the 15th Amendment and the previous rights of citizenship it had outlined. Through regular conventions, organizations such as NACWC led the work of local and state clubs and activists around the nation. With encouragement and support, members lived out the motto, "Lifting as We Climb." The collective nature of their gatherings promoted comradery and provided a way for black suffragists and activists to use their voice, debate one another, and set a unified agenda not only promoting the black individual, but also working to improve life for all black Americans.

Lobbying for the Vote

Photograph of Theodora Youmans wearing suffrage tunic, 1916, The Wisconsin Historical Society, Madison, WI, https://www.wisconsinhistory.org/
WISCSONSIN HISTORICAL SOCIETY, WHS-1927

A ny social or political movement lasting as long as the struggle for women's suffrage is sure to undergo change. As the push to secure voting rights for women unfolded slowly, activists realized their tactics needed to evolve with the world around them. The second decade of the twentieth century not only saw the influx of new and youthful suffragists to the movement, but also saw the United States become a society marked by technological advances, modern consumerism, and progressive thought. While some of the strategies developed in the early years of their movement remained in use, suffragists strengthened and altered many over time to remain relevant to modern society. By combining long-standing activities such as personal appeals to lawmakers with modern public spectacle, activists increased their visibility and made it clear they were here to stay.

While the tactics used by suffragists in the early years of the movement may appear safe and conservative, their lunchrooms and automobile tours certainly pushed the boundaries of their world. Their actions challenged the firmly established political and social hierarchy of the time, and in speaking out for their rights, they sought to make a permanent place for themselves in the male-centered activity of voting. Not only were these desires bold, so was their insistence that they carry out their work in public. According to popular thought, a respectable woman stayed in the home where she could guide the moral well-being of her family. Suffragists worked to prove that wrong. They gave lectures and attended conventions, met in public halls and churches, solicited door-to-door support for petitions, and polled men and women on their opinion of female voting rights.[1]

One of the oldest public techniques used by suffragists was lobbying. Over their seventy-two-year campaign they never stopped pressuring officeholders to change the existing laws limiting women's opportunities and barring their rights as citizens. At the Seneca Falls Convention, attendees adopted resolutions to pressure lawmakers and educate the public.[2] As the century went on activists in states around the nation regularly met with their legislators, asking them to grant women the right to vote. These efforts proved mildly successful, and by 1900 four states and territories had enfranchised women.[3] While traditional lobbying remained a mainstay until the passage of the 19th Amendment, it became clear more visible and public action was needed to supplement conventional methods. Many suffragists believed if they wanted to be seen and heard by lawmakers, they needed to go big or go home.

Adopted by conservatives and radicals alike, the suffrage movement greatly benefitted from the exposure created by public demonstrations. Unlike private meetings or debates, these events gave suffragists an opportunity for great visibility. Exposed to the public, press, and politicians, they appeared in small or large numbers, depending on the situation, drawing attention to themselves and the suffrage cause. They set their own agendas, determined their course of action, and claimed public space in a way they had not done before. Often comprised of professionals, college graduates, workers, and middle- and upper-class women, large events symbolized the deep desire for suffrage stretching across the fabric of society. They also provided candy for the eye. At parades, banners, floats, and automobiles decorated in bright colors and slogans dotted routes as far as the eye could see. And at pageants, elaborate costumes and outfits told stories chronicling women's history and demand for the vote.[4]

In 1916, suffragists effectively brought together aspects of these public demonstrations and traditional lobbying to appeal to lawmakers during the Republican National convention in Chicago. To grab attention, the National American Woman Suffrage Association (NAWSA) invited suffragists from around the nation to join them for a massive demonstration. Grabbing media attention, suffragists caused a commotion as they converged upon the city. After assembling together, they set out on a march culminating at the site of the lawmakers' meeting. Among those invited were members of the Wisconsin Woman Suffrage Association. Frustrated after several failed attempts to secure voting legislation in their own state, the women of Wisconsin shifted their attention to the national movement. Their president, Theodora Youmans saw the opportunity as a chance to lift the morale of her over-worked and under-rewarded members.[5]

On June 7, 1916, the women of Wisconsin traveled to Chicago to join their fellow suffragists. To help create excitement for the event, Youmans commissioned an artist to design special colorful tunics for her state's activists to wear. Made of fabric in suffrage yellow, "WISCONSIN" was stenciled in bold black letters down the front. While the outfit most certainly caught the eye of many, only activists planning to join the demonstration could acquire it. Sold exclusively to participants, a tunic along with coordinating hat and a round-trip train ticket could be purchased for only $3.10. On the day of the event, most of the Wisconsin contingent gathered together in Milwaukee and marched down Grand Avenue to the railroad depot where they boarded their train. Special "suffrage cars" carrying marchers from Madison, Waukesha, and Kenosha joined the procession—ensuring that the media paid attention from the moment the activists began their journey.[6]

Arriving in Chicago, members of both NAWSA as well as the Congressional Union, met the women of Wisconsin. Although the two national legions did not often see eye to eye, this occasion carried enough importance to draw both groups together. In the past, the Republican Party had endorsed the principles of suffrage, but they had not yet supported the passage of a constitutional amendment. Suffragists hoped this event would change their minds, and they pulled out all the stops during planning.[7] With NAWSA drawing thousands of activists from around the country, live elephants symbolizing the Republican Party lined up and hopes were high as suffragists donned sashes or special regalia such as Wisconsin's tunics.[8]

Unfortunately, when the train from Wisconsin arrived in Chicago, suffragists from the Badger State were met with more than just comrades. A torrential storm also greeted the activists. Undeterred by the weather, the suffragists carried on with their plans. Marching down Michigan Avenue under the banners of NAWSA and the Congressional Union, the group of demonstrators made their way to the site of the Republican convention. As they did, heavy rain and whipping wind pelted the suffragists.[9] Watching on were men who had first ridiculed the marchers, but then fell silent in admiration as the women stayed in their ranks despite the torrential weather.[10] At the front of the march, activists carried their most important weapon—copies of resolutions to present to lawmakers. Wet, cold, and tired, the activists arrived at the convention's doors where four suffragists, representing all of the women who had braved the storm, carried them inside.[11] For decades suffragists had made appeals to lawmakers, but unlike the discreet work of the nineteenth century, dramatic spectacle filled the scene in 1916. Rather than quietly lobby their lawmakers as usual, this day, suffragists made sure the legislators and the nation took notice.

In the end, suffragists only partially received what they requested. The Republican Party included a suffrage plank in their national platform, but rather than support a federal amendment as suffragists hoped, they instead crafted a statement supporting a state-by-state approach.[12] In response, NAWSA called an emergency convention in September and invited both presidential candidates. The Republican nominee did not show but had already distanced himself from his party and endorsed a federal amendment granting women's suffrage. Woodrow Wilson, the Democratic nominee and the soon-to-be winner, did attend. When the time came for him to speak, he pledged his support of suffrage, but then added, "we will not quarrel in the long run as to the method of it."[13] Foreshadowing his future foot-dragging to support a federal amendment, Wilson's words disappointed suffragists. Nevertheless, appearing at their convention at all signaled progress. By combining old tactics with new ones, female voting rights became a serious issue in American politics, and suffragists found new ways to reach lawmakers who had never before given them a second look.

Swimming for Suffrage

Photograph of National Women's Life-Saving League members at Sheepshead Bay, New York, July 16, 1914, Library of Congress Prints and Photographs Division, Washington, DC, https://www.loc.gov/pictures/

Every four years athletes from around the world gather at the Summer Olympics. Soccer players go toe-to-toe on the field, and runners give it their all on the track. In the pool, the fastest women in the world wear swimsuits and caps meant to reduce drag and allow for the fastest times possible. Today, the formfitting suits seen at the competitive level, or at public pools and beaches, barely turn heads, but in the early 1900s, women daring to appear publicly in swim garments hinting at their female form made a bold statement. Often the individuals who wore these new-fangled swimsuits were the same women demanding the right to vote.

In the last quarter of the nineteenth century, public opinion about women and athletics began to change. Colleges began offering exercise programs for female students, and girls played basketball in bloomers and sweaters.[1] Soon women could be seen on tennis courts, swinging golf clubs, and riding bicycles as they sought greater freedom. By the turn of the twentieth century, sporting among women had become so popular that female athletic clubs popped up around the country. In places like Providence, Rhode Island, New York City, and Chicago, women's athletic clubs featured gymnasiums, bowling alleys, billiard rooms, and swimming pools. This foray into sports not only challenged stereotypes depicting women as physically weak, but actually proved them the strong, powerful individuals suffragists championed.[2]

In the water women pushed the limits. For decades their options for swimwear had been limited to heavy and modest bathing costumes covering most of their bodies. Decked out in stockings, skirts, and full-coverage tops, excursions to the beach involved more sinking than swimming, as their bathing suits absorbed water and weighed them down. In 1910, professional Australian swimmer Annette Kellerman shocked the American public when she appeared in the United States in a one-piece, fitted suit showing off her figure. Similar designs had already appeared in England, and soon competitive American swimmers adopted the style to improve their performance.[3] One such proponent of bathing suit reform was Charlotte Epstein, the Jewish American woman considered the nation's mother of swimming. Not just a mover and shaker in the water, however, Epstein also grabbed opportunities to use the visibility of the organizations she led to endorse women's suffrage.[4]

In 1911, Epstein joined the National Women's Life-Saving League, eventually serving on its board of directors, and by 1913 she had become the chairman of the League's Athletic Branch. In this role she directed all the organization's local competitions in New York and worked to devise spectacular events and swimming contests not only pushing female swimmers to the limits of their speed and skill, but also demanding proficiency in running and life-saving. Many of these programs attracted skilled swimmers clad in the new streamlined suits of the day, and Epstein earned a reputation for outstanding leadership.[5]

In July 1915, one of the League's local outdoor swimming competitions highlighted the organization's advocacy of suffrage. Taking place at Manhattan Beach in New York, about fifty women gathered to compete in the competition. If spectators anticipated the swimwear as the spectacle of the day, they thought wrong. After traditional swimming contests, the *New-York Tribune* reported, the meet concluded with an eye-catching "suffrage rescue race."[6] According to the newspaper, the race occurred in connection with a local suffrage group, and "the water women are all good suffragists."[7] Lining up to start, competitors wore "Votes for Women" sashes and prepared to dive into the water. Fifty yards off shore a dummy served as their target. Dressed in a white dress, white shoes, stockings, silk gloves, white cap, and a red sash reading "Anti-Suffrage," the mannequin had to be towed safely to shore by the first member of the Life-Saving League to reach it. As a spokesperson told the newspaper, "We want to save the anti-suffragists from political voicelessness and we will help them along in any way we can."[8] In a fast sprint to the dummy, Jewish American swimmer Rita Greenfield grabbed the mannequin and brought it safely to shore. Showing her own true suffrage colors, Greenfield later told the press she would "much rather have drowned it."[9]

Although the event raised eyebrows with its novelty, swimming suffragists were not isolated to the Life-Saving League. In fact, local clubs around the nation took to the water to show their support of suffrage, as well as athletics for women. In 1912, a dozen women in Canton, Ohio, shocked swimmers at a local beach. When the women arrived, they wore bathing suits showing off their bare legs, donned yellow caps, and waded out into the water where they held their suffrage meeting. They swam along the life lines, decorating them with yellow posters urging other swimmers to support voting rights for women.[10] In 1915, suffragists in New York, New Jersey, and Pennsylvania planned to include swimming in one of their largest publicity events. Throughout New Jersey's campaign for state suffrage that year, a large wooden torch called the "Torch of Liberty" passed from city to city in the tri-state area to drum up interest in the cause. That August plans began for a symbolic swim of the torch across the Delaware River by a young activist. Plans were foiled, however, when the torch went missing and suffragists' focus shifted to simply locating the iconic item.[11]

Throughout these events, athletes demonstrated that suffrage and swimming went hand in hand. While the sight of women in form-fitting swimwear turned heads on its own, with the issue of suffrage attached, it made for a public demonstration capable of catching the eye and shocking many people. Once attention was grabbed, the swimmers in the water communicated the desire of many women for change in their lives. When suffragists of the Life-Saving League staged their "rescue race" in 1915, women had just emerged into the world of competitive swimming. By the 1920s, they had not only helped secure the opportunity for women to vote, but they had also broken into Olympic competition. Speaking to the *Woman's Home Companion* in 1924, Glenna Collett, the top female golfer in the United States, summed it up best when she said, "American women, in the first quarter of the twentieth century, have won two rights: the right of exercising the suffrage and the right of participation in sport."[12] Both were major victories for women's rights, and in many ways women's expansion of physical exercise played an important role in making suffrage a reality for both female swimmers and spectators.

Falling into Line

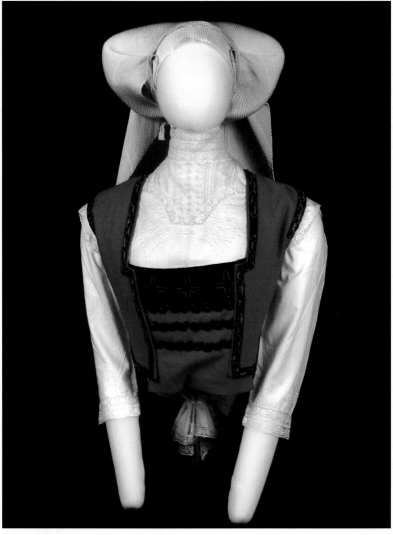

Norwegian Headdress and Vest, 1913, Wisconsin Historical Society, Madison, WI, https://www.wisconsinhistory.org/

From Cinco de Mayo to St. Patrick's Day, American citizens take pride in celebrating their heritage. Whether through food, drink, or dance, the traditions of ancestors often pass from generation to generation. One example is the traditional Norwegian headdress and vest seen on the facing page, made by Thea Johanna Stondahl Nelson of Wisconsin around 1913.[1] The daughter of Norwegian immigrants, the American-born Nelson created the outfit for a very specific purpose. In March of that year she travelled to Washington, DC, to join thousands of activists in what became one of the most famous public demonstrations the suffrage movement would undertake. Marching down Pennsylvania Avenue, Nelson proudly wore the costume of her ancestry. While her pride on any given day may have reflected many aspects of Norwegian culture, on this day her costume represented the progress her ancestral home had already made in granting women the right to vote. While full universal suffrage would not be passed in Norway until a few months after the parade, at the time of the procession, middle-class women across the European nation already held the right to vote in parliamentary elections, and all female citizens could vote at the local level.[2]

While Norway's suffrage movement made great strides in the early years of the twentieth century, the movement in the United States experienced growing pains. As members of the older generation passed away, the National American Woman Suffrage Association (NAWSA) and its state and local affiliates struggled to find their footing. With leadership made up significantly of nonworking, wealthy white women, the organizations often struggled to connect with professional women, African Americans, and union organizers linked to the working classes. Younger, energetic women slowly began to come into the fold however, and in 1912 a rising militant leader named Alice Paul joined the national organization. Borrowing techniques from the British suffrage movement, Paul hoped to infuse drama and new energy into the tired group.[3]

Soon after becoming involved, Paul began pressuring NAWSA to begin a program calling for an amendment to the federal constitution. Part of her vision included a permanent congressional committee to work toward legislation in the nation's capital. The organization approved the committee in 1912, and Paul became its head. Almost immediately, the committee began making plans for a large suffrage parade in Washington, DC, the next year. If all went as planned, the event would create enthusiasm for a federal amendment, grab the attention of lawmakers, and energize state and local suffragists around the nation. With the newly elected president of the country scheduled to be inaugurated on March 4, organizers set their sights on the day prior for their parade. Not only would politicians, dignitaries, the public, and press be in town, but the new president would also be sure to get the message.[4] As plans for the parade began to unfold, leaders at NAWSA became wary for fear the event would be too militant and unladylike. Despite these concerns, leaders eventually came to support the event, knowing the potential it held for exposure and impact.[5]

Although shocking to many people, the 1913 parade was not the first time American suffragists had taken to the streets. While activist had used formal marches before, and would continue to after, these events focused mainly on moving groups of suffragists from one destination to another in a formal manner—much like a military unit. While they may have involved some individuals or groups independently choosing to carry banners, or wear sashes and coordinating outfits, the overall focus remained on presenting one physically large unit. Suffrage parades, however, brought a higher level of spectacle for the public. These organized processions were highly choreographed and designed celebrations meant to shock, awe, and entertain. Typically, they consisted of a series of purposeful displays, performances, and floats building upon each other to tell a story. When advertised correctly, the public came out in droves to watch. In 1908, a few hundred women staged a parade in California. By 1912, a handful of similar events dotted locations across the country, and for the next few years they remained a regular form of demonstration. Unlike small meetings or debates, parades could bring large amounts of suffragists together at one time. Taking to public thoroughfares, activists knew they would be seen, which would draw attention to them and their message— precisely what happened in 1913.[6]

Throughout the planning process, organizers wanted to ensure that the 1913 parade's beauty and visual effect remained front and center. With that in mind, they focused much of their energy on issues related to artistry and pageantry. The parade was divided into several sections including delegations from states where females already voted, working women representing numerous businesses and professions, and a section depicting the past seventy-five years of the struggle for women's rights. A series of segments depicting countries where women's suffrage had already been secured also featured prominently in the parade. Made up of immigrants or women with ancestral connections, each section featured marchers wearing the national costume of the country they represented. Surely, Nelson's costume could be seen marching past onlookers alongside other proud Norwegians and Norwegian Americans. Floats were interspersed throughout the marching units, and banners and costumes such as Nelson's brought a sense of pageantry to the affair. Those not dressed in special costume were encouraged to wear white, a traditional color associated with purity and temperance. The color also served as the perfect backdrop for the parade's official colors—purple, green, and white of the British militant movement. Against a sea of white, the bold colors easily stood out.[7]

Although organizers focused most of their attention on pageantry and not size during the planning of the parade, five thousand participants arrived in the nation's capital to take part. The suffragists who appeared represented the wide variety of women toiling around the nation for voting rights. Participants included white women and women of color; individuals who identified not only as Americans but with dozens of other ancestral nations; citizens representing economic classes ranging from the very wealthy to the working class; professionals; and the college educated. Falling into line, the marchers prepared to dazzle onlookers, attract recruits, and most importantly, grab the attention of lawmakers with their celebration of women's suffrage. Very intentionally, they walked with dignity and conveyed the serious, respectable demeanor of responsible voters.[8]

In a symbolic move, the parade set out on the afternoon of March 3, following the same path President Wilson's inaugural parade would take the next day. Inez Milholland led the march. Dressed in flowing white robes and resembling Joan of Arc, Milholland gallantly led the procession atop a white horse as three hundred thousand onlookers crowded the sides of the street. It did not take long for what began as a joyous event for suffragists to turn into a scene of violence. As the activists marched along their path, the crowd became irate at their demands and their boldness to appear in public. Male and female bystanders alike verbally abused and physically assaulted parade marchers. In some instances, men even jumped on floats in an attempt to accost terrified female riders.[9] As the crowd pushed in from the sides of the street, they swamped the activists, spitting on them and pelting them with lit cigars, as the local police stood idly by.[10] At times, Milholland even had to charge rioters with her horse so marchers could move ahead. And at one point, sympathetic male students from the Maryland Agricultural College attempted to create a physical barrier between the suffragists and the mob.[11] Only when troops of cavalry from Fort Meyers arrived to take control of the situation could activists finish their march.[12]

Unfortunately, the rioting of onlookers was not the only disdainful action of the day. Before the public reared its ugly head, suffragists had shown their own unseemly side. As marchers arrived, delegations of African Americans from the National Association of Colored Women and Howard University's Delta Sigma Theta sorority were informed that they would be relegated to the rear of the parade. According to organizers, they did not want to offend white southern suffragists refusing to march alongside African Americans.[13] Whatever the reason, leadership clearly did not intend to let black suffragists march alongside their white counterparts. When Ida Wells-Barnett, president of Chicago's Alpha Suffrage League, attempted to line up with her fellow Illinois suffragists she was quickly informed to move to the rear of the march. Angry at the blatant disregard for her right as a woman, Wells-Barnett told delegates, "I shall not march at all unless I can march under the Illinois banner."[14] Although she disappeared before the parade began, as the procession got underway she emerged from the crowd and slipped into the Illinois delegation, marching alongside her white colleagues.

The suffrage parade of 1913 was monumental in size and also in what it represented. In one day, the event brought many issues to the forefront of the suffrage movement. Bringing together women from many races, social classes, and ways of life, the 1913 parade not only displayed solidarity for the cause, but it also represented the changing attitudes spreading through society. Despite increased levels of equality at the event, a racist sentiment still infected the suffrage movement to the bone, and inequality persisted for women of color, including native peoples and immigrants. Often, suffrage leaders used southern white women as their excuse for discrimination against blacks; in reality, the racist feelings stemmed from both sides of the Mason-Dixon line. For native communities, activists like Marie Louis Bottineau Baldwin, a Chippewa law student, agitated for her people. In 1913, she joined in the Washington parade, but it would not be until 1924 that native peoples born in the United States were granted full citizenship.[15] The rioting crowds also proved that many people still saw women's public actions as highly inappropriate.

Even with disapproval swirling from many people, when the inaction of the Washington, DC, police was investigated, the episode brought tremendous publicity to suffragists, and the new congressional committee and their more radical tactics gained momentum. Activists knew that to make headway and push acceptance, they had to continue to bravely wade into the public arena and demand their rights as citizens. They entered into a new era of public demonstration, one marked by increased spectacle and outrageousness. The suffrage parade of 1913 garnered national attention in a way the movement had not seen before. As suffragists from national, state, and local organizations fell into line, they realized that sometimes public boldness would be the only way to grab the attention their cause needed.

Jailed for Freedom

"Jailed for Freedom" Pin, 1917, National Woman's Party, Washington, DC,
http://nationalwomansparty.org/learn/national-womans-party/

In history books, peaceful protests often come up when discussing the resistance campaigns of Mahatma Gandhi, or the nonviolent protests encouraged by Martin Luther King Jr. These men practiced civil disobedience as a way of protesting the unjust treatment of their fellow men. Through marches, demonstrations, fasting, sit-ins, and countless other actions they drew attention to societal injustices and worked for more equality in the world. During the twentieth century, suffragists used similar demonstration techniques in their fight for the right to vote. As the end of the 1910s drew near, the anxiety, frustration, and impatience of activists reached a boiling point. Women had worked in earnest to secure voting rights for nearly seventy years. For suffragists aligned with Alice Paul and the National Woman's Party, they grew tired of waiting and believed the time had come to increase their level of agitation on the federal government. Putting their own health, safety, and reputations aside, many of these suffragists risked arrest and imprisonment to secure voting rights for themselves and others.[1] In 1917, that was exactly what happened to many women, black and white, who took a stand outside of the White House. For those who spent time behind bars, the "Jailed for Freedom" pin seen on the facing page became a badge of honor.

Although Alice Paul had begun her suffrage work in the United States with the National American Woman Suffrage Association (NAWSA), it did not take long after the 1913 parade in Washington, DC, for the activist to part ways with the conservative organization. Favoring more militant but peaceful action and agitation, Paul and fellow suffragist Lucy Burns formed the organization that would become the National Woman's Party (NWP). They began employing a variety of publicity stunts to call for the right to vote, but by 1917 their techniques of lobbying, petitioning, and parading became stale. They believed that to secure a federal suffrage amendment they needed to escalate the pressure on President Wilson.[2]

To make their demands of support as apparent to Wilson as possible, members of the NWP decided to begin a picketing campaign in front of the president's home. Many years earlier suffragists in New York tried this form of public demonstration, and in Britain, picketing proved an effective form of protest. Activists in labor disputes also relied on the technique to make their demands heard, and suffragists took note of their success. Following those examples, on January 10, 1917, the first group of women arrived. Stationing themselves on the sidewalks out front, these suffragists became the first people in history to picket the White House.[3] They carried flags featuring the NWP's tricolors of gold, purple, and white and hoisted banners above their heads with messages such as, "Mr. President, What Will You Do for Woman Suffrage?" Wanting their banners to do the speaking for them, the pickets stood motionless and silent in protest; earning them the nickname, the Silent Sentinels. Because of the novelty, authorities at first seemed unsure what to do about the women who appeared daily, rain or shine. For the first few months, police remained passive, and President Wilson courteously raised his hat to the women standing on either side of the gates.[4]

The tide changed, however, when the United States entered World War I. With their country's entrance into the conflict some women viewed the picketing as unpatriotic and chose to abandon the public demonstrations. Large portions of the group's membership were also Quakers, pacifists who did not support the war effort. These women believed the global conflict only magnified the need to continue picketing. They wondered how other women could idly stand by while the president sent troops overseas to fight for democracy while denying women the right to vote at home. To them, this represented the ultimate act of hypocrisy. Rather than reduce their picketing in the face of war, these suffragists turned up the heat. Their banners with thought provoking messages had already been essential elements of their campaign, and in the face of the global conflict, they became an even greater source of tension. Swapping out benign messages for sharper ones, banners soon appeared reading "Democracy Should Begin at Home." Others referred to "Free Russia," where women had received the vote, in comparison to "Kaiser Wilson," who did nothing. Onlookers, including servicemen in uniform, grew more agitated with the pickets, and the government's anger flared.[5]

Although the activists remained silent and peaceful, mob violence soon broke out, and on June 22, 1917, arrests began.[6] The crowds attacking demonstrators and destroying their signs were not the target of police, however. Instead, the authorities jailed and imprisoned suffragists on the flimsy charge of obstructing sidewalk traffic. While their banners may have been inflammatory, the women remained within their rights. At first those arrested were dismissed from custody without sentence, but as the picketing and violence continued, the district courts began penalizing the activists with jail time. Gradually their terms increased from a few days to several months.[7]

Imprisoned in places like the Occoquan Workhouse in Virginia, suffragists began to protest the illegality of their incarceration, the bad conditions, and the brutality of their treatment. They insisted the courts acknowledge that they were not "traffic obstructers," and that politics was the real motivation behind their arrests. When they drafted a letter to the district commissioners demanding political prisoner privileges, they received no response. Instead, authorities grew irritated and impatient with their repeated demands and increased jail time for newly arrested suffragists, including Alice Paul, who received seven months in prison.[8] That autumn, jailed activists backed up their insistence on the political nature of their imprisonment with action. They refused to do their assigned sweatshop sewing and manual labor and refused to eat until their political status was acknowledged.[9]

At the Occoquan Workhouse, tensions escalated, peaking in November in an incident known as the "Night of Terror." During the night of November 15, guards used bodily force against a group of newly arrived suffragists. They beat, pushed, and threw women into their cells when they refused to cooperate. One woman was knocked unconscious and another was handcuffed with her arms above her head. The next day sixteen of the suffragists began a hunger strike. In response, prison workers instituted an assaultive regimen of force feeding. Under physical restraint prison staff shoved feeding tubes down throats and up noses, and steel gags pried open jaws. As word of the abusive treatment made its way out of the prison, a public outcry erupted, and at the end of November suffrage prisoners were ordered to be released.[10]

In the aftermath of the 1917 arrests, the NWP staged a mass meeting in Washington, DC, to recognize the women who had served time in prison. Alice Paul had a pin produced representing a jail door, based on a similar one worn by British suffragists. During the ceremony these "Jailed for Freedom" pins were presented to the former prisoners as a badge of honor.[11] It would have been easy for the arrests and mistreatment to dissuade suffragists from further public demonstration. Instead, it fueled them on as they continued picketing and publicly burning copies of President Wilson's speeches and image. By March 1919, a total of 218 suffragists from twenty-six states had been arrested. Of those, ninety-seven spent time in jail.[12] Writing about the experience years later, African American suffragist Mary Church Terrell reflected on the importance of the events: "We helped picket the White House as a protest against the disfranchisement of women. There is no doubt that this gesture on the part of determined women called attention to the injustice perpetrated upon them by denying them the suffrage and hastened the passage of the nineteenth amendment."[13]

Throughout the picketing, members of NAWSA had distanced themselves from the imprisoned suffragists and the NWP. By focusing heavily on keeping themselves separated from the other suffrage group, however, they failed to recognize the injustice being served to fellow activists. Instead, they made every effort to support World War I while pushing for a suffrage amendment as a reward for their patriotic efforts. Although the factions did not see eye to eye and repeatedly separated themselves, all efforts toward a suffrage amendment ultimately worked together to bring about change. Just one day after the head of the Senate Committee on Woman Suffrage visited the Occoquan Workhouse in 1917, the committee issued a favorable report on creating a federal amendment. In September, the House of Representatives established a committee on suffrage, and just four months later, the House passed a constitutional amendment granting women the right to vote. Members of the NWP claimed these advances were due to their picketing efforts. NAWSA believed them a result of the work undertaken by their organization.[14] No matter who held responsibility, going forward, members of the NWP used the experience of the arrests to spread the call for the ratification of the 19th Amendment. In February 1919, they began a "Prison Special" tour, where speakers outfitted in prison dress used stories of their experiences to increase local support for the ratification effort.[15] Over many years, suffragists from all factions utilized public demonstrations to bring attention to their cause. The experiences proved exhilarating, bonds were formed, and spirits lifted. Through the efforts of many women, public demonstrations helped keep the suffrage cause in the public eye, and when pieced together, they created a bigger impact than any one demonstration could have done on its own.

Part VIII

MILESTONES

Significant moments and events mark any social or political movement, no matter how short or long. Sometimes these milestones are acknowledged the moment they happen, while in other instances hindsight allows the recognition of their importance only after the fact. The women's suffrage movement in the United States played out for more than seventy years. During those long decades, many leaders and participants came and went while the movement saw highs and lows. In the nineteenth century, the progress of suffragists happened slowly, and new developments did not occur often. While a small handful of states and territories in the American West granted women the right to vote, no major victories took place east of the Mississippi River until well after 1900. When victories in those early years were won, suffragists basked in the glory as long as possible. By the second decade of the twentieth century the movement entered a new stage of life, with breakthrough moments happening at a much quicker rate than ever before. With support from major political parties, new roles for women in government, and a long-awaited endorsement from the president of the United States, suffragists began to feel the winds of change blowing in their direction.

40

Winning in the West

South Pass City State Historic Site, town established around 1867, Lander, WY, http://wyo parks.state.wy.us/

PHOTO BY JAMES A. JANKE

A rriving in South Pass City, Wyoming, visitors feel as if they have stepped back in time.[1] The dirt roads. The nearby gold mine. The local saloon where a sarsaparilla or game of billiards awaits. With seventeen of the town's twenty-three original structures restored, the mind easily imagines a covered wagon pulling off the Oregon Trail. As the ambiance and flavor of the Old West seeps from every building, the town's stories of boom and bust come as no surprise to visitors at the historic site. What they might not anticipate, however, is that South Pass City also has strong ties to women's suffrage and is directly linked to one of the movement's first major milestones. Just as the town's connection to suffrage surprises visitors today, in 1870, news of the first victory for women's voting rights surprised many people in the United States. In fact, it came about so quietly that very little was known about it outside of Wyoming until the territory's legislature had already granted women the right to vote.[2]

In 1867, gold was discovered on the southeastern end of the Wind River Mountains in Wyoming. As word spread of the find, gold seekers flocked to the area. South Pass City was quickly laid out, and as the population exploded, so did the community. Within one year, more than 250 buildings had gone up, including saloons, hotels, and businesses.[3] The Carissa, South Pass City's principal mine, produced more than $15,000 of gold by 1868 when only hand processing was available. When technological developments sped up the mining process, the region began producing gold even faster, eventually turning out about $7 million worth of the precious material.[4] With the potential lure of fortune, the town quickly attracted about one thousand residents, becoming one of the bustling cities of the region. Like many mining communities however, the excitement and boom died out as quickly as it began. South Pass City's hustle and bustle peaked around 1870, and by 1872 the population had fallen to only a few hundred people.

So how did a boom town in the gold mining west become forever linked with the suffrage movement? The answer lies in the hands of a local saloon-keeper named William Bright. Although born and raised in Virginia, Bright served in the Union Army throughout the Civil War. After the close of the war, Bright and his wife, Julia, moved to Salt Lake City in 1865. Shortly after, news spread about the discovery of gold in South Pass City. Hoping to strike it rich, Bright set out for the young community. Upon his arrival he staked sev-

eral mining claims and then turned a profit by selling them to the many min-
ers flocking to the area. By 1868, Bright and his family settled into South Pass
City, where he opened a local saloon and got involved in Democratic politics.[5]

That same year, the United States government incorporated Wyoming as a
territory. President Ulysses S. Grant appointed fellow Republicans to top positions of power with a territorial legislature set for election the following fall.
In advance of the election, the newly appointed Republican attorney general
made a legal ruling stating that no one in Wyoming could be denied the right
to vote based on race. As an area populated mainly with Democrats, many
white citizens grew suspicious that the ruling was an attempt by Republicans
to secure black votes in the upcoming election. Whether true or not, when
officials counted ballots, Wyoming elected only Democrats—among them,
William Bright. Not only had Bright secured a seat representing South Pass
City in the territorial government, but he also served as president of the upper house of the legislature, known as the Council. This meant he would run
Council meetings and decide which bills to vote on and when.[6]

When the legislature met in October of 1869, they hinted at things to come
when taking measures to guarantee equal pay for teachers, no matter their sex.
They also assured married women property rights separate from their husbands; and late in the session, Bright introduced yet another bill dealing with
women's rights. In a move not anticipated outside of the territory, he lobbied
for women in Wyoming to be allowed to vote.[7] After passing through both
houses of the legislature, the bill landed on Governor Campbell's desk. Many
people expected the governor, an ardent Republican, to veto the bill. After
letting the legislation sit for four days, however, Campbell signed the bill into
law, making Wyoming the first jurisdiction to amend its laws granting women
the explicit right to vote.[8] In 1890, when the territory applied for statehood
however, it was suggested that it might not be given state status if it insisted
on continuing to enfranchise its female citizens. In response Wyoming's legislature declared, "We will remain out of the Union a hundred years rather than
come in without the women."[9] When push came to shove, Wyoming won.
On July 10, 1890, they secured federal statehood with women's voting rights
intact. Once again, Wyoming led the nation in ensuring its female citizens
could cast ballots for state and local elections at the polls, as well as for federal
elections of the president and congress.

If the same incidents happened today, social media and the modern press would guarantee many people would know about the events in Wyoming; but sometimes milestones come without much warning. While the topic of women's voting rights had swirled in public discussion since the 1840s, and the governments of Kansas and New York considered suffrage provisions, Wyoming was simply not on the radar of most people. The territory had a sparse population, and men greatly outnumbered women. Additionally, at the time, no major suffrage campaigns had occurred outside of Kansas. Even so, as national suffrage organizations in the East were in disarray following the passage of voting rights for black men, women's suffrage made quiet headway in the West.[10] With Wyoming leading the way in 1870, the territory of Utah adopted suffrage for women just a few months later. In 1883 Washington Territory gave its female citizens the vote, and four years after that, the territory of Montana did the same. Colorado came on board in 1893 and Idaho in 1896. In between, many other western territories and states considered similar measures, while no states east of the Mississippi River granted suffrage until after 1910.[11]

The reasoning behind the West's precociousness on the topic has been long debated. In the case of Wyoming, suffrage for women was not a new idea. The territories of Washington and Nebraska had debated the topic in 1854 and 1856. After the close of the Civil War, an unsuccessful bill had even been introduced in the US Senate to enfranchise women in all federal territories. By the time Wyoming took up the issue, many of its legislators had moved to the territory from other regions where the question had already been discussed.[12]

Some people have argued that western areas gave women political power as a way of civilizing an untamed land. Others insist frontier governments granted women the vote as a reward for proving their ability to endure the same difficult conditions as men. More likely, the issue of women's suffrage came down to practical politics. In Utah, for example, Mormons remained confident women's votes would help preserve Mormon traditions, including polygamy. In areas populated with black and Chinese males, racism came into play when white citizens expressed disdain that men of other races could vote when white women could not. Many western politicians also believed suffrage could be used as an advertising gimmick to entice more women to the region.

Some easterners even saw the territories as a good place to test the controversial idea of women's suffrage because territorial voters did not have the same influence on federal issues. In the midst of all of these factors, suffragists themselves even pushed for campaigning in the west to test out strategies and tactics later used elsewhere.[13]

No matter the reason William Bright chose to introduce women's suffrage legislation in his territory, the simple fact is it passed. The granting of women's voting rights in Wyoming confirmed for the suffrage movement that its goal could be met. With a new confidence, suffragists around the country dug in for the many years of hard work to come. The first domino had been knocked over, and with its tumble, a saloonkeeper from South Pass City set a very long string of events in motion.

Progressing in Politics

Campaign Bandana, 1912, Woodrow Wilson Presidential Library and Museum, Staunton, VA, http://www.woodrowwilson.org/

In January 2009, Barack Obama began his first of two terms as president of the United States. As the first black leader of the nation, Obama made history, instilling a new sense of hope in many black communities around the country. For the LGBTQ community and its supporters, Obama's evolution on the topic of same-sex marriage proved crucial to their cause. As a presidential candidate in 2008, Obama openly stood against same-sex marriage. Four years later he changed his position and came out in support of the measure. Momentum in the gay rights movement had been building in the country for decades. Where proponents had made headway in gaining broader political support for some human rights and civil liberties throughout the 1970s, 1980s, and 1990s, not until 2012 did the Democratic Party officially back the legalization of gay marriage. With the support of a major political party, the movement surged forward, leveraging the influence needed to bring about legal change. In a similar manner, the women's suffrage movement toiled for many years without the endorsement of any major political party.[1] In 1912, things changed. Campaign bandanas like the one seen on the facing page became visible as the race for the presidency got underway. Emblazoned with words like, "Battle Flag," the Progressive Party indicated they knew they were in for a fight. In a move unlike his previous actions, then-nominee and past-president Theodore Roosevelt threw his support toward the suffrage cause, making it part of his battle plan. This move made the Progressive Party the first major backer of voting rights for women at the national level.[2]

Prior to 1912, only six states had granted women the right to vote.[3] To achieve even this small handful of victories, suffragists had launched countless hard-fought campaigns around the country. Although they tirelessly lobbied legislators, pursued support of politicians, and achieved victory at the state level, no major political party would back the suffrage cause. That Theodore Roosevelt was the politician to bring about the first national endorsement may seem odd. For many people Roosevelt is not remembered as a women's rights man. Instead, his name recalls images of the American West, war heroes, and hypermasculinity. In the Spanish-American War, he led a group of volunteer cavalry in the charge up San Juan Hill, and with an eye to American military strength and commerce, he oversaw the construction of the Panama Canal.

Looking more closely at Roosevelt's life and political record, however, it becomes clear that his convictions concerning the roles and rights of men and women were not always black and white. Although he obsessed over inspiring modern men to act as he thought they should, his theories on women often fell into shades of gray.[4] His Harvard senior thesis of 1880, titled "Practicability of Equalizing Men and Women before the Law," endorsed the theory of equal rights for women as a matter of justice. At the same time, however, he argued that women still needed a heavy dose of protection from men. As governor of New York and president of the United States, he indicated his disdain for abusive men when he called for the harsh punishment of rapists. And when serving as police commissioner of New York City, he put women into executive positions at the police department.[5] All the while, Roosevelt continued to revere women for their traditional roles as mothers and wives, believing their moral superiority placed them in a respected position in society.

Despite his instinct to acknowledge the strengths of women, Roosevelt's views on suffrage remained indefinite for many years. In an 1898 letter to Susan B. Anthony he said, "I have always favored allowing women to vote, but . . . I do not attach the importance to it that you do. I want to fight for what there is the most need of and the most chance of getting."[6] By the next year he must have sensed an increase in public demand because he recommended women's suffrage on school related topics during his inaugural address as governor of New York. Within five years, however, Roosevelt's willingness to work on the issue had all but faded. He even admitted that he had become only "lukewarm" in his support of women's suffrage because he did not believe it an important issue that Congress would pass. When asked by suffragists in 1908, near the end of his presidency, to recommend a federal amendment in his annual message to Congress, Roosevelt politely refused.[7]

Within five years, however, Roosevelt did an about-face. After being out of office for three years, he attempted to secure the Republican Party nomination for president yet again. The competition was stiff however, and William Howard Taft beat out Roosevelt while Woodrow Wilson became the nominee of the Democrats. Not one to be defeated, Roosevelt quickly founded the Progressive Party, which offered a reformist view on social issues. As expected, the party selected him the presidential nominee and women across the country quickly became active in the campaign. Jane Addams, a noted social reformer, activist, and suffragist even seconded his nomination at the party's convention.[8] With three major candidates now vying for votes, the election of 1912 became highly competitive. Setting themselves apart from both Republicans and Democrats, the Progressive Party chose to endorse women's suffrage as part of their party's presidential platform—the first time a major party had done so in the history of the nation. Like his opponents, Roosevelt believed a woman's main duty was to care for the home and family. Unlike them, he did not believe this responsibility excluded them from participating in public life.[9]

So, what made 1912 different? Why the sudden change of heart to endorse suffrage? Although individual women had been active in political campaigns for years, by 1912 a critical mass of females eager and willing to work for presidential candidates existed. Also, six states had now enfranchised women, turning more than one million females in those areas into potential voters. With the outcome of the election uncertain and Roosevelt's appeal splitting the Republican Party, those 1.3 million votes looked very attractive to Progressives.[10] As Roosevelt himself had admitted, in the past he was not willing to back a cause with no chance of support. With the tides changing, however, Roosevelt's practical instincts kicked in and the Progressive Party put suffrage on the national agenda. An astute politician, Roosevelt may have seen the writing on the wall. Recognizing the inevitable success of the movement, it stood to reason that the number of potential female voters would only grow going forward. If he anticipated yet another presidential run in 1916 or 1920, advocating for suffrage in 1912 could ensure female votes for him in the future.[11]

Despite his support of the suffrage cause, when the ballots were tallied in November, Roosevelt lost the election in a landslide to Woodrow Wilson. While his endorsement of women's suffrage may not have won him many votes, it became an important moment for the movement.[12] Change did not come overnight, but Roosevelt's support proved the tide was shifting. With the public's awareness of equal suffrage on the rise, the question soon began to shift from a state issue to one of national debate. In the meantime, Kansas, Oregon, and Arizona all granted women the right to vote in 1912. The next year a record number of suffrage bills were introduced into state legislatures, setting the stage for more referenda asking men to extend the vote to women. By 1916, both the Republican and Democratic platforms included support for women's voting rights at the state level.[13] While it would take until 1920 for suffragists to finally reach their goal, Progressives helped push them closer. When the Progressive Party presented its support at its national convention in 1912 it stated, "We believe that the women of the country, who share with the men the burden of government in times of peace and make equal sacrifice in times of war, should be given the full political right of suffrage both by State and Federal action." Eight years later, Congress came to agree.

A Move Eastward

Ballot Box, 1912, Chicago History Museum, Chicago, IL, https://www.chicagohistory.org/
CHICAGO HISTORY MUSEUM, ICHI-32106

In April 1912, Chicago's voters filled out a special ballot printed with two boxes: "FOR the Extension of Suffrage to Women" and "AGAINST the Extension of Suffrage to Women."[1] Once voters checked the one best representing their opinion, they slipped the paper into the ballot box seen on the facing page.[2] With no legal standing, this vote simply served as a way to gauge current sentiment on the topic of women's suffrage. Since Wyoming's success in securing voting rights for women, activists and elected officials around the nation periodically asked citizens similar questions. The information collected proved crucial for suffragists needing to know and understand what people thought about the topic. It also allowed them to form a stronger plan of attack to best use time, energy, and money. Even with this data on hand however, suffragists struggled to secure voting rights for women outside of the American West before 1913.

In Illinois, residents had been working for women's suffrage since 1869, the year of Wyoming's victory. When a state Constitutional Convention convened the next year, it included a referendum calling for women's suffrage, and activists' hopes soared. Even though this attempt to amend the state's constitution failed, Illinois' suffragists did not lose hope. In 1891, women won a small victory with the passage of a law granting them the right to vote in school district elections. After this success, Catharine McCulloch, a noted lawyer and suffragist, took charge of the Illinois Equal Suffrage Association's work to lobby the state legislature. Persistence, visibility, and spectacle easily describe her approach. She arranged automobile tours to draw attention from the state press and special trains packed with suffragists made trips from Chicago to the state capitol in Springfield. On one occasion, suffragists even lowered petitions pasted on yard-wide muslin streamers from the galleries and into the aisles of the state legislature during a dramatic appeal to lawmakers.[3]

As the lawmaking body of the state considered bill after suffrage bill but continued to vote them down, McCulloch conducted a survey of the Illinois bench and bar. When she published her findings in 1901, she found that the responding lawyers and judges reported greatly favoring the extension of voting rights to women.[4] Pointing out this inconsistency with their actions did not change lawmakers' minds, however. In response, McCulloch initiated and gained approval for a special vote to measure public sentiment on the topic during the April 1912 elections in Chicago. Commenting on the vote, McCulloch said, "Even if men decide against suffrage it will do the cause no harm. If they vote in favor of it—as I have no doubt they will—it will help immeasurably

when we go before the legislature the next time."[5] McCulloch's confidence in
the outcome typified her attitude and positive outlook. After counting the special ballots, however, the results showed just over 135,000 voters disapproved
of women voting, while only around 71,000 approved.[6]

With this information in hand, the Illinois Equal Suffrage Association did
a tactical about-face when preparing to lobby the state legislature during the
1913 session. Where the group had previously been brash, bold, and loud
under McCulloch's leadership, the group now unleashed a quiet and subdued
campaign aimed at neutralizing the most controversial aspects of the earlier
crusades. They arranged no large meetings, no trainloads of supporters, and
no obvious displays of force.[7] Leading to this major shift, McCulloch stepped
down from her role as legislative chair and a new conservative president
named Grace Wilbur Trout took the reins of the organization.

Convinced McCulloch's brash tactics would never succeed, Trout and
three other women worked alone in the state capital. Rather than bring in
additional support that might draw too much attention, the women quietly
worked in a tight-knit fashion to bring about change. Additionally, rather
than criticize opponents, the suffragists now worked to convert adversaries
into friends. Trout stressed the need for her brand of diplomacy with a soft
word here and a pointed question there.[8] From her observations, spectacle
brought publicity, and publicity aroused opposition—the thing she most
wanted to avoid. Working in this quieter way, the suffragists implemented
a special card index. Each card contained the name of a legislator with data
regarding their politics and personal lives. These cards were then filed for
reference, so activists could more easily approach lawmakers for suffrage
support in a way that appealed to them personally.[9]

Another major difference between Illinois's 1913 suffrage campaign and
previous ones was what exactly suffragists requested and how. In the past,
activists pushed for an amendment to the state's constitution that would provide full suffrage to women. Without fail, these attempts had ended in defeat.
This time suffragists embraced an entirely new approach. Rather than ask
legislators to approve a constitutional amendment granting full suffrage, activists instead asked them to create a state bill providing women with limited
suffrage to vote in national and municipal elections. Where the amendment
process could become burdensome and required many steps and approvals,
a state bill could be created by the state's legislature then directly voted on by

the lawmaking body. While this approach meant sacrificing the ability to vote in elections for state representatives and governor, suffragists hoped it would increase their chances to vote for presidential electors and local offices.[10]

With several members of the newly created Progressive Party recently elected to the state Congress, suffragists made an appeal for their support. When they found out Progressives already intended to introduce a women's suffrage bill as a party measure, Trout convinced them it would be more beneficial for the suffrage association to sponsor the bill than to have it represented by any political party. Keeping it nonpartisan would also make it more appealing to both Republicans and Democrats sympathetic to the suffrage cause. In addition to the backing of Progressives, suffragists also secured the support of Democratic governor Edward Dunne by assuring him the measure would not require a constitutional amendment.[11]

Over the next few months, Trout and her small team worked nonstop. When fires popped up, they quickly put them out. And even without using shock tactics, widespread support in the Chicago and Springfield press grew. Through their efforts, suffragists proved to state lawmakers that the public strongly favored the enfranchisement of women. In May the suffrage bill passed through the Illinois Senate and was introduced to the House of Representatives. Despite several attempts by various lawmakers to kill it, the bill slowly made its way through multiple readings. When the announcement came that the legislation would be brought up for a final vote on June 11, Trout's team got busy meeting with state representatives. Many pledged their support and several even agreed to serve as captains during the voting session, making sure other lawmakers were in their seats and ready to vote each time the bill came up for consideration. On the day of the vote, Trout's team kept track of each legislator who arrived at the capitol. For any suffrage supporters missing in action, activists personally sent cabs to bring them to the state house. As Trout guarded the doors to make sure no supporters left the room, the votes were taken, and with a final count of eighty-three to fifty-eight, lawmakers approved the women's suffrage bill.[12]

With the bill's passage in 1913, Illinois became the first state east of the Mississippi River to grant its female citizens the right to vote for presidential electors. In many ways this victory served as a turning point for the movement. For decades, suffragists had toiled for the cause, but an invisible barrier persisted across the center of the country. By passing limited suffrage for women,

Illinois's legislature knocked down the wall.[13] The success also provided a new model for establishing voting rights for women. Prior to the victory, all previous successes had been achieved through state constitutional amendments for full suffrage rights. The approach in Illinois however, provided an example of an alternative route that did not require a constitutional amendment. Instead, by seeking direct legislation, women in Illinois had gained the ability to vote for presidential electors—giving them a voice in selecting the nation's highest leader. After 1913, a wave of states approved either full or limited suffrage for women through the direct legislative action modeled by Illinois. In most states this path was simply more likely to succeed—a point proven by the fact that only four more states granted women's suffrage through state constitutional amendments before the federal approval of the 19th Amendment. When New York granted women the franchise in 1917, Carrie Chapman Catt, president of the National American Woman Suffrage Association said, "New York women never could have won their great suffrage victory . . . if Illinois had not first opened the door in 1913."[14] In hindsight, many suffragists came to agree. The victory in Illinois moved the wave of success eastward, and it quickly became clear the movement was gaining ground. It would only be a matter of time before all women in the nation would be provided with the opportunity to vote.

Walking into History

Shoe, worn by Jeannette Rankin, around 1916, Montana Historical Society, Helena, MT, http://mhs.mt.gov/

JEANNETTE RANKIN SHOE FABRIC, LEATHER, BROCADE, CA. 1916 MONTANA HISTORICAL SOCIETY COLLECTION, 2006.01.01

A typical stroll through the shoe section of most stores involves sightings of tennis shoes, hiking boots, and sandals in every color imaginable. Every shoe is different, and many have a unique purpose. Sometimes a specific type of footwear is chosen based on the wearer's activities of the day. Other times the selection reflects the individual's personality and style. In the most basic terms, shoes provide protection and allow the freedom and mobility for the wearer to go where they want. The shoe seen on the previous page is no exception.[1] Made in the 1910s, this evening shoe, with its brocade covering, reflects the wearer's stylish and bold choices. She had strong convictions and forged a path as she walked into history—a path not yet taken, when in a landmark 1916 vote Jeannette Rankin became the first woman elected to Congress.[2]

Born in 1880 outside of the western Montana community of Missoula, Jeannette Rankin was the oldest of seven children born to a successful rancher and businessman. Like many of her future peers, Rankin's family was white and upper-middle class. And from an early age she displayed the personality traits the national press later used to define her. Just as they noticed, her family and friends described her as an independent, hardworking child with a good dose of stubbornness and independence. At the same time however, she could be painfully shy, while also showing a willingness to cooperate.[3]

After attending public school Rankin graduated from the University of Montana in 1902 with a degree in biology. She then taught briefly in rural Montana schools before giving up the profession to serve a short apprenticeship as a seamstress. Her restlessness only grew when in 1904 her father passed away. As her mother withdrew from household duties, Rankin took on the responsibility of caring for her younger siblings. At the age of twenty-eight she once again looked for her calling in life. She packed her bags and headed to the New York School of Philanthropy where she studied briefly before returning west to try her hand as a social worker.[4] In her first professional position at the Washington Children's Home Society in Spokane, Rankin discovered her interests lay more in policy issues than on-the-ground social work. It was her desire to learn how to push for better legislation on children's issues, jails, and food supplies that led her to the University of Washington in 1909. Her experience as a social worker also convinced her that women needed to vote if the social justice programs of the time were to succeed.[5]

In 1909, Rankin hit a turning point in her life when she became involved in Washington State's suffrage campaign. Through the work, Rankin found the passion she had been searching for and not only deepened her commitment to women's voting rights, but also became a firm believer that the quest for peace should be incorporated into the suffrage question.[6] After the women of Washington achieved victory in 1910, Rankin headed back to her home state of Montana to put her newly honed suffrage skills to work. In 1911, she urged the state legislature in her home state to grant women the right to vote. Over the next five years she worked tirelessly for women's voting rights not only in Montana, but also around the country as a field secretary for the National American Woman Suffrage Association. In 1914, she was ecstatic when Montana granted full voting rights to its female citizens.[7]

By 1916, Rankin's experiences had improved her skill and confidence as a speaker, writer, and organizer. Looking for her next move she realized as a Westerner, she was not a shoo-in for national suffrage leadership. Although states in the east failed time and again to secure voting rights for their female citizens, easterners had always dominated the leadership of the national suffrage movement and there were no signs of change in the future. Still yearning for meaningful work however, the suffrage movement inspired Rankin to work for women's political equality on a larger scale.[8]

After investigating potential support from Montana suffragists that now held the right to vote, Rankin threw her hat in the ring for one of the state's seats in the US House of Representatives. Running as a progressive Republican, Rankin had two big advantages: first, her reputation as a successful suffragist; second, her brother Wellington had political connections and the resources to finance her campaign. Although some national suffrage leaders worried her failure may hurt their cause, Rankin continued with a campaign true to herself. Pledging to work for a constitutional suffrage amendment, she also emphasized social welfare issues. A longtime pacifist, Rankin was also upfront with voters that she did not support the country's potential involvement in the European war raging across the Atlantic Ocean. Although Rankin did not come in first place, she easily gained enough votes for second, earning her a seat. While national suffrage leaders let out a sigh of relief that she had not lost, Rankin prepared for legislative duty.[9]

On April 2, 1917, members of the 65th Congress were sworn into special session. Among the representatives to take the oath of office that day was Jeannette Rankin. A modest woman in most ways, fashionable clothing proved one of her few vices. Dressed in a dark-blue silk suit, Rankin walked into the session with confidence. In her hands she carried a bouquet of yellow and purple flowers given to her earlier in the morning at a suffrage breakfast.[10]

That same day, President Woodrow Wilson asked Congress to declare war on Germany. As an ardent pacifist Rankin had long stood against the nation's entry into war. As Congress prepared to vote on the president's request, suffrage leaders again held their breath. The National Woman's Party urged Rankin to vote her conscious, while NAWSA pressured her to cast a vote in favor of war, fearing a vote in opposition would make suffragists appear weak. When the moment came Rankin uttered but a few words. "I want to stand by my country, but I cannot vote for war. I vote no."[11]

Her experience as a suffragist had given Rankin the confidence to do what she felt was right even in the face of criticism, and even when her beliefs did not align with fellow activists. In the following years Rankin would often say that she "ran for woman suffrage and got elected to Congress."[12] Staying true to her word, in the fall of 1917 she pushed for the creation of a committee on women's suffrage. When the special committee reported out on a potential constitutional amendment in January 1918, Rankin opened the very first House Floor debate on the subject. "How shall we answer their challenge gentlemen," she asked. "How shall we explain to them the meaning of democracy if the same Congress that voted for war to make the world safe for democracy refuses to give this small measure of democracy to the women of our country?"[13]

Rankin's term in Congress ended in March 1919, meaning she was not in the legislative body to see the passage of the 19th Amendment. Although not present for the fateful vote, Rankin had already made history. She had taken the first step for women to find a role in national politics. In the following years women who had been suffragists, along with some who had not, slowly found their way into electoral politics. In 1916, Joseph M. Carey, governor of Wyoming, described the situation in his state, "It is true that woman is not much of a seeker after office, but she has been greatly benefitted by having the door opened to her, to enter if she will."[14] On the national level Jeannette Rankin had the courage to walk through that door. Following her lead, women in the future pushed boundaries and took bold initiatives.[15] Prior to 1917, no female representation existed in Congress, but by the start of the twenty-first century women advanced to roles of party leadership. While the acceptance of women in political power began slowly, and continues to evolve today, one woman had to take the first step toward change, and Jeannette Rankin courageously led the way.

Tipping the Scale

Top Hat, worn by President Woodrow Wilson, made by Cooksey & Co., London, circa 1903, The President Woodrow Wilson House, Washington, DC, http://www.woodrowwilsonhouse.org/
COURTESY OF THE WOODROW WILSON PRESIDENTIAL LIBRARY, STAUNTON, VA

Outside the White House, groups of women stood in the cold and the rain. Tired and exhausted, day after day they hoisted their banners and signs demanding the right to vote. In response, the president tipped his hat politely as he drove past. Woodrow Wilson was no newcomer to the political stage when radical suffragists began their picket in January 1917. The American public had just elected him to his second term in office, but much like the tip of his hat, his stance on women's suffrage had been distant and reserved. Through decades of lobbying for the right to vote, suffragists learned that presidential support would be crucial if they wanted to achieve a federal women's suffrage amendment. As the leader of the nation, the commander in chief had a unique ability to rally unified support around a cause. In Wilson's case, his evolution from suffrage denouncer to suffrage supporter was a slow burn. Through the persistent action of suffragists and the changing attitudes of society, Wilson gradually shifted his stance, which helped to tip the congressional scale in favor of women's voting rights.

That Woodrow Wilson did not support women's voting rights early in his career should not come as a surprise. Born in Staunton, Virginia, in 1856, and raised in Augusta, Georgia, Wilson's upbringing instilled in him a strong adherence to conservative traditions, including the belief that women's proper place was in the home.[1] Throughout his life he placed his mother, wives, and daughters on the pedestals he believed they deserved. In turn they adored and coddled him, providing comfort and serving as confidantes.[2] Needless to say, not all the women in Wilson's life shared his idea of what the ideal woman should be—a homemaker, helpmate, and hostess, not a colleague or partner in public life.[3] Putting his feelings into words, in 1884 he mused about a Woman's Congress meeting of the Association for the Advancement of Women in Baltimore. Writing about the event he described the "chilled, scandalized feeling" he felt when he would "see and hear women speak in public."[4] Ironically, after earning degrees from Princeton, the University of Virginia Law School, and Johns Hopkins University, he accepted a teaching position at Bryn Mawr, a newly established college for women. Although his wife Ellen noted that it seemed "absurd" and "unnatural" that he should stoop to teaching girls, Wilson's time at Bryn Mawr launched him into a distinguished career as a teacher and scholar.[5] By the age of forty-six he had become the president of Princeton University and gained a national reputation as a leading political thinker. Wilson then began to consider his next move. When conservative Democrats persuaded him to run for governor of New Jersey in 1910, he not only won, but he also displayed political independence by bucking the conservatives who nominated him and by endorsing a progressive platform.[6]

Within two years, the Democratic Party nominated Wilson as their candidate in the presidential election of 1912 and a historic campaign ensued. The nominee pool included a current president (William H. Taft), a former president (Theodore Roosevelt), and a future president (Woodrow Wilson), and fierce words flew all around. After a whirlwind campaign season where candidates stumped around the nation, the unexpected happened when the nation elected the two-year governor from New Jersey. Although Wilson was known to advocate for a strong central government and reform legislation on issues like labor rights, his progressive views at the time did not encompass suffrage. Always the good politician however, Wilson knew better than to publicly denounce the issue and risk isolating voters. Instead, he simply dodged the topic whenever possible, even as the suffrage movement entered the height of its activity. In fact, during the campaign of 1912 he rarely spoke publicly on the issue. When a militant suffragist interrupted his speech on October 19, demanding to know what he thought about the vote, he claimed it was a state matter and "not a question that is dealt with by the National Government at all."[7]

While Wilson believed suffrage should be handled by the states and not by the federal government, many suffragists began to think otherwise. After years of waging a slow state-by-state battle, activists began to realize that the push for a federal amendment would be necessary to succeed. And if they had any hope of advancing it through Congress, they knew they needed the support of the nation's most influential leader. With that in mind, activists began planning how to persuade the new president to support their cause. Suffragists knew that to turn Wilson into a supporter meant a lot of hard work. Not only did Wilson's own upbringing predispose him to a less than supportive position, but he also had close relationships with many southern Democrats, fellow lawmakers who insisted women's suffrage was a states' rights issue, not a federal one. This did not slow suffragists down, however, and activists acted quickly. As Wilson's train pulled into the nation's capital the day before his inauguration, he noticed right away the lack of people and reporters there to greet him. When he inquired about the small crowd, he was told that everyone was watching the suffrage parade. Indeed, thousands of marchers had taken to the streets of Washington, DC, to demonstrate for women's voting rights. Thousands more watched from the sidelines. Although Wilson hoped to avoid the hot button topic, suffragists made it clear from day one that it would be impossible to ignore them. Throughout the remainder of his first term, radical and conservative suffragists alike bombarded Wilson with pleas for support. When they captured his ear, they made their case again and again. The president had no intention of making any quick moves, however, and he stood his ground. Despite their efforts, he still insisted that the federal government had no business wading into the matter.[8]

Although Wilson believed suffrage would be the cause of disaster in the American home, in August 1914 his own homelife took a drastic turn. His beloved wife, Ellen, passed away, leaving the president in a state of helplessness. In January he met Edith Galt, a widow who seemed the perfect match for the statesman. By December 1915, the couple had married. The day he announced their engagement he also announced that he would travel to his resident state of New Jersey and cast a vote in favor of women's suffrage. Despite outward appearance, the president had not yet had a change of heart. Rather, he hoped his pro-suffrage vote would boost his image heading into the 1916 presidential election. Knowing the legislation had a slim chance of passing, Wilson's vote reflected little of his personal attitude toward suffrage. On the other hand, his meaningless ballot may have helped him win back favor from the progressive voters he had isolated when imposing racial segregation in the federal civil service. At the same time, Wilson knew it would not hurt to appeal to the women who could vote within their states. As a cherry on top, his ballot may have even helped repair some of the negative fallout from his seemingly quick marriage.[9]

In voting for women's suffrage in New Jersey, Wilson also silently communicated his continued support for a state-by-state approach rather than a federal one. In a time when few states had granted women the right to vote, Wilson knew this would keep the issue out of his federal administration. Slowly, however, he began to crack. In April 1917, just one month after beginning his second term, the United States entered World War I. A few months earlier, frustrated radical members of the National Woman's Party (NWP) began picketing the white house. At first Wilson seemed amused by their antics. As the stress of the war began to weigh on him, however, his amusement gave way to agitation. Very soon, suffragists were being arrested and imprisoned with little resistance from the White House. When Wilson pardoned suffrage prisoners in July 1917 (hoping to avoid bad press by getting the news of their ill-treatment off the front page of newspapers), Edith questioned her husband's sympathetic action toward the "demons in the workhouse."[10]

While radical suffragists continued to push Wilson to his breaking point, conservative members of the National American Woman Suffrage Association (NAWSA) took a different approach. They threw themselves into war work, making the argument that a federal suffrage amendment would be all the payment necessary for their invaluable patriotic efforts. To make themselves even more appealing to the president, conservatives embraced him when radicals denounced him. And when the picketers took outlandish actions, NAWSA made sure to distance themselves as much as possible from their counterparts. Over time, these two tactics inadvertently worked together to bring Wilson around to supporting their cause. It also did not hurt that Wilson's middle daughter, Jessie, had become a fervent suffragist, undoubtedly sharing her views with her father. Perhaps more importantly, however, World War I itself played a major role in pushing Wilson toward federal support. As a leader in the Allied cause, the United States had taken on a new role of global leadership, and the country had become a guardian of democracy. As such, Wilson knew it was important for the nation to demonstrate to the world the democratic principles of freedom and equality.[11]

As a wave of state suffrage victories swept the nation in 1917, Wilson could no longer deny that public sentiment was changing. As a president who had always touted the necessity to represent the will of the people, Wilson's years of foot dragging came to an end. In January 1918, Woodrow Wilson finally endorsed a federal suffrage amendment. In urging Congress to act, Wilson acknowledged that he saw suffrage as a reward. Referring to the selfless war work American women had undertaken, he said, "It is high time that some part of our debt of gratitude to them should be acknowledged and paid, and the only acknowledgement they ask is their admission to the suffrage. Can we justly refuse?"[12] Going forward, Wilson never wavered. As the debate for the amendment dragged on in the Senate, he again leveraged his power, appealing to Democrats still holding out. While his persuasive argument to pass the legislation as a war measure seemed to be heard by many in his party, his appeals fell on deaf ears in the South. Fearful of women's suffrage creating more black voters, most southern lawmakers resisted the president's

call to action. In the end, Wilson's words of encouragement finally brought
the needed number of senators on board and the amendment passed. After
the final ratification, NAWSA took full credit for Wilson's conversion while
the NWP claimed it happened due to their actions. Wilson himself took im-
mense pride in women gaining the right to vote, almost seeming to forget the
years of anguish he had caused suffragists working to convert him to their
cause. While no one can say for sure if Wilson became a whole-hearted advocate of women's rights, or if he simply bowed to the political pressure around
him, his official stance on suffrage had changed. Rather than continue to
glibly tip his hat, Wilson had finally provided the breakthrough suffragists
needed. Through his endorsement and congressional pressure, the congressional scale tipped in favor of voting rights for women.

Mother Knows Best

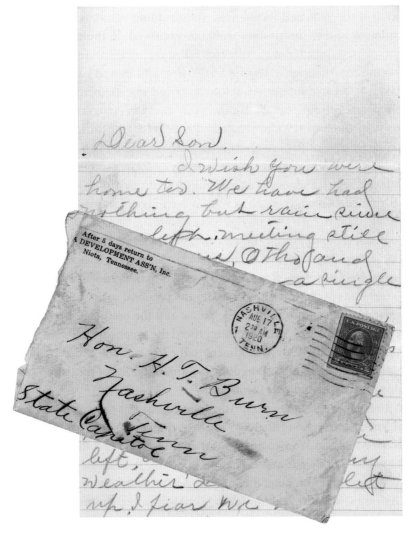

Letter, to Rep. Harry T. Burn from his mother, August 1920, C. M. McClung Historical
Collection, Knox County Public Library, Knoxville, TN, cmdc.knoxlib.org/cdm/
HARRY T. BURN PAPERS, MCCLUNG HISTORICAL COLLECTION

In 1878, what would later become the 19th Amendment was introduced for the first time to Congress. Named for the legendary suffrage leader who had served as its author, the measure was first known as the Susan B. Anthony Amendment and aimed to prohibit the denial of voting rights based on sex. After its introduction into Congress, the proposal sat until 1887 when the Senate finally considered the measure and quickly rejected it. Over the next thirty-three years, suffragists turned their attention to working at the state and local levels while holding out hope that a federal amendment to the Constitution would be approved. In the meantime, suffragists achieved scattered victories for full and partial voting rights around the nation. As victories were won in the west and moved eastward, politicians slowly became supporters of the cause, and women themselves became involved in electoral politics. By the time the 19th Amendment came up for its final vote in 1919, the Senate had rejected it four times in thirty-two years. The House of Representatives had only voted on the measure twice.[1]

In 1918, President Woodrow Wilson finally endorsed women's suffrage and encouraged fellow Democrats in Washington, DC, to do the same. As more states granted women the right to vote, Wilson urged Congress to discuss an amendment for women's voting rights once again. In January 1919, the House of Representatives approved the measure, but the Senate still held out. Frustrated, suffragists got to work lobbying for the support of lawmakers, hoping to turn at least two votes from "no" to "yes." In May, President Wilson called Congress into special session to consider the proposal again. This time, with considerable pressure from both the public and the president, the House of Representatives and the Senate both approved the proposition. Before it could officially become the 19th Amendment to the Constitution however, another major hurdle needed to be cleared. By law, three-fourths of the nation's states needed to ratify, or approve, the measure.[2]

With forty-eight states comprising the country at the time, suffragists would need thirty-six of them to approve the new amendment. Both the National American Woman Suffrage Association and the National Woman's Party got to work right away. They reached out to state governors asking them to consider the amendment and put pressure on the president to deliver on his support. The timing was poor however, and most state legislatures were out of session; some would not meet again until the following year unless the governor called them in for a special assembly. This did not slow suffragists down. They knew that the longer the amendment sat, the more momentum it would lose, something they could not afford to risk.[3] By the summer of 1920, their advocating had paid off and thirty-five states had approved the amendment, while six had rejected it. If suffragists could win the approval of just one more state, they would, at long last, achieve their goal. When Delaware unexpectedly defeated the amendment in early June, all eyes turned to Tennessee. Knowing the state had granted their female citizens partial voting rights just two months before Congress passed the 19th Amendment, suffragists had high hopes.[4]

Despite their optimism, suffragists knew not to take Tennessee for granted. If they had learned anything in the long struggle for the vote, it was that appearances could be deceiving and there are no guarantees. With the state's Democratic governor, Albert H. Roberts, up for reelection, he realized supporting the amendment could cost him the crucial votes needed to retain office. At the same time, the national Democratic Party applied pressure to support ratification of the measure. After receiving a telegram from President Wilson urging him to support the amendment, Governor Roberts finally agreed to call a special session of his legislature, but not until August, after the state's Democratic primary.[5]

At the time of the special session, suffragists and anti-suffragists from around the state and nation swarmed into Nashville. Battling head to head for support, they worked tirelessly to secure committed votes from lawmakers for their cause. On August 13, the state's Senate came into agreement with Governor Roberts and approved the measure, leaving the final showdown to the Tennessee House of Representatives. When the morning of Monday, August 18, 1920, arrived, the city was practically buzzing. Suffrage-yellow could be seen everywhere, but just as prevalent was the red rose of anti-suffrage. Countless residents from Nashville and Davidson County packed the lawn, galleries, and hallways of the statehouse as lawmakers arrived on Capitol Hill. Everyone knew this day was a historic moment and hoped to get a glimpse of the action.[6]

For many legislators the night before proved exhausting and stressful. They sat through late night conferences and many were awoken by individuals looking to capture their ear. Suffragists and anti-suffragists tallied up committed support among the House of Representatives. They knew that when the time came, the votes would be extremely close. The next morning the House of Representatives was a scene of chaos. The press box was jammed with re-porters; the galleries were filled with activists from both sides; and lawmakers wearing yellow or red roses in their lapels anxiously waited for the debate and vote. When Representative Harry T. Burn walked in, he sported a red rose on his jacket and made his way to the left side of the chamber. Soon after, a page delivered a small yellow envelope to his seat in the third row.[7]

At 10:35 a.m. the Speaker of the House banged his gavel to signal the start of the session. As debating and speeches took place for the first hour, the room grew warm and agitated. In the third row, Representative Burn read the letter delivered to him, refolded it, and slipped it into the inner breast pocket of his suit. Wild action then occurred as members of the House first voted whether to table the issue (which would kill the resolution) or consider it for approval. Disagreement on the final tally required the House to vote twice at this point. After two exhausting rounds of voting, the issue barely remained on the table, but a final vote had been approved to either ratify or reject the 19th Amend-ment. Lawmakers in support of the measure were eager to vote, and those against suffrage for women grew annoyed at the failed attempt to table the issue. For those activists keeping track in the room, the number of expected "aye" versus "nay" votes seemed to shift slightly as voting began. Any more changes in position could easily alter the outcome of the vote.[8]

As the final vote continued, the tally seemed to bounce back and forth like the ball in a game of tennis, with spectators in the galleries and lawmakers on the floor growing more excited by the minute. As Representative Burn heard his name called, it is hard to know what was going through his head. Person-ally, he favored giving women the right to vote, but he also knew most of his constituents did not support women's suffrage. In all earlier instances he had pledged to vote against the 19th Amendment and wore a red anti-suffrage rose to the session.[9] In his jacket pocket, however, sat the letter he read earlier that morning. Addressed to Hon. H. T. Burn at the Tennessee State Capitol, the letter came from his mother; a strong supporter of women's suffrage. As he read the pages earlier in the session he was met with these words: "Dear Son . . . Hurrah and vote for suffrage and don't keep them in doubt. . . . I've been waiting to see how you stood but have not seen anything yet. . . . Don't forget to be a good boy and help Mrs. Catt . . . With lots of love, Mama."[10] As Burn opened his mouth to cast his vote the word that came forth changed from "nay" to "aye." When roll call finished, the final count was recorded as forty-nine votes in favor of ratification with only forty-seven against.[11]

The capitol exploded with both cheers of joy and cries of defeat. Accused of taking a bribe, Burn released a statement to the press the following day. The explanation of his changed vote was quite simple, "I know that a mother's advice is always safest for her boy to follow."[12] Seventy-two years after women at the Seneca Falls Convention adopted the "Declaration of Sentiments," twenty-six million American women secured the opportunity to vote. The moment did not mean the work begun by the movement was done, however. While celebrated wildly by activists at the time, and often praised today, the ratification of the 19th Amendment was not an ultimate victory; it was only one milestone in a longer journey. Although the amendment stated that states could not discriminate against voters based on sex, that left countless women of color still barred from the polls. Like African American men, black women often found themselves blocked from the ballot box by poll taxes and other racial barriers, while American Indians and Asian immigrants were largely excluded from citizenship altogether.[13] With their initial goal reached, suffragists, always primed for the next campaign, prepared for their next steps in the journey of the franchise and women's rights.

Part IX

LEGACY

Legacy—its entry in a variety of dictionaries defines it as anything handed down from the past, as from an ancestor or predecessor. Indeed, after the ratification of the 19th Amendment, the broader push for women's rights continued, often feeling the touch of the former words, actions, successes, and faults of suffragists. From its earliest years, the fight for women's voting rights had always been just one of many causes making up a much larger movement. With the 19th Amendment secure, opportunities arose for activists to continue chipping away at old and new initiatives. African American women, who came up shorthanded after the 1920 elections, continued their own struggle for the ballot and looked to expand broader civil rights for all men and women of color. Women as a gendered class also set their sights on fuller equality under the law, pushing and pulling in many directions for decades. However, inheritance comes in many forms. While some legacies are beautiful heirlooms, others can be brutal reminders of the past. In the twenty-first century, women continue to push for equality. As they do, the lessons of suffrage echo in their ears, just as they did for the activists of many colors and creeds that opened the door for broader women's rights in the century prior.

Under the Watchful Eye

Broadside, 1919–1929, Jane Y. McCallum Papers, Austin History Center, Austin, TX,
https://library.austintexas.gov/ahc/about-us

Suffragists rejoiced as news of the ratification of the 19th Amendment spread across the country. After decades of investing time, energy, and sweat into the fight, sex no longer stood as a barrier to voting rights in the United States. With this goal accomplished, what was next? Anticipating the void in activity left by its success, the National American Woman Suffrage Association (NAWSA) took steps to prepare women to become active educators of new voters. In doing so, it drew on many of the same tactics that had worked in the past. Just as suffrage clubs used posters to help women obtain the right to vote, later female political organizations such as the League of Women Voters used similar techniques to get women to the polls and put their right into action. With its eye-catching imagery and ominous message, the Texas League of Women Voters used the poster on the previous page during one of its early campaigns. Looking to get as many female voters to the polls as possible, the set of eyes implores the viewer to heed the poster's command. And with its simple, but straight forward message, a sense of urgency grows in the viewer for fear that inaction will let down the entire state.

As early as 1919, Carrie Chapman Catt, head of NAWSA, sensed a suffrage victory close at hand. Spurred by her instincts, when suffragists gathered at the organization's fiftieth national convention in St. Louis, Catt proposed the creation of a "league of women voters to finish the fight and aid in the reconstruction of the nation."[1] She knew that once suffrage was obtained, women would need encouragement and guidance in their new roles as voters. While the national organization still had work ahead of it in securing the 19th Amendment, some affiliated organizations heeded her advice and began work on the next step of their journey. In many states where female voting rights had already been won, suffrage organizations reorganized themselves and adopted the new name, League of Women Voters. The next year, on February 14, 1920, just six months before the ratification of the 19th Amendment, NAWSA moved forward as well.

Certain that ratification was just around the corner, NAWSA reorganized itself as the League of Women Voters of the United States, planning to ensure that new voters would take their hard-won right seriously and use it wisely.[2] Made up of leagues formed from dissolved suffrage organizations, the League of Women Voters followed a hierarchical structure similar to what had been instituted by suffragists. The national league lead from the top down, with state and local branches supporting its efforts. With its familiar structure and a pool of suffragists looking for their purpose, it did not take long for the idea of the league to spread. In fact, by 1924, 346 grassroots branches had popped up around the nation.[3] While these affiliated leagues shared some finances and common goals with the national organization, in their day-to-day work they retained most of their autonomy and authority over their individual programming. The members believed strongly that voters should play a critical role in democracy and through a variety of nonpartisan programs the league educated both female and male citizens about government and social reform legislation.

On Saturday, August 28, 1920, church bells rang and factory whistles blew across the country marking the 19th Amendment's ratification. Behind the planning of these celebrations were branches of the League of Women Voters.[4] Their rejoicing quickly turned to serious work, however. Designed to help twenty million women carry out their new civic responsibility, the November 1920 elections loomed as a test of the league's abilities. Not only did the League of Women Voters want to demonstrate that its work was effective, but many former suffragists had something to prove as well. If women turned out to the polls in large numbers, they believed it would confirm that their efforts had not been in vain, and that they had been right all along—women did indeed want the right to vote. When Election Day arrived, about ten million American women went to the polls, just over one-third of the eligible female electorate. For league members and former suffragists, this turnout came as a disappointment. Even with the excitement of the 19th Amendment's recent passage, two out of every three women stayed home. Trying to explain the results, Catt, now the head of the league, insisted it was not a lack of enthusiasm. Instead, she argued that with such a short timeframe between ratification and the election, women struggled to have enough time to register. She also argued that because voting was new for many women, they simply had not yet learned the behavior. She assured the critics that the League of Women Voters would help to educate the new female electorate and bring the voting numbers up.[5]

At the time of the national league's organization, activists in the Lone Star State were already concerned about low voter turnout and had efforts well under way to get more women to the polls. After the Texas Equal Suffrage Association dissolved in October of 1919, the group reorganized itself as the Texas League of Women Voters.[6] Like other league branches around the nation, it operated as a nonpartisan entity and did not endorse or oppose specific candidates or political parties. Instead, it encouraged members and the public to study political issues and positions in order to form their own opinions. In 1918, Texas granted women the right to vote in primary elections; and when federal suffrage passed two years later, the need for educated voters only increased. In addition to running citizenship classes to educate new voters about how to register and vote, the league also published a monthly newspaper, the *New Citizen*. A steep learning curve was not the only thing that worried the league, however. Like many other southern states, Texas practiced aggressive voter suppression. The institution of "white primaries" meant no person of color could vote in primary elections. Additionally, the state required eligible voters to pay a poll tax in order to cast their ballots. On top of keeping many minorities and African Americans (who were unable to pay such fees) from the polls, the league worried the taxes discouraged white women from voting as well.[7]

To combat this potential hurdle, the Texas League of Women Voters launched multiple campaigns in 1919 and the 1920s encouraging women to pay poll taxes and show up to vote. In addition to posters that gave warnings such as "Women! The Eyes of Texas Are Upon You," numerous articles hit local newspapers and informational meetings were held. If exercising the right to vote did not interest women, the league also made it clear that poll taxes helped support the school fund. In essence, by making tax payments on time, qualified teachers would be encouraged to stay in the schools and voters could feel good about playing a vital role in securing proper education for children.[8] The league also tried to encourage the payment of poll taxes by removing barriers such as traveling to courthouses in order to do so. For instance, in 1920 a Poll Tax Tea was hosted in El Paso. In addition to beverages and refreshments, attendees could pay their poll tax to an official taking payments and issuing receipts on site.[9] As the decade continued, the league's concern with Texas's poll tax requirement persisted, and in 1924, during an aggressive campaign in January, it issued a special voter's calendar highlighting all election dates and other important political days of the year. Circled boldly on the calendar, January 31 was the last day for paying poll taxes.[10] Like other branches around the nation, Texas's league members wanted to see more women casting ballots, and they wanted to ensure that when those voters made it to the polls, they were well informed about the process, their civic responsibilities, and the issues.

Just as it did in 1920, today the League of Women Voters continues its invaluable work as a nonpartisan organization. Through its educational out-

reach, it has helped millions of women and men become informed participants in government through publications, classes, and other programs. The
league has also carried out successful legislative work. It proved vital in the
passage of the Sheppard-Towner Act of 1921, providing federal aid for maternal and childcare programs. In the 1930s, league members worked successfully toward the enactment of the Social Security and Food and Drug Acts.
And following World War II, it helped lead efforts to establish the United
Nations and ensure American participation.[11] Despite these huge successes,
women's turnout at the polls remained surprisingly low as the twentieth century progressed. It was not until the early 1960s that the number of women
voting in national elections equaled the number of male voters. And not until
1980 did the percentage of women voters surpass that of men.[12] For some
former suffragists, the success of the 19th Amendment came as a letdown.
Large numbers of activists did not break into political office as many had
hoped. Rather, under the direction of Carrie Chapman Catt many of the most
promising suffragists funneled their energy into educational work rather than
direct political action.

Activists had not closed their eyes to their cause, however, they had simply
inherited struggles that suffragists faced for years. For decades suffragists
worked in a divided nature, often disagreeing. In the moment when women
were faced with the question, "What's next?" it came as no surprise that no
unified answer existed. Instead, organizations and activists responded in the
best ways they knew how. For NAWSA, preparing voters for what lie ahead
was the answer. Unfortunately, the good work the league achieved in its early
years might have inadvertently convinced male politicians that, as many had
suspected, women were not really interested in politics after all.[13] Under their
watchful eye, male lawmakers did not observe women throwing themselves
into the political arena. Instead, they saw these new voters take up the mantle
of reform work, something they had done in the past, and something politicians viewed as the natural work of women. In many ways, NAWSA's choice to
become the League of Women Voters filled a great need. And in other ways it
perpetuated the divided nature suffragists had created in the past. As former
NAWSA members settled into their new role, the National Woman's Party
set its sights on continuing the push for greater equality. As had happened in
the past, the two groups did not see eye to eye and a unified front of activism
splintered before it even began.

47

Bridges of Hope

Edmund Pettus Bridge, constructed 1939, United States Civil Rights Trail, Selma, AL, https://civilrightstrail.com/attraction/edmund-pettus-bridge/

On March 3, 1913, suffragists took to the streets of the nation's capital to demonstrate their demand for women's voting rights. Onlookers jeered, and some became violent toward the marchers. Despite local law enforcement's presence, police officers did nothing to protect the activists. Ironically, at the same time, many suffragists failed to protect their own. When Ida B. Wells and other black suffragists attempted to march alongside their state comrades, leadership told them to move to the rear of the parade. Rather than stand up for their sisters in arms, white suffragists complied without question, segregating their friends and allies to a place of dishonor. Fifty-two years later, in 1965, a new suffrage campaign was underway. Once again activists took to the road. Putting foot on pavement, marchers crossed the Edmund Pettus bridge in Selma, Alabama, protesting the voting rights continually denied to blacks. This time, however, African Americans were at the head of the line. This was their march, their rights, and their time. When violence broke out against the peaceful protest, a wave of disgust washed across many Americans, both black and white. Within a short time, President Lyndon B. Johnson signed into action the Voting Rights Act of 1965, finally addressing the injustice that had gone on for far too long.

From the earliest days, racism was present in the organized women's suffrage movement. The passage of the 14th and 15th Amendments divided the cause, prompting many white suffragists to abandon black men and women who had worked as their allies for years. Often, African American women found themselves unwelcome in organizations such as the National American Woman Suffrage Association (NAWSA). The signals became mixed in the early twentieth century when such organizations saw a benefit in adding black women to their ranks as a way of increasing numbers. Their treatment remained unequal, however, and suffrage leadership walked a thin line trying to keep African American activists appeased while also playing to the sympathies of racist white members who insisted black women had no need for the vote. After the passage of the 19th Amendment, it came as no surprise when white suffragists abandoned their black sisters. While some African American women succeeded in registering to vote, racist officials, especially in the American South, began utilizing the same discriminatory tactics against black women that they had used to keep black men from the polls since the nineteenth century. Within a short time, many African American women had their voting privileges stripped away.

To keep them from the voting booth, African Americans (whose population suffered a high rate of poverty and illiteracy due to centuries of oppression) were forced to jump through hoops that whites were not. In order to cast
a ballot, they had to pay poll taxes they often could not afford. Literacy tests
were given as a requirement of voting, and when that did not work, intimidation and physical violence came into play.[1] As many black women struggled
to implement their political right as voters, white women ignored their plight.
Shortly after the election of 1920, the National Association for the Advancement of Colored People testified before Congress, bringing evidence of the
violent suppression of black citizens' votes in the South. When this attempt
for protection proved futile, they turned to former suffragists for help.[2] Alice
Paul, head of the National Woman's Party, insisted, however, that theirs was a
race issue, not a woman's issue. Her organization had already become deeply
engrossed in moving forward with the larger women's rights cause and had no
time to bother with such problems.[3] At the 1921 convention of the League of
Women Voters, African American women reached out to the newly formed
organization. Almost as if the past repeated itself, white southern delegates
threatened to walk out if the "negro problem" was debated. The league's
compromise allowed the black women to speak before the delegation, but the
organization took no action to assist the disenfranchised citizens.[4]

Abandoned by the government and white female activists, the drive to
reclaim voting rights for many African Americans lie in the future. As time
passed, American society and politics began to shift. Changes occurred in the
US Supreme Court and science began telling a truth many African Americans
already knew—the difference between blacks and whites was only skin deep.
As the Cold War unfolded following World War II, the United States found it
hard to credibly advocate freedom for people of color around the globe while
they discriminated against their own population at home.[5] As African American women in the political arena strengthened their coalitions with black
men, grassroots activism for racial equality popped up around the nation. By
the mid-1950s, the civil rights movement had burst onto the national scene;
among its leaders were the daughters and granddaughters of black suffragists.[6]
As time passed, the movement saw successes. In 1954, the Supreme Court
outlawed "separate but equal" schools in their ruling of *United States v. Brown.*
The following year, Rosa Parks made a bold statement when she refused to give
up her seat to make room for a white man on a bus in Birmingham, Alabama.
The event sparked a year-long bus boycott in the city. Soon to follow were

lunch counter sit-ins and struggles for blacks to have access to white schools, swimming pools, libraries, and hospitals. As the movement swelled in the mid-1960s, African Americans set their sights on equality at the polls.[7] For many years individual state laws unfairly denied blacks their right to vote. With a sense of urgency and growing momentum for equality across the races, the time seemed ripe to make their voices heard at the federal level.

In June 1964, tensions came to a boil when one black and two white voting rights activists were murdered in Mississippi by a group of white men. As the case unfolded, it became clear that the state would refuse to prosecute the accused conspirators.[8] Demonstrating their outrage about the murders and the denial of voting rights to blacks, on Sunday, March 7, 1965, six hundred peaceful marchers gathered in Selma, Alabama, intending to march to the state capitol in Montgomery. Heading East on US Route 80, the large group only made it the six blocks to the Edmund Pettus Bridge before things went awry. As the protestors crossed the bridge, they were met by state and local lawmen who violently attacked them. Marchers were trampled, dragged, and bloodied with billy clubs and whips. As tear gas rained down, the police who should have been protecting the marchers, instead, drove them back to Selma.[9] The televised attacks seared what has become known as "Bloody Sunday" into the minds of citizens around the country. As a result, public support grew for the voting rights activists, and on March 21, the march resumed with court protection. Speaking on his ruling, Federal District Court judge Frank M. Johnson Jr. said, "The law is clear that the right to petition one's government for the redress of grievances may be exercised in large groups . . . and these rights may be exercised by marching, even along public highways."[10] When the marchers resumed, more than three thousand people set out from Selma—a large increase from the original six hundred. Walking twelve miles a day and sleeping in fields along the way, the group of protestors had grown to twenty-five thousand strong by the time it reached the state capitol in Montgomery on March 25.[11]

In the wake of the violence, President Lyndon B. Johnson called for comprehensive voting rights legislation at the federal level. In a speech before Congress, he outlined the devious ways officials denied African Americans the vote and expressed the vital need for legal intervention. By July 9, both the Senate and House of Representatives had passed what would become the Voting Rights Act of 1965. On August 6, with Martin Luther King Jr. and other civil rights leaders present, Johnson signed it into law. Once enacted, the Voting Rights Act prohibited the denial to vote on account of race or color. It also outlawed the use of literacy tests, provided for federal oversight of voter registration in certain areas, and authorized the US attorney general to investigate the use of poll taxes in state and local elections. Additionally, the legislation required any jurisdictions considering the addition of new voting procedures to obtain preclearance from an authorized federal entity before doing so.[12]

As one of the most far-reaching pieces of civil rights legislation in US history, the Voting Rights Act of 1965 was immediately challenged in the court system. Between 1965 and 1969, the Supreme Court issued several decisions upholding its constitutionality. And in 1970, 1975, and 1982, the act was readopted and strengthened. Very quickly, activists could see the impact of the law. By the end of 1965, one-quarter of a million new black voters had been registered around the nation; and by the end of the next year only four out of every thirteen southern states had fewer than 50 percent of African Americans registered to vote.[13] Despite these success stories, many areas of the nation still saw weak enforcement of the law, and over time, government officials have continued to turn a blind eye to discriminatory practices.

While black voting rights were supposedly secured by the events of 1964 and 1965, barriers continue to plague many communities today. Restrictive registration requirements have cropped up, and voter identification cards barre eligible voters from the polls. In other ways, limited early voting options and inadequate polling resources in black, Hispanic, and other minority neighborhoods discourage many voters from casting ballots.[14] Loopholes in the law continue to allow racism, xenophobia, and discrimination based on ethnicity, national origin, and incarceration to play a role in continued disfranchisement. In the face of such realities, recent accusations of voter suppression, such as the occurrences during the 2018 Georgia gubernatorial election, demonstrate that voting rights are a continuing debate today. There is no denying that equality is far from being reached and more work lies ahead for many citizens and their allies. While the Voting Rights Act of 1965 represented the political and emotional peak of the modern civil rights movement, today, the Edmund Pettus Bridge (now a National Historic Landmark) stands as a beacon of inspiration to black rights activists around the nation and world. In its beauty a sense of hope arises. And in its brutal history a sense of determination stirs. Just as the marchers of 1965 overcame the physical trestle in Alabama, activists today continue to push through the barriers in front of them. One step at a time they create bridges and coalitions in the fight for equality.

Taking the Next Step

Charm Bracelet, assembled by Alice Paul, 1972, The National Museum of American History, Washington, DC, http://americanhistory.si.edu/

After Congress approved the 19th Amendment in June 1919, it had to be ratified by three-quarters of the states before enactment could begin. It was not long before suffragists began tallying up the count as more and more legislatures across the country approved the measure. To keep track of the amendment's progress, the National Woman's Party (NWP) created a "ratification flag," sewing on a new star each time a state approved the amendment. When final victory was reached in August 1920, Alice Paul unfurled the banner from the balcony of the organization's headquarters in triumph. Fifty-two years later Paul tasked herself with a similar project. The bracelet seen on the previous page is one of four created by Paul in the 1970s. After working to secure voting rights for women, Paul and the NWP pivoted, focusing on full equality for women. In 1972, when Congress passed the Equal Rights Amendment (ERA), designed to guarantee protection against sexual discrimination for women, Paul began her first bracelet. With each state that approved the measure, Paul added a charm.[1] Unlike the 19th Amendment, which saw relatively quick ratification after its passage in Congress, the ERA faced another fate entirely.

Following the 1920 election, the women of the suffrage movement set off in new directions. While Carrie Chapman Catt transformed the National American Woman Suffrage Association into the League of Women Voters, Alice Paul's NWP stayed intact, but with new ambitious goals. For these activists, winning suffrage was just the first of many steps toward achieving equal legal, social, and economic rights for women.[2] Knowing the quest for women's rights would be an ongoing struggle, Paul drafted the text of the ERA in 1923. In simple words Paul put forth the wishes of the NWP in the amendment's original text: "Men and women shall have equal rights throughout the United States and every place subject to its jurisdiction."[3] When the amendment was introduced to Congress that December, however, it was immediately opposed by the League of Women Voters and most other women's organizations working for labor and social welfare reform. Fearing the passage of the ERA would strike down previous labor laws protecting women specifically, many former suffragists refused to support the measure. And when Paul and the NWP refused to aid African Americans in working to protect the vote for women of color, they, too, had little reason to get behind another amendment they believed would provide no safeguards for them.[4]

Because the ERA fell short in considering the needs of working women and African Americans, it was destined to fail. With little support outside the NWP, the legislation did not even come up for debate after its introduction into Congress in 1923. It continued to languish unconsidered every year until 1970.[5] The divide over the ERA had become so wide, in fact, that for many years it split the feminist movement into factions. As the twentieth century progressed, however, the events of the civil rights movement energized black and white activists alike. As women examined their own situation more closely, it became apparent that a considerable amount of unfinished business had accumulated since 1920. The inequality of wages had become glaringly obvious, equal opportunities for women in the workplace were non-existent, and housewives wanting a life outside the home felt trapped. When the groundbreaking book *The Feminine Mystique* hit bookshelves, it struck a nerve. Arguing that women in American society were being programmed into a kind of homemaker primarily concerned with consumerism, Betty Friedan's book served as a catalyst to reenergize the women's rights movement.[6]

When the National Organization for Women (NOW) formed in 1966, it began moving on a variety of issues. Among them, the ERA, which had been gathering dust for decades. By 1970, activists succeeded at forcing a hearing on the amendment in Congress. By that time the wording had been altered by Paul to read, "Equality of rights under the law shall not be denied or abridged by the United States or by any state on account of sex." Within two years Congress approved the measure, and like the 19th Amendment, it was sent to the states for ratification. Hoping to push the process as quickly as possible, women's organizations of every kind came together to work for the measure. They raised money, generated public support, and even staged marches in key states around the country. Many women who had never done anything political in their lives came out of the woodwork to assist with door-to-door canvassing, walk-a-thons, and meetings. As organization's like NOW swelled to historic sizes, women's magazines, newspapers, and many other mainstream publications featured stories about the ERA and its progress. Within just three years, thirty-four of the thirty-eight states needed had ratified the amendment.[7] Unlike the 19th Amendment, however, the ERA was up against a ticking clock. Lawmakers had set a limit to the ratification period, meaning that all thirty-eight required states had to sign on by 1977.

Certainly, no movement is without its opponents. In short order a strong group of conservative Christian women formed the STOP ERA movement. These women feared a statement like the ERA in the Constitution would give the government too much control over citizens' personal lives. They charged that its passage would lead to men abandoning their families, the decriminalization of rape, unisex bathrooms, gay marriage, and women being drafted.[8] In a flash of showmanship (much like suffragists had employed) they even highlighted their status as mothers and wives at protests by wearing aprons and utilizing props like homemade pies. In the interest of balanced reporting, the media gave equal attention to such arguments, and the group's claims prompted fear and doubt in many people around the country.[9] On top of public opinion, many politicians considered the legislation too controversial and failed to assist in generating support in state legislatures. As concern grew about the rapid change happening in society, the early ratification momentum came to a screeching halt. After 1974, only the state of Indiana ratified the amendment before activists secured a three-year extension on the deadline. When the time limit was reached in 1982, no other states had signed on with their support. The ERA was dead in the water, only three states shy of federal ratification.[10]

Following the passage of women's suffrage, Alice Paul dedicated the remainder of her life to fighting for full women's equality, and as each of the first thirty-four states to ratify the ERA approved the measure, she added a charm to one of her four bracelets. On July 9, 1977, Paul passed away at the age of ninety-two, knowing the chances of the amendment's passage were slim. Despite the grim outlook, activists carried on with Paul's strength of conviction and continued to advocate for the amendment until its final denial in 1982. Although the ERA had been reintroduced in every session of Congress since the deadline passed, no major movement took hold. In 2018, however, the ERA again made headlines. Although the deadline passed thirty-six years earlier, on May 30, Illinois became the thirty-seventh state to ratify the Equal Rights Amendment. A year earlier, Nevada had also approved the legislation. In June 2019, the topic of the ERA even made it to the stage during a Democratic debate between potential candidates for the party's 2020 presidential nominee. Directing her comments to former Vice President Joe Biden, Senator Kamala Harris of California stated, "That's why we need to pass the ERA, because there are moments in history where states fail to preserve the civil rights of all people."[11] Bolstered by the #MeToo movement and an energized female political body, interest in the decades-old ERA resurfaced. With a renewed concern for the amendment, legal strategists began arguing that the passage of the deadline may not be a deal breaker to the amendment's ratification. Some asserted that because other amendments had no time limit, the ERA should not have had one either. Other strategists contended that Congress simply needed to extend the deadline as it did before.

Perhaps one of the strongest arguments lies in the example of the passage of the 27th Amendment in 1992. Concerned with congressional salaries, the amendment had originally been proposed in 1789 and took more than two centuries to win states' ratification. ERA backers are optimistic that this example indicates that there may be hope for them when a thirty-eighth state comes on board.[12] If the ERA is to succeed now, activists need to look at the lessons of the past. Suffragists demonstrated that focusing on a single issue could prove successful over time, and activists of the 1970s proved the necessity of collaborating with other social movements. In an era filled with groups like Black Lives Matter, #MeToo, and the Women's March, perhaps activists will come together once again to create the momentum needed to push the ERA through to its final victory and bring women one step closer to equality.[13]

49

Going Global

Pussyhat, made by Kiki Smith, 2017, Smith College Historic Clothing Collection, Smith College, Northampton, MA, https://schistoricclothing.com/
PHOTOGRAPH BY STAN SHERER

Throughout the course of their movement, suffragists became masters of visual statement. By using sashes, banners, costumes, and a host of other articles, they drew attention to themselves and their cause. The use of such visual pomp was not just about catching the eye of onlookers, however. Once noticed, the messages these objects communicated proved just as important as the item itself. Sometimes these ideas were straightforward, carried out through printed slogans like "Votes for Women." Other times, the bold colors of suffrage carried their message of unity. In 2017, the suffrage movement had been over for more than ninety years, however, the use of visual symbols was alive and well. That year, the pink hat seen on the facing page arrived at the Women's March in Boston atop the head of one of the many demonstrators who flooded capital cities across the country. Joining countless other women to fight back against the words of a male politician, the pussyhat quickly became a symbol of female solidarity and political resistance. Made by the thousands, the unassuming knitted hat represented the everyday woman's fight and continued demands of justice and equality in the face of continuing sexism.

The presidential campaign of 2016 had been one for the history books. Making it past the primaries, the nation not only saw the first woman emerge as the nominee of a major political party, but it also witnessed the primary election of a candidate without a political background. Hillary Clinton, the Democratic Party's nominee, faced a federal investigation for the misuse of a private email server during her time as secretary of state. The Republican Party's nominee, Donald Trump, brought a rhetoric to the campaign that elevated personal attacks over policy development. Outside of the heated debates, violence rose among the public, and media coverage exploded. Even before the primaries ended, Trump had taken low blows at women, insulting the looks of Republican primary candidate Carli Fiorina as well as the wife of Republican senator Ted Cruz. With the November election less than a month away, *The Washington Post* broke a story on October 7, 2016, that sent shock waves through many women in the country. Audio and video coverage had surfaced of presidential candidate Donald Trump and television host Billy Bush in 2005. Taped aboard a bus on their way to film an episode of the television show *Access Hollywood*, Trump described his unsolicited attempt to seduce a married woman. Bragging of his wealth and power, Trump added, "I don't even wait. And when you're a star, they let you do it. You can do anything. Grab them by the pussy. You can do anything."[1]

The derogatory comments relaying what many legal experts would describe as sexual assault drew sharp comments and disgust from many women, while others dismissed the remarks as indiscretions of the past. Trump himself brushed off the incident as nothing more than "locker-room banter."[2] In the weeks following the release of the footage, politicians, the public, and the press wondered if the video would impact the outcome of the looming election. No one can know for sure what effect it had on the final vote, but when ballots were tallied Trump came out the winner. Very quickly, activists promoting equity, justice, and dignity organized. Plans were underway for a series of protests across the nation on January 21, 2017, the day after the inauguration of President-Elect Donald Trump. Known as the Women's March, the collective's laundry list of advocacy issues included human rights, women's rights, immigration reform, health care reform, reproductive rights, the environment, LGBTQ rights, racial equality, freedom of religion, workers' rights, and tolerance.[3]

With excitement of the Women's March growing, a group of women in California conceived an idea. What if the demonstrators attending the marches could make a unique visual statement to help activists be better heard? Through conversations during knitting classes at the Little Knittery, a local yarn store in Los Angeles, friends Jayna Zweiman and Krista Suh came up with an idea. Suh planned to attend the march in Washington, DC, and would need a cap to keep her head warm in the winter air. Zweiman, who was recovering from an injury, would not be able to attend but wanted to find a way to have her voice heard even though she could not physically be there. Together, the two came up with the idea of creating a sea of pink hats to make a bold statement of collective solidarity and to allow those who could not make the trip to participate. Little Knittery owner Kat Coyle designed a simple open-source pattern that would allow people of all knitting levels to be part of the action. The name Pussyhat Project was chosen due to the design, which had the appearance of a cat with two ears projecting from the top. Using the play on words of "pussycat" and "pussyhat," the group directly made the link to Trump's now-infamous bragging about the freedom he felt to grab women by the genitals. It also hoped the project could assist in destigmatizing the word "pussy" and transform it into a word of empowerment rather than one of denigration.[4]

Shared across the internet on social media platforms, the pussyhat design and concept took off. Although the project launched at the end of November, leaving less than two months for women to hear about the hat and begin work, everyday women embraced the idea. For centuries women had taken to needle and yarn during times of political strife. During major wars, such as the American Revolution, Civil War, and both world wars, knitting became a political activity of women. Through their efforts, many items were supplied to the military and soldiers. In the years following the 9/11 attacks, knitting was again taken up as a political action when artists began incorporating textile pieces into politically charged public art. Additionally, everyday crafters turned the hobby into a form of political action when women began using it to rebel against "the sleek, the mass-produced, the male."[5] During the rapid push of the Pussyhat Project, women across the nation downloaded the pattern for free and began buying up all the pink yarn they could find. They knitted on their couches, they knitted in coffee shops, and, importantly, they often knitted together. Through their efforts, volunteers not only made hats for themselves, but they also sent thousands to a Virginia collection center preparing to distribute them for free to marchers. Others sold their handiwork online, donating proceeds to Planned Parenthood.[6] When the day of the event arrived on January 21, 2017, the Women's March drew more than five hundred thousand participants to Washington, DC, creating a sea of pink. In more than six hundred sister marches around the globe, like the one held in Boston, more than three million additional people demonstrated their solidarity for women's rights in protest of the incoming Trump Administration.[7] Alongside their hats, they held homemade signs and banners carrying messages of frustration as well as words of hope. Following the lead of the peaceful demonstration practices used by civil rights activists in the 1960s and suffragists in the 1910s, no arrests were made.

In a small amount of time, the pussyhat stood up as a symbol that unified marchers in Washington, DC, and at gatherings around the globe. Women, men, transgender, nonbinary, and a host of other individuals joined together to create one voice letting the presidential administration know that they believed in an equitable and tolerant world, safe for everyone in the human race.[8] For individuals who had fallen into feelings of despair and dread following the election, the pussyhat allowed them to begin recovery and healing. It empowered makers, reminding them that they were not alone, and it gave ordinary people a creative outlet for their political frustration.[9] Following the march's 2017 success, the Women's March organization continued with its work to prove that women's rights are human rights. The 2018 protest in January adopted the catchy slogan, "Power to the Polls," focusing on registering more women to vote and to elect women and progressive candidates to public office. This time around far fewer pussyhats were present than in the year before. Intended to be a play on words, some people saw the hats as vulgar. Others believed that the chosen color pink (intended to represent femininity) excluded women of color whose genitals are better represented by other shades. Even the name itself created an outcry for its exclusion of nonfemale allies, as well as individuals who identify as female but might not have been born with female genitalia.[10] Responding to these sentiments, founders of the Pussyhat Project made it clear that their intent had not been exclusion or offense. They invited "anyone, of any gender and color to create a hat in the way that represents them best."[11]

Today, a visit to many museums and historic collections across the globe provides the opportunity to view one of the pussyhats from the historic marches of 2017. Researchers diving into the Smith College Historic Clothing Collection in Northampton, Massachusetts, will find the hat seen on on the first page of this chapter, knitted by professor of theatre Kiki Smith. Halfway across the country, visitors to the Michigan State University Museum may encounter one of the many pussyhats made by activists in their state. Even a visit to the Victoria and Albert Museum (V&A) in London, England, may provide the opportunity to view one of the most notable pussyhats from the Women's March of 2017—one made by Jayna Zweiman, the cofounder of the Pussyhat Project, who had been unable to attend the march. As she had hoped, Zweiman found a way to participate even though she could not physically be at the event in the nation's capital. Although she made numerous hats during the lead-up to the march, the one at the V&A was personally sent to a longtime friend to wear on the big day. But why have such an iconic pussyhat from the United States in London? Looking to document important global events in real time, the V&A's Rapid Response Team seeks out just such items. While the hat had only been worn two months earlier when it was unveiled in their galleries in March 2017, it had already reached the level of icon, making it a logical addition to the museum's permanent collection. In the blink of an eye, the pussyhat had become an internationally recognized symbol of solidarity for women's rights. It reached countless people, brought the everyday woman into political activism, and supported ongoing conversations about the definitions of womanhood, gender identity, and equality.[12] Through inexpensive materials and the work of many hands, what had started out as a small unassuming item took the narrative of women's rights global and proved that sometimes pussies do fight back.

Reckoning with the Past . . . and Future

Sculpture—*Portrait Monument to Lucretia Mott, Elizabeth Cady Stanton, and Susan B. Antony*, Adelaide Johnson, 1920, United States Capitol, Rotunda, Washington, DC, https://www.visit thecapitol.gov/

ARCHITECT OF THE CAPITOL

Walking into the rotunda of the US Capitol building, visitors cannot help but feel the sense of importance around them. Positioned in the center of the structure beneath the Capitol dome, the rotunda is sometimes referred to as the heart of the building. Branching off in either direction from the majestic hall are the north and south corridors—one leading to the US House of Representatives, the other to the US Senate. As a place of honor, the rotunda has been the site of the lying in state of numerous American politicians, and is home to some of the nation's most beautiful pieces of artwork. John Trumbull's epic paintings of the American Revolution hang on the walls, and numerous statuary works depicting historic figures, such as President Abraham Lincoln and civil rights leader Martin Luther King Jr., have places of honor as well. Almost exclusively the depictions are male dominated, making the marble *Portrait Monument to Lucretia Mott, Elizabeth Cady Stanton, and Susan B. Anthony* stand out not only for its size, but also for its depiction of three women. With three busts rising from the eight-ton block of white marble, the sculpture pays honor to three important pioneers of the women's suffrage movement. Because of its rough-hewn look and the mysterious fourth protrusion behind the three women, in the recent past, speculation has swirled that the unfinished portion was left by the artist with the intent that the first female president would later be added.[1] While rumors tend to grow, the true meaning behind the work is something even greater.

In mid-April 1920, Alice Paul invited sculptress Adelaide Johnson to the National Woman's Party headquarters to discuss an idea. Years earlier Johnson had sculpted three individual busts of suffrage pioneers Lucretia Mott, Elizabeth Cady Stanton, and Susan B. Anthony for display in the Woman's Building at the 1893 World's Columbian Exhibition. After their completion Johnson hoped they could be displayed at the US Capitol. But great friction between Johnson and the National American Woman Suffrage Association (NAWSA), who had been involved with their initial execution and financing, made the issue nearly impossible. Now with the ratification of the 19th Amendment inching nearer, Paul had an interest in making that original intent happen. In fact, she had a much grander vision. She hoped to have the busts presented at the Capitol as part of a great ceremony to celebrate the end of the suffrage movement. As the two women talked at length, Johnson suggested that rather than use the original busts, she create new ones. In the twenty-seven years since she sculpted the originals, her technique had been refined, and she was certain she could produce better likenesses. With Paul's approval of initial funding, Johnson set out, making plans to head across the ocean to Italy where she could source the finest marble for the artwork.[2]

Born in rural Illinois in 1859, Johnson may have seemed an unlikely choice, but she was certainly up for the challenge. She studied art at the St. Louis School of Design, earning accolades for her work. After moving to Chicago, she suffered a serious accident when she fell down an elevator shaft while heading to her studio. After recovering from her injuries, she took the $15,000 from her insurance settlement and financed a trip to Europe, where she continued studying sculpture in Italy.[3] By the time the National Woman's Party commissioned her, Johnson had spent the greater part of her life refining her craft.

Although Paul had asked Johnson for three busts, the artist decided that combining them into one piece of artwork would be more effective than to again create three individual pieces. She had done that in the past, and she intended this new piece to take on a larger meaning. As a loyal suffragist and women's rights advocate, Johnson regarded the continued refinement of the suffrage busts as her life's work, and she planned to put her heart and soul into the creation of the newest piece. After selecting the perfect eight-ton block of marble from which her creation would emerge, Johnson, with the assistance of stone carvers and finishers, spent the remainder of 1920 in Carrara, Italy, working diligently on the sculpture. On November 11, 1920, Alice Paul sent a letter to voters stating, "Now that the suffrage victory is finally established by the voting of women this November, let us pause, before entering upon our next work, to honor the pioneers who made today's victory possible." In the letter she announced that on February 15, 1921, the statue would be placed in the Capitol with a glorious ceremony. She also noted that the National Woman's Party needed to raise $20,000 for the event—a large portion no doubt needed to cover the cost of the sculpture itself, as well as its transport across the ocean.[4]

At the time Paul sent her letter she had been in discussions with Congress for several months concerning the artwork. As of November, they had not yet officially accepted it as a gift. Nonetheless, plans to deliver the piece to the Capitol pushed on. By the time the piece arrived on February 4, it had traveled by ship, train, and wagon. With nowhere to go, the piece sat for a week outside of the Capitol under the steps. Finally, on February 10, members of the congressional Fine Arts Commission approved the gift. The next day the sculpture was hoisted on temporary ramps up the steps and into the rotunda.[5]

Not only did February 15 mark the day of the unveiling, but it was also the 101st anniversary of Susan B. Anthony's birth. Just as Paul had promised, the ceremony was indeed grand, drawing attendees from more than seventy different women's organizations.[6] As guests arrived, a monument covered by yellow cloth greeted them. Once the official acceptance took place, the room darkened as two young women dressed as Greek goddesses dropped the veil and an opera singer began the refrains of "Oh, Lord of Hosts." At the same time a brilliant spotlight shone on the statue. In the true fashion of suffrage spectacle, the National Woman's Party made sure the unveiling took on as much drama as possible. Within minutes, however, life went back to normal and workmen began removing all evidence of the occasion. As people were still coming forward to look at the monument, the workers started to cover it back up.[7]

Congress had never intended for the monument to permanently stay in the rotunda. Instead, it quickly moved below to the crypt. At the time, the lower level served more as a storage area than anything else, but visitors were escorted down if they wished to see the sculpture. Unfortunately, a good look at the piece could not be had. When moved below, it had been placed against a wall, hiding Johnson's provocative inscription, "Woman, first denied a soul, then called mindless, now arisen declared herself an entity to be reckoned."[8] When questioned about the move, politicians responded with vague answers. They claimed the piece was too heavy to sit in the rotunda. Others argued the sculpture did not have the artistic merit for such a place of honor. Some simply said it was too big. As for Johnson's original inscription, it was removed without her knowledge. The country may have been ready for women to have the opportunity to vote but not for them to have such a strong voice or presence in the nation's place of lawmaking.

While the piece remained on continuous view in the crypt, even being moved to the center of the room when the area became a permanent place for art display, many people felt the sculpture deserved a place of prominence. For decades the same excuses were given to dismiss the issue. After years of demands that it be moved back to the rotunda, however, legislation to move the sculpture finally passed the Senate in 1995 before being killed in the House of Representatives. A year later, the legislation passed both houses, but without funding. After almost $75,000 of private funds were raised, the *Portrait Monument* again took its place in the Capitol's heart.[9]

On Mother's Day weekend in May 1997 the sculpture ascended the stairs. Placed in the rotunda, a new generation of visitors now has the opportunity to view Johnson's masterpiece. Together, the three figures, placed in a triangular shape, signify the special trinity the three formed. It also shows the progression of time. Because of her early initiative in the movement, Mott is seen in an advanced position. Since Stanton worked with Mott to hold the first Woman's Rights Convention in Seneca Falls, she comes next. Anthony, arriving last, is situated in the back but very near Stanton, communicating the close work the women shared. Although visitors and Capitol guides have speculated the unfinished protrusion at the back was reserved for the first female president, Johnson had no such intentions. The rough-hewn appearance around the edges as well as the unfinished projection represented the struggles, difficulties, and obstacles women faced in the past.[10]

As a woman who knew suffrage was only one step in the journey of women's rights, Johnson left a gift for the women of the future. The three suffragists represented in her statue remind everyone of the past struggles and triumphs women have achieved. Just as portions of her artwork appear unfinished, so, too, is the work ahead. Although politicians may have been unprepared for women to take such a place of honor at the nation's home of lawmaking, slow progress is being made. Before the ratification of the 19th Amendment, Jeannette Rankin succeeded at becoming the nation's first female member of the House of Representatives. While the numbers of women in office following the passage of the 19th Amendment did not increase quickly, it has steadily grown in amount and diversity. Shirley Chisholm became the first black woman elected to Congress, in the 1960s. In the 1980s, Geraldine Ferraro made history as the first woman nominated for vice president on a major ticket. And in the 2000s, Condoleezza Rice became the first black woman to serve as the US national security advisor and then the US secretary of state. Since 2008, the presidential primaries and presidential election have included women in some way. Sarah Palin was nominated as John McCain's Republican running mate in 2008. The same year, Hillary Clinton faced Barrack Obama in the Democratic primaries. While Clinton's run for president in 2016 ended in defeat, the outcome of the election has spurred more women into political action. In 2018, 255 female candidates ran for office around the nation.

Among those elected were women who identify as Native American, Latino, black, white, Asian American, immigrants, and refugees. Johnson's *Portrait Monument* represents all these women and encourages more to add their names to future ranks of female politicians and activists. As the artist recognized, the successes suffragists achieved were only part of the work needed in the future. As the nation's politicians and visitors to the Capitol cast their eyes on her sculpture, one can only hope that they also come to understand her words and carry forth the sentiment that women are indeed "an entity to be reckoned" with.[11]

Appendix

Significant Women's Suffrage Victories in the United States before the Ratification of the 19th Amendment

1869
The territory of Wyoming is established with full suffrage for women.

1870
The territory of Utah adopts full suffrage for women.

1883
The territory of Washington adopts full suffrage for women.

1887
The territory of Montana adopts full suffrage for women.

1890
The state of Wyoming is admitted with full suffrage for women.

1893
The state of Colorado grants full suffrage for women.

1896
The states of Idaho and Utah grant full suffrage for women.

1910
The State of Washington grants full suffrage for women.

1911
The state of California grants full suffrage for women.

1912
The states of Arizona, Kansas, and Oregon grant full suffrage for women.

1913
The territory of Alaska adopts full suffrage for women.

The state of Illinois adopts presidential and municipal suffrage for women.

1914
The states of Montana and Nevada grant full suffrage for women.

1917
The state of New York grants full suffrage for women.

The states of North Dakota, Nebraska, and Rhode Island adopt presidential suffrage for women.

The state of Arkansas grants women the right to vote in primary elections.

1918
The states of Michigan, Oklahoma, and South Dakota grant full suffrage for women.

The state of Texas grants women the right to vote in primary elections.

The state of Indiana adopts presidential suffrage for women.

1919
The states of Maine, Missouri, Iowa, Minnesota, Ohio, Wisconsin, and Tennessee adopt presidential suffrage for women.

1920
The state of Kentucky adopts presidential suffrage for women.

Notes

INTRODUCTION

1. Barbara Stuhler, *For the Public Record: A Documentary History of the League of Women Voters* (Westport, CT: Greenwood Press, 2000), 25–26.

2. Letter from Abigail Adams to John Adams, March 31–April 5, 1776. Massachusetts Historical Society, June 30, 2019, https://www.masshist.org/digitaladams/archive/doc?id=L17760331aa.

3. Marjorie Spruill Wheeler, ed., *One Woman, One Vote: Rediscovering the Woman Suffrage Movement* (Troutdale, OR: NewSage Press, 1995), 29.

4. Wheeler, *One Woman, One Vote*, 32.

5. Wheeler, *One Woman, One Vote*, 32.

6. Wheeler, *One Woman, One Vote*, 32.

7. "Suffrage," Merriam-Webster, March 3, 2019, https://www.merriam-webster.com/dictionary/suffrage.

8. "The Women Suffrage Timeline," Women Suffrage and Beyond: Confronting the Democratic Deficit, March 7, 2019, http://womensuffrage.org/?page_id=69.

9. John Mack Fraragher et al., *Out of Many: A History of the American People* (Upper Saddle River, NJ: Pearson Prentice Hall, 2006), 358.

10. Jessica D. Jenkins, "Marching Shoulder to Shoulder: New Life in the Connecticut Woman Suffrage Movement," *Connecticut History* 50, no. 2 (Fall 2011): 133.

11. Jenkins, "Marching Shoulder to Shoulder," 133.

12. Office of History and Preservation, Office of the Clerk, US House of Representatives. *Women in Congress: 1917–2006* (Washington, DC: US Government Printing Office, 2006), 21.

13. Ellen M. Plante, *Women at Home in Victorian America: A Social History* (New York: Facts On File, 1997), ix–x.

14. Wheeler, *One Woman, One Vote*, 14–15.

15. Wheeler, *One Woman, One Vote*, 15.

CHAPTER 1. LAYING A STRONG FOUNDATION

1. Provenance Note—In 1903, Susan B. Anthony presented her personal library of feminist and antislavery literature to the Library of Congress. The collection, now known as the Susan B. Anthony Collection, contains inscribed volumes presented by admirers, the official reports of the national suffrage conventions, addresses made at congressional hearings after 1869, and files of reform periodicals such as the *Woman's Journal*. In many of the 272 volumes, Anthony wrote notes about the donor or author. The collection also includes thirty-three scrapbooks of newspaper clippings, programs, handbills, and memorabilia. The scrapbooks began at the suggestion of her father, in 1855, and document changes in public opinion toward Anthony and the suffrage movement. Throughout this book the author will include provenance notes related to the highlighted treasures, when possible. In some instances, the information has been worked into the body of the chapter rather than a note. Ideally, collecting institutions would have a recorded provenance for every item in their collection, but in reality, that is rarely the case. In many instances the history of the object is not known.

2. Leonard N. Beck, "The Library of Susan B. Anthony," *The Quarterly Journal of the Library of Congress* 32, no. 4 (October 1975): 324–35.

3. Beck, "The Library of Susan B. Anthony," 324–35.

4. Eileen Hunt Botting and Christine Carey, "Wollstonecraft's Philosophical Impact on Nineteenth-Century American Women's Rights Advocates," *American Journal of Political Science* 48, no. 4 (October 2004): 720.

5. Jennifer A. Lemak and Ashley Hopkins-Benton, *Votes for Women: Celebrating New York's Suffrage Centennial* (Albany: State University of New York Press, 2017), 8–9.

6. Botting and Carey, "Wollstonecraft," 707–9.

7. Botting and Carey, "Wollstonecraft," 718.

8. Botting and Carey, "Wollstonecraft," 717.

CHAPTER 2. PAWNS OF POLITICS

1. "It Happened Here—New Jersey. The Petticoat Politicians of 1776: New Jersey's First Female Voters," New Jersey Historical Commission, accessed September 5, 2018, https://www.nj.gov/state/historical/it-happened-here/ihhnj-er-petticoat-politicians.pdf.

2. Jan Ellen Lewis, "Rethinking Women's Suffrage in New Jersey, 1776–1807," *Rutgers Law Review* 63, no. 3 (August 2011): 1017.

3. Bob Blythe, "Stories from the Revolution," National Park Service, accessed September 5, 2018, https://www.nps.gov/revwar/anout_the_revolution/voting_rights.html.

4. Lewis, "Rethinking," 1019.

5. Lewis, "Rethinking," 1019–21.

6. Susan L. Ditmire, "Petticoat Electors," GardenStateLegacy.com, Issue 7, March 2010, https://gardenstatelegacy.com/files/Petticoat_Electors_Ditmire_GSL7.pdf.

7. "It Happened Here."

8. Ditmire, "Petticoat Electors."

9. Alexander Keyssar, *The Right to Vote: The Contested History of Democracy in the United States* (New York: Basic Books, 2000), 44.

10. Allan J. Lichtman, *The Embattled Vote in America: From the Founding to the Present* (Cambridge, MA: Harvard University Press, 2018), chap. 4.

CHAPTER 3. CHANGE BEGINS WITH EDUCATION

1. Provenance Note—After being used by students at Sarah Pierce's Litchfield Female Academy, this globe was owned and used by John Catlin in his boarding school in Northfield, Connecticut, a village within the town of Litchfield. Charles H. Woodruff, who donated the globe to the Litchfield Historical Society, attended Catlin's school in the winter of 1845/1846 and remembered the globe being used during his time as a student in Northfield. Woodruff's mother, Henrietta Seymour, had been a student of Sarah Pierce from 1819–1823 during the globe's use at the school.

2. Jennifer A. Lemak and Ashley Hopkins-Benton, *Votes for Women: Celebrating New York's Suffrage Centennial* (Albany: State University of New York Press, 2017), 4.

3. Eleanor Flexner and Ellen Fitzpatrick, *Century of Struggle: The Woman's Rights Movement in the United States* (Cambridge, MA: The Belknap Press of Harvard University Press, 1996), 14.

4. Nancy Faust Sizer and Theodore Ryland Sizer et al., *To Ornament Their Minds: Sarah Pierce's Litchfield Female Academy 1792–1833* (Litchfield, CT: The Litchfield Historical Society, 1993), 9.

5. "The Ledger," The Litchfield Historical Society, accessed February 4, 2018, http://litchfieldhistoricalsociety.org/ledger/studies/history_lfa.

6. "Litchfield Female Academy History," The Ledger, accessed February 4, 2018, http://litchfieldhistoricalsociety.org/ledger/studies/history_lfa.

7. Sizer and Sizer, *To Ornament*, 9–10.

8. Sizer and Sizer, *To Ornament*, 13.

CHAPTER 4. CREATED EQUAL

1. Jennifer A. Lemak and Ashley Hopkins-Benton, *Votes for Women: Celebrating New York's Suffrage Centennial* (Albany: State University of New York Press, 2017), xxiii.

2. Rosalyn Terborg-Penn, *African American Women in the Struggle for the Vote, 1850–1920* (Bloomington: Indiana University Press, 1998), 13.

3. Winifred Conkling, *Votes for Women! American Suffragists and the Battle for the Ballot* (Chapel Hill, NC: Algonquin, 2018), 34–35.

4. Lemak and Hopkins-Benton, *Votes for Women*, 14.

5. Terborg-Penn, *African American Women*, 14.

6. Marjorie Spruill Wheeler, ed., *One Woman, One Vote: Rediscovering the Woman Suffrage Movement* (NewSage Press, 1995), 37.

7. Lemak and Hopkins-Benton, *Votes for Women*, 14.

8. Wheeler, *One Woman, One Vote*, 38.

9. Lemak and Hopkins-Benton, *Votes for Women*, 11.

CHAPTER 5. "AIN'T I A WOMAN?"

1. Provenance Note—According to a notation on the back of the cabinet card, it was purchased on April 21, 1870, in Washington, DC, from Sojourner Truth. The writer of the note only identified themselves with initials, however, so their identity is not known. In 1870, Truth was in Washington, DC, working to secure land grants for former slaves. While in the nation's capital, she met with President Grant at the White House.

2. Nell Irvin Painter, "Representing Truth: Sojourner Truth's Knowing and Becoming Known," *The Journal of American History* 81, no. 2 (September 1994): 463–64.

3. Eleanor Flexner and Ellen Fitzpatrick, *Century of Struggle: The Woman's Rights Movement in the United States* (Cambridge, MA: Belknap Press of Harvard University Press, 1996), 84–86; Rosalyn Terborg-Penn, *African American Women in the Struggle for the Vote, 1850*–1920 (Bloomington: Indiana University Press, 1998), 14–16; Jennifer A. Lemak and Ashley Hopkins-Benton, *Votes for Women: Celebrating New York's Suffrage Centennial* (Albany: State University of New York Press, 2017), 36–37; Ann Bausum, *With Courage and Cloth: Winning the Fight For a Woman's Right to Vote* (National Geographic Society, 2004), 20–21; Painter, "Representing Truth," 461–92; Teresa Zackondnik, "The 'Green-Backs of Civilization': Sojourner Truth and Portrait Photography," *American Studies* 46 no. 2 (Summer 2005): 117–43; "Sojourner Truth; Abolitionist, Suffragists, Lower East Sider," Tenement Museum Blog, accessed February 24, 2018, http://tenement.org/blog/sojourner-truth-abolitionist-suffragist-lower-east-sider/.

4. Winifred Conkling, *Votes for Women! American Suffragists and the Battle for the Ballot* (Chapel Hill, NC: Algonquin, 2017), 48–50.

5. Flexner and Fitzpatrick, *Century of Struggle*, 85.

6. Terborg-Penn, *African American Women*, 15.

CHAPTER 6. DRESSING THE PART

1. Provenance Note—For many years this bloomer costume was stored inside a trunk and held in the Homer National Bank in Homer, New York. Along with the bloomer costume was documentation indicating Meriva Carpenter, a resident of Homer (also the birthplace

of Amelia Bloomer), originally owned the garment. The bank was unsure of how long it had been stored at their facility or why. In 1994, the bank notified the Cortland County Historical Society of the costume and transferred it to the museum's collection.

2. Laura J. Ping, "Clothes as Historical Sources: What Bloomers Reveal about the Women Who Wore Them," *AHA Today Blog*, accessed February 11, 2018, blog.historians.org/2017/02/clothes-historical-sources-bloomers-reveal-women-wore/.

3. Jennifer A. Lemak and Ashley Hopkins-Benton, *Votes for Women: Celebrating New York's Suffrage Centennial* (Albany: State University of New York Press, 2017), 26.

4. Linda Welters and Anny Lillethun, eds. *The Fashion Reader* (Oxford: Berg, 2007), 31.

5. Lemak and Hopkins-Benton, *Votes for Women*, 27.

6. Eleanor Flexner and Ellen Fitzpatrick, *Century of Struggle: The Woman's Rights Movement in the United States* (Cambridge, MA: Belknap Press of Harvard University Press, 1996), 79.

7. Phyllis G. Tortora and Keith Eubank, *Survey of Historic Costume: A History of Western Dress* (New York: Fairchild Publications, 2005), 307.

8. Robert E. Riegel, Elizabeth Cady Stanton, and Mary S. Bull, "Woman's Rights and Other 'Reforms' in Seneca Falls: A Contemporary View," *New York History* 46, no. 1 (January 1965): 55.

9. Ann D. Gordon, ed., *The Selected Paper of Elizabeth Cady Stanton and Susan B. Anthony*, vol. 6 (New Brunswick, NJ: Rutgers University Press, 2013), 34.

CHAPTER 7. ORGANIZING A NATION

1. Kim Anderson, "Gertrude Weil," *History for All the People, A State Archives of North Carolina Blog*, accessed June 30, 2018, https://ncarchives.wordpress.com/2018/03/16/international-womens-day-2018-gertrude-wil.

2. "Gertrude Weil," Jewish Women's Archives, accessed June 30, 2018, https://jwa.org/womenofvalor/weil.

3. Leonard Rogoff, *Gertrude Weil: Jewish Progressive in the New South* (Chapel Hill: University of North Carolina Press, 2017), 107.

4. Wheeler, Marjorie Spruill, ed., *One Woman, One Vote: Rediscovering the Woman Suffrage Movement* (Troutdale, OR: NewSage Press, 1995), 10.

5. Eleanor Flexner and Ellen Fitzpatrick, *Century of Struggle: The Woman's Rights Movement in the United States* (Cambridge, MA: The Belknap Press of Harvard University Press, 1996), 208.

6. Flexner and Fitzpatrick, *Century of Struggle*, 208.

7. Wheeler, *One Woman, One Vote*, 14.

8. Wheeler, *One Woman, One Vote*, 14.

9. Wheeler, *One Woman, One Vote*, 14.

10. Andrew W. Robertson, ed. *Encyclopedia of US Political History*, vol. 1 (Washington, DC: CQ Press, 2010), 406.

11. Jessica A. Bandel, "Portraits of War: Gertrude Weil," North Carolina Department of Natural and Cultural Resources, accessed June 30, 2018, https://www.ncdr.gov/blog/2017/03/16/portraits-war-gertrude-weil.

12. Heather Geisberg Pennington, "Gertrude Weil: 1879–1971," The Encyclopedia of Jewish Women, accessed July 11, 2019, https://jwa.org/encyclopedia/author/pennington-heather.

CHAPTER 8. WHAT'S OLD IS NEW AGAIN

1. In April 2016, President Barrack Obama designated the Sewall-Belmont House and Museum as the Belmont-Paul Women's Equality National Monument. As a National Monument, the site is owned by the National Park Service, while it continues to serve as a museum and headquarters for the National Woman's Party, an education nonprofit.

2. "Overview," National Woman's Party at the Belmont-Paul Women's Equality National Monument, accessed March 31, 2018, http://nationalwomansparty.org/learn/overview/.

3. "Presidential Proclamation"—Establishment of the Belmont-Paul Women's Equality National Monument, April 12, 2016, https://obamawhitehouse.archives.gov/the-press-office/2016/04/12/presidential-proclamation-establishment-belmont-paul-womens-equality.

4. "National Woman's Party," National Woman's Party at the Belmont-Paul Women's Equality National Monument, accessed March 30, 2018, http://nationalwomansparty.org/learn/national-womans-party/.

5. Marjorie Spruill Wheeler, ed., *One Woman, One Vote: Rediscovering the Woman Suffrage Movement* (Troutdale, OR: NewSage Press, 1995), 16.

6. Andrew W. Robertson, ed., *Encyclopedia of US Political History*, vol. 1 (Washington, DC: CQ Press, 2010), 407.

7. "Who is Alice Paul?" National Woman's Party at the Belmont-Paul Women's Equality National Monument, accessed March 31, 2018, nationalwomansparty.org/learn/who-is-alice-paul/; and Robertson, *Encyclopedia*, 407.

8. Robertson, *Encyclopedia*, 407.

9. Wheeler, *One Woman, One Vote*, 278.

10. Brooke Kroeger, *The Suffragents: How Women Used Men to Get the Vote* (Albany: State University of New York Press, 2017), 199.

11. Kroeger, *Suffragents*, 199.

CHAPTER 9. SCANDINAVIANS FOR SUFFRAGE

1. This photograph depicts members of the Scandinavian Woman Suffrage Association (SWSA) marching in the national Suffrage Red Letter Day parade on May 2, 1914, in Minneapolis. Just one of many organizations participating, SWSA had its own section of

the parade. Members demonstrated the separate nationalities represented by SWSA while alerting onlookers to their unified support of the American suffrage cause.

2. Elinor Lerner, "Jewish Involvement in the New York City Woman Suffrage Movement," *American Jewish History* 70, no. 4 (June 1981): 443.

3. Lerner, *Jewish Involvement*, 444–46.

4. Anna Marie Peterson, "Adding 'A Little Suffrage Spice to the Melting Pot': Minnesota's Scandinavian Woman Suffrage Association," *Minnesota History* 62, no. 8 (Winter 2011/12): 289.

5. Barbara Stuhler, *Gentle Warriors: Clara Ueland and the Minnesota Struggle for Woman Suffrage* (Saint Paul: Minnesota Historical Society Press, 1995), 67.

6. Anna Peterson, "Making Women's Suffrage Support an Ethnic Duty: Norwegian American Identity Constructions and the Women's Suffrage Movement, 1880–1925," *Journal of American Ethnic History* 30, no. 4 (Summer 2011): 12.

7. Peterson, "Suffrage Spice," 289.

8. Peterson, "Ethnic Duty," 16.

9. Peterson, "Ethnic Duty," 12–14.

10. Peterson, "Suffrage Spice," 295.

11. "Swedish Play Will Be Given by Suffragists," *Star Tribune*, February 25, 1917; "National Dances to Be Feature of Dramatic Festival," *Star Tribune*, February 27, 1917.

12. "A Woman Citizen Building," *Woman Citizen* (October 27, 1917), 413.

CHAPTER 10. VOTES FOR JUSTICE

1. Quinn Chapel started in 1844 as a prayer group, holding services at members' homes. In 1847, after being formally admitted to the African Methodist Episcopal Church, they made their home in a building in downtown Chicago. In 1871, the Great Chicago Fire destroyed the structure. The congregation then held services in a series of temporary locations until purchasing their current site on 24th Street and Wabash Avenue. In 1872, the current structure was built at that location.

2. Quinn Chapel AME Church, "About Us," accessed April 3, 2018, http://quinnchicago .org/about-us/.

3. "Miss Anthony's Lecture," *Chicago Tribune*, August 29, 1865.

4. National Register Nomination, "Historic Quinn Chapel of the African Methodist Episcopal Church," accessed April 4, 2018, https://archive.org/stream/ NationalRegisterNominationsForChicago/QuinnChapelA.m.e.ChurchNrNom_djvu.txt.

5. "Negro Women Plan Club to Aid Suffragist Fight," *Chicago Tribune*, January 6, 1913.

6. Wanda A. Hendricks, *Gender, Race, and Politics in the Midwest: Black Club Women in Illinois* (Bloomington: Indiana University Press, 1998), 89–90.

7. Beth Tompkins Bates, *Pullman Porters and the Rise of Protest Politics in Black American, 1925–1945* (Chapel Hill: University of North Carolina Press, 2001), 69.

8. Rosalyn Terborg-Penn, *African American Women in the Struggle for the Vote, 1850–1920* (Bloomington: Indiana University Press, 1998), 99.

9. Hendricks, *Gender, Race, and Politics*, 90.

10. Anne M. Knupfer, *Toward a Tenderer Humanity and a Nobler Womanhood: African American Women's Clubs in Turn-of-the-Century Chicago* (New York: New York University Press, 1996), 52.

11. Terborg-Penn, *African American Women*, 99.

12. Marjorie Spruill Wheeler, ed., *One Woman, One Vote* (Troutdale, OR: NewSage Press, 1995), 264.

13. National Register, "Historic Quinn Chapel."

14. Terborg-Penn, *African American Women*, 81–106.

CHAPTER 11. ONE OF MANY COGS

1. This quilt belonged to William Agnew Johnston and Lucy Browne Johnston of Topeka, Kansas. The Johnstons were active in the Kansas Equal Suffrage Association (KESA) and the Men's Equal Suffrage League of Kansas (MESL), two organizations critically allied in the 1912 ratification of the Woman's Suffrage Amendment to the Kansas constitution. Lucy Johnston was president and campaign manager of KESA from 1911–1912, during the final push for ratification. Her husband, William Agnew Johnston, was chief justice of the Kansas Supreme Court and an active member of MESL of Kansas, an organization that canvassed the state for woman's suffrage.

2. Jennifer Gilbert, *The New England Quilt Museum Quilts* (Concord, CA: C & T Publishing, 2011), 45.

3. Kansas Memory, Object record—1937.11.9, Kansas Historical Society, accessed March 18, 2018, http://www.kansasmemory.org/item/224721.

4. Holly J. McCammon, "Stirring up Suffrage Sentiment: The Formation of the State Woman Suffrage Organizations, 1866–1914," *Social Forces* 80, no. 2 (December 2001): 449–51.

5. Marjorie Spruill Wheeler, ed., *One Woman, One Vote: Rediscovering the Woman Suffrage Movement* (Troutdale, OR: NewSpage Press, 1995), 66–68.

6. Ida Husted Harper, ed., *The History of Woman Suffrage*, vol. 5 (National American Woman Suffrage Association, 1922), 193.

7. "Women's Suffrage," Kansapedia, Kansas Historical Society, accessed March 18, 2018, https://www.kshs.org/kansapedia/women-s-suffrage/14524.

8. Martha B. Caldwell, "The Woman Suffrage Campaign of 1912," *Kansas Historical Quarterly* 12, no. 3 (August 1943): 300–302.

9. "Suffrage Prizes Offered," *Ottawa Daily Republic*, February 14, 1912.

10. "Bucklin Girl Wins Suffrage Prize," *Topeka Capital*, November 3, 1912.

CHAPTER 12. "VOTES FOR WOMEN"

1. E. Lee Eltzroth, "Woman Suffrage," *New Georgia Encyclopedia Online*, accessed December 22, 2017, https://www.georgiaencyclopedia.org/articles/history-archaeology/woman-suffrage.

2. Ann Bausum, *With Courage and Cloth: Winning the Fight for a Woman's Right to Vote* (Washington, DC: National Geographic, 2004), 25.

3. Bausum, *Courage and Cloth*, 25, 28.

4. Terborg-Penn, *African American Women in the Struggle for the Vote, 1850–1920* (Bloomington: Indiana University Press, 1998), 96.

5. Eltzroth, "Woman Suffrage."

6. "Opening Concert Given by Sousa for Auto Lovers," *Atlanta Constitution*, November 12, 1913.

7. "The Political Rights of Women," *Atlanta Constitution*, November 16, 1913.

8. Eltzroth, "Woman Suffrage."

CHAPTER 13. LOYALTY, PURITY, AND LIFE

1. This purple, gold, and white tri-color flag is part of the Connecticut Woman Suffrage Association (CWSA) collection held at the Museum of Connecticut History. Although the organization adopted and used the green, purple, and white colors of the British movement, some members of the CWSA also held membership in the state's branch of the Congressional Union, later to become the National Woman's Party. Within the state, the two organizations did not always align in terms of tactical philosophy but still worked closely together to bring about change.

2. Philip Bump, "Red vs. Blue: A History of How We Use Political Colors," *Washington Post*, November 8, 2016.

3. Kenneth Florney, *Women's Suffrage Memorabilia: An Illustrated Study* (Jefferson, NC: McFarland, 2013), Kindle edition, chap. Colors, para. 3.

4. Margaret Finnegan, *Selling Suffrage: Consumer Culture and Votes for Women* (New York: Columbia University Press, 1999), 93.

5. Marisa Iati, "Why Did Women in Congress Wear White for Trump's State of the Union Address?" *Washington Post*, February 6, 2019.

6. Iati, "Why Did Women."

7. Allison LaCroix, "The National Woman's Party and the Meaning behind Their Purple, White, and Gold Textiles," *National Woman's Party at Belmont-Paul Women's Equality National Monument Blog*, accessed January 3, 2018, http://nationalwomansparty.org/the-national-womans-party-and-the-meaning-behind-their-purple-white-and-gold-textiles/.

8. Iati, "Why Did Women."

CHAPTER 14. THE WAR OF THE ROSES

1. Jennifer A. Lemak and Ashley Hopkins-Benton, *Votes for Women: Celebrating New York's Suffrage Centennial* (Albany: State University of New York Press, 2017), 134.

2. Eleanor Flexner and Ellen Fitzpatrick, *Century of Struggle: The Woman's Rights Movement in the United States* (Cambridge, MA: Belknap Press of Harvard University Press, 1996), 288.

3. "Red Rose as Antis' Badge," *New York Times*, May 4, 1914.

4. "Antis Call Fight for Votes Sex War," *New York Times,* April 16, 1914.

5. "Anti-Suffrage Rose Named 'Mrs. Doge,'" *New York Times*, April 6, 1915.

CHAPTER 15. THE SPIRIT OF 1776

1. Karen M. DePauw and Jessica D. Jenkins, *The House of Worth: Fashion Sketches, 1916–1918* (Mineola, NY: Dover Publications, 2015), 10.

2. Today only two campaign wagons used by suffragists are known to exist. In addition to the wagon featured here, the other wagon is part of the collection of the Smithsonian; it was used for rallies, speaking engagements, and to help distribute the *Woman's Journal*, a popular suffrage publication. "Woman Suffrage Wagon," National Museum of American History, Behring Center, accessed July 21, 2018, http://americanhistory.si.edu/collections/search/object/nmah_1444301.

3. During the closing days of the 2013 session of the New York State Legislature, both houses passed a resolution to honor the centennial of the "Spirit of 1776" wagon's first trip for organizing purposes. July 1, 2013, was designated as "Spirit of 1776" Wagon Day in New York. For more information about the resolution see the *New York History Blog*, https://newyorkhistoryblog.org/2013/07/02/spirit-of-1776-wagon-recognized-by-legislative-resolution/.

4. Jennifer A. Lemak and Ashley Hopkins-Benton, *Votes for Women: Celebrating New York's Suffrage Centennial* (Albany: State University of New York Press, 2017), 120.

5. Marguerite Kearns, "The Spirit of 1776," *New York Archives* (Fall 2013): 28.

6. Kearns, "Spirit," 29.

7. Kearns, "Spirit," 29.

8. "Votes for Women," Huntington History, accessed July 21, 2018, https://huntingtonhistory.com/2018/07/03/votes-for-women/.

9. Kearns, "Spirit," 29.

10. Lemak and Hopkins-Benton, *Votes for Women*, 121.

CHAPTER 16. IDENTITY ERASED

1. Patricia Vettel-Becker, "Sacajawea and Son: The Visual Construction of America's Maternal Feminine," *American Studies* 50, no. 1/2 (Spring/Summer 2009): 27–28.

2. Vettel-Becker, "Sacajawea and Son," 30.

3. Andrew Guilford, ed., *Preserving Western History* (Albuquerque: University of New Mexico Press, 2005), 205–6.

4. Ella E. Clark and Margot Edmonds, *Sacajawea of the Lewis and Clark Expedition* (Berkeley: University of California Press, 1979), 94.

5. Tracy J. Prince and Zadie Schaffer, *Notable Women of Portland* (Charleston, SC: Arcadia Publishing, 2017), 30.

6. Albert Furtwangler, "Reclaiming Jefferson's Ideals: Abigail Scott Duniway's Ode to Lewis and Clark," *Pacific Northwest Quarterly* 98, no. 4 (2007): 165.

7. Vettel-Becker, "Sacajawea and Son," 34–35.

8. Wanda Pillow, "Searching for Sacajawea: Whitened Reproductions and Endarkened Representations," *Hypatia* 22, no. 2 (2007): 6.

CHAPTER 17. MARTYR FOR THE CAUSE

1. Rosemary Betterton, *An Intimate Distance: Women, Artists, and the Body* (New York: Routledge, 1996), 48.

2. Ann Bausum, *With Courage and Cloth: Winning the Fight for a Woman's Right to Vote* (Washington, DC: National Geographic, 2004), 27, 29.

3. Bausum, *Courage*, 11–12; Ann Marie Nicolosi, "The Most Beautiful Suffragette: Inez Milholland and the Political Currency of Beauty," *Journal of the Gilded Age and Progressive Era* 6, no. 4 (July 2007): 286–309.

4. Kathleen Kelly, "Joan of Arc's Birthday: Reflections on NY Suffrage History," *New York History Blog*, accessed January 12, 2018, http://newyorkhistoryblog.org/2014/01/05/on -joan-of-arcs-birthday-reflections-on-ny-suffrage-history/.

5. Nicolosi, "The Most Beautiful Suffragette," 291–92.

6. "Vassar Girls' Field Day," *New York Times*, May 9, 1909.

7. Linda J. Lumsden, *Inez: The Life and Times of Inez Milholland* (Bloomington: Indiana University Press, 2004).

8. Nicolosi, "The Most Beautiful Suffragette," 306–8.

CHAPTER 18. THE MODERN SHOPPER

1. Jan Whitaker, *The World of Department Stores* (New York: Vendome Press, 2011), 253.

2. Macy's Herald Square has served as the headquarters for Macy's Department Store since 1902. In 1978, the building was added to the National Register of Historic Places as a national historic landmark.

3. "LaForge, Margaret Getchell (1841–1880)," Encyclopedia.com, accessed November 5, 2018, https://www.encyclopedia.com/women/encyclopedias-almanacs-transcripts-and -maps/laforge-margaret-getchell-1841-1880.

4. "Company History," Macy's, accessed November 5, 2018, https://www.macysinc.com/about-us/macysinc-history/overview/default.aspx.

5. Jessica Sewell, "Sidewalks and Store Windows as Political Landscapes," *Perspectives in Vernacular Architecture* 9 (2003): 90. Prior to 1911, the following states had enfranchised their female citizens—Wyoming (1890), Colorado (1893), Idaho (1896), Utah (1896), and Washington (1910).

6. "Company History," Macy's.

7. Sewell, "Sidewalks," 86.

8. Margaret Finnegan, *Selling Suffrage: Consumer Culture and Votes for Women* (New York: Columbia University Press, 1999), 95–125.

9. William R. Leach, "Transformation in a Culture of Consumption: Women and Department Stores, 1890–1925," *Journal of American History* 72, no. 2 (September 1984): 338.

10. Finnegan, *Selling Suffrage*, 67–69.

11. Macy's Advertisement, *The Sun*, November 3, 1912.

12. Sewell, "Sidewalks," 86.

13. Leach, "Transformation," 339.

14. "Society," *Muncie Sunday Star*, May 2, 1915.

CHAPTER 19. POSTERS AS PUBLICITY

1. Kenneth Florey, *Women's Suffrage Memorabilia: An Illustrated Guide* (Jefferson, NC: McFarland, 2013) Kindle edition, Chap. Posters-Art and Propaganda, para. 2.

2. Jessica Sewell, "Sidewalks and Store Windows as Political Landscapes," *Perspectives in Vernacular Architecture* 9 (2003): 85.

3. Margaret Finnegan, *Selling Suffrage: Consumer Culture and Votes for Women* (New York: Columbia University Press, 1999), 54.

4. Sewell, "Sidewalks," 85.

5. Robert P. J. Conney Jr., "California Women Suffrage Centennial: A Brief Summary of the 1911 Campaign," *California Secretary of State*, accessed November 10, 2018, https://www.sos.ca.gov/elections/celebrating-womens-suffrage/california-women-suffrage-centennial/.

6. "Suffrage League Offers Prize," *Oakland Tribune*, May 13, 1911.

7. "State Convention at Long Beach—Suffragists Offer a Poster Prize," *San Francisco Chronicle*, May 14, 1911, and "Oakland Suffragists to March Across Bay," *The San Francisco Examiner*, June 3, 1911.

8. "Picture to Plead Votes for Women," *San Francisco Call*, June 17, 1911.

9. "Suffrage Poster to Go on Display—Art to Aid Women in Fight for Vote," *Oakland Tribune*, August 19, 1911.

10. Conney, "California Women."

11. Alison K. Hoagland and Kenneth A. Breisch, eds., *Constructing Image, Identity, and Place: Perspectives in Vernacular Architecture* (Knoxville: The University of Tennessee Press, 2003), 85.

12. In 2019, the California Women Suffrage Centennial issued a reprint of Bertha Boye's "Votes for Women" poster to honor the 100th anniversary of women winning the right to vote in California.

13. Finnegan, *Selling Suffrage*, 55.

CHAPTER 20. ALL BUTTONED UP

1. Kenneth Florey, *Women's Suffrage Memorabilia: An Illustrated Guide* (Jefferson, NC: McFarland, 2013) Kindle edition, Introduction, paras. 1–4.

2. Florey, *Women's Suffrage*, chap. Buttons and Badges—American, paras. 1–2.

3. Florey, *Women's Suffrage*, chap. Buttons and Badges—American, paras. 2–12.

4. "Women's Suffrage," Arizona State Library, Archives and Public Records, accessed November 20, 2018, https://azlibrary.gov/dazl/learners/research-topics/women's suffrage.

5. Heidi Osselae, "Women's Suffrage and Arizona's Quest for Statehood," Prescott Corral, accessed November 20, 2018, www.presscottcorral.org/TT9/9pages24-30.prf.

6. "Arizona Women's Suffrage Anniversary," Arizona Women's Hall of Fame, https://www.azwhf.org/Arizona-womens-suffrage-movement-anniversary/ (accessed 20 November 2018).

7. Osselaer, "Women's Suffrage."

8. "Woman Suffrage Is Lively Issue in Campaign," *Copper Era and Merenci Leader*, October 4, 1912.

9. "Political Parties Brought to Showdown," *Arizona Republic*, September 28, 1912.

10. Florey, *Women's Suffrage*, chap. Buttons and Badges—American, para. 3.

11. Florey, *Women's Suffrage*, Intro., para. 4.

CHAPTER 21. A RECIPE FOR SUCCESS

1. Nina Martyris, "How Suffragists Used Cookbooks as a Recipe for Subversion," The Salt, accessed November 15, 2018, https://www.npr.org/sections/thesalt/2015/11/05/454246666/how-suffragists-used-cookbooks-as-a-recipe-for-subversion.

2. Martyris, "How Suffragists."

3. Cathleen Nista Rauterkus, *Go Get Mother's Picket Sign: Crossing Spheres with the Material Culture of Suffrage* (Lanham, MD: University Press of American, 2010), 61–63.

4. Martyris, "How Suffragists."

5. Rauterkus, *Go Get Mother's*, 63.

6. Shanna Stevenson, "The Fight for Washington Women's Suffrage: A Brief History," Washington State Historical Society, accessed November 15, 2018, http://www.washingtonhistoryo.org/research/whc/milestones/suffrage/.

7. Kenneth Florey, *Women's Suffrage Memorabilia: An Illustrated Guide* (Jefferson, NC: McFarland, 2013) Kindle edition, chap. Cookbooks, para. 5.

8. Florey, *Women's Suffrage*, para. 6.

9. "Would the Enfranchised Woman Lose Interest in Her Home?" *Labor Journal*, September 16, 1910.

10. "Suffragists Can Cook—To Prove It They Have Written Cookbook," *Seattle Star*, June 10, 1910.

11. Stevenson, "The Fight."

12. Florey, *Women's Suffrage*, para. 8.

CHAPTER 22. SUFFRAGE ON THE SILVER SCREEN

1. Advertisement, *Daily Ardmoreite*, April 18, 1915.

2. Margaret Finnegan, *Selling Suffrage: Consumer Culture and Votes for Women* (New York: Columbia University Press, 1999), 101.

3. Mary Mallory, "Hollywood Heights: *Your Girl and Mine* Promotes Women's Suffrage," *Daily Mirror*, accessed November 1, 2018, https://ladailymirror.com/2015/10/19/mary-mallory-hollywood-heights-your-girl-and-mine-promotes-womens-suffrage/.

4. Finnegan, *Selling Suffrage*, 100–101.

5. Matthew Wills, "How Women's Suffrage Has Been Represented in American Film," *Daily JSTOR,* accessed November 1, 2018, https://daily.jstor.org/how-womns-suffrage-has-been-represented-in-american-film/.

6. Wills, "How Women's Suffrage."

7. Finnegan, *Selling Suffrage*, 104.

8. Mallory, "Hollywood Heights."

9. Mallory, "Hollywood Heights."

10. Andrew A. Erish, *Col. William N. Selig, the Man Who Invented Hollywood* (Austin: University of Texas Press, 2012), 204.

11. Erish, *William N. Selig*, 204.

12. Erish, *William N. Selig*, 204.

13. Finnegan, *Selling Suffrage*, 105.

14. Finnegan, *Selling Suffrage*, 101.

CHAPTER 23. CATCHING FIRE

1. "Abolition and Women's Rights," *The Pluralism Project*, Harvard University, accessed September 2, 2018, http://pluralism.org/religions/christianity/christinaity-in-america abolition-and-womens-rights/.

2. Jennifer A. Lemak and Ashely Hopkins-Benton, *Votes for Women: Celebrating New York's Suffrage Centennial* (Albany: State University of New York Press, 2017), 7.

3. "Abolitionist Women at Pennsylvania Hall," The Library Company of Philadelphia, accessed September 2, 2018, https://librarycompany.org/2013/05/17/abolitionist-women -at-pennsylvania-hall/.

4. Beverly C. Tomek, "Pennsylvania Hall," *The Encyclopedia of Greater Philadelphia*, accessed September 2, 2018, http://philadelphiaencyclopedia.org/archive/pennsylvania -hall/#16556.

5. "Abolitionist Women at Pennsylvania Hall."

6. Tomek, "Pennsylvania Hall."

7. Susan Ware, *American Women's History: A Very Short Introduction* (Oxford: Oxford University Press, 2015), 46.

8. Lemak and Hopkins-Benton, *Votes for Women*, 7, 17–18.

9. Nancy A. Hewitt, "Abolition and Suffrage," *Not for Ourselves Alone*, PBS, accessed September 2, 2018, http://www.pbs.org/stantonanthony/resources/index.html?body =abolitionists.html.

10. Hewitt, "Abolition and Suffrage."

CHAPTER 24. CONVERTING TO THE CAUSE

1. Located in Columbia City, Indiana, this window was donated to the Whitley County Historical Museum by the Columbia City United Methodist Church.

2. Eleanor Flexner and Ellen Fitzpatrick, *Century of Struggle: The Woman's Rights Movement in the United States* (Cambridge, MA: Belknap Press of Harvard University Press, 1996), 174.

3. Flexner and Fitzpatrick, *Century of Struggle*, 174.

4. "Early History," Woman's Christian Temperance Union, accessed September 7, 2018, https://wctu.org/history.html.

5. "Biography," Frances Willard House Museum and Archives, accessed September 6, 2018, https://franceswillardhouse.org/frances-willard/biography/.

6. Flexner and Fitzpatrick, *Century of Struggle*, 175.

7. Jennifer A. Lemak and Ashley Hopkins-Benton, *Votes for Women: Celebrating New York's Suffrage Centennial* (Albany: State University of New York Press, 2017), 88.

8. Margaret Finnegan, *Selling Suffrage: Consumer Culture and Votes for Women* (New York: Columbia University Press, 1999), 29.

9. "Woman's Suffrage," Frances Willard House Museum and Archives, accessed September 7, 2018, https://franceswillardhouse.org/frances-willard/women's-suffrage/.

10. Lemak and Hopkins-Benton, *Votes for Women*, 88.

11. Marjorie Spruill Wheeler, ed. *One Woman, One Vote: Rediscovering the Woman Suffrage Movement* (Troutdale, OR: NewSage Press, 1995), 127.

12. Rosalyn Terborg-Penn, *African American Women in the Struggle for the Vote, 1850–1920* (Bloomington: Indiana University Press, 1998), 85–86.

13. Aileen S. Kraditor, *The Ideas of the Woman Suffrage Movement, 1890–1920* (New York: W. W. Norton, 1981), 59.

14. Flexner and Fitzpatrick, *Century of Struggle*, 177.

15. "Woman's Suffrage," Frances Willard House Museum and Archives.

CHAPTER 25. MEN FOR SUFFRAGE

1. John Engstrom, "100 Years of the Brattle," The Brattle Theatre, accessed August 26, 2018, http://www.brattlefilm.org/brattlefilm/first100.html.

2. Brooke Kroeger, *The Suffragents: How Women Used Men to Get the Vote* (Albany: State University of New York Press, 2017), 3.

3. Kroeger, *Suffragents*, 3.

4. RG 101, Connecticut Woman Suffrage Association, Connecticut State Library, Hartford, CT.

5. Woman's Franchise League records, Archives and Special Collections, Ball State University Libraries.

6. Ida Husted Harper, ed., *The History of Woman Suffrage*, vol. 5 (New York: J. J. Little & Ives, 1922), 674.

7. Brooke Kroeger, "How the Suffragists Used a Few Good Men to Help Get the Vote," *What It Means to Be American Blog*, accessed August 26, 2018, http://www.whatitmeans tobeamerican.org/engagements/how-the-suffragists-used-a-few-good-men-to-help-get -the-vote/#.

8. Johanna Neuman, *Gilded Suffragists: The New York Socialites Who Fought for Women's Right to Vote* (New York: Washington Mews Books, 2017), 94.

9. Elida Kocharian and Trula J. Rael, "The Harvard Men's League for Women's Suffrage," *The Crimson*, October 5, 2017, https://www.thecrimson.com/article/2017/10/5/harvard -men-for-suffrage/.

10. "Harvard Men's League for Woman Suffrage," *Crimson*, December 2, 1911, https:// www.thecrimson.com/article/1911/12/2/harvard-mens-league-for-woman-suffrage/.

11. "Explains Exclusion of Mrs. Pankhurst," *Boston Globe*, November 29, 1911.

12. Kocharian and Rael, "Men's League."

13. "Mrs. Pankhurst's Lecture to Be Given in Brattle Hall This Afternoon at 4:30 O'clock," *The Crimson*, December 6, 1911, https://www.thecrimson.com/article/1911/12/6/mrs -pankhursts-lecture-pmrs-emmeline-pankhurst/.

14. "Mrs. Pankhurst Speaks to Harvard Students," *Cambridge Chronicle*, December 9, 1911.

15. Kroeger, *Suffragents*, 6–9.

16. Neuman, *Gilded Suffragists*, 99.

CHAPTER 26. IF YOU SCRATCH MY BACK, I'LL SCRATCH YOURS

1. Jessica D. Jenkins, "Marching Shoulder to Shoulder: New Life in the Connecticut Woman Suffrage Movement," *Connecticut History* 50, no. 2 (Fall 2011): 131.

2. "Five Bands for Suffrage Parade," *Hartford Courant*, May 2, 1914.

3. Allison Lange, "Working Women in the Suffrage Movement," Crusade for the Vote, accessed August 30, 2018, http://www.crusadeforthevote.org/working-women-movement/.

4. Steve Thornton, "A Feeling of Solidarity: Labor Unions and Suffragists Team Up," ConnectictHistory.org, accessed September 1, 2018, https://connecticuthistory.org/a-feeling-of-solidarity-labor-unions-and-suffragists-team-up/.

5. Carol Nichols, *Votes and More for Women: Suffrage and After in Connecticut* (New York: The Haworth Press, 1983), 12–15.

6. Thornton, "Feeling of Solidarity."

7. Thornton, "Feeling of Solidarity."

8. "In Their Own Words," *Hartford Courant*, February 16, 1997.

9. "In Their Own Words," *Hartford Courant*.

10. "In Their Own Words," *Hartford Courant*.

11. "Labor and Women's Suffrage," Washington State Historical Society, accessed September 1, 2018, http://www.washingtonhistory.org/files/library/laborpanels.pdf.

12. Robin Miller Jacoby, "The Women's Trade Union League and American Feminism," *Feminist Studies* 3, no. 1/2 (Autumn 1975): 130.

13. Jacoby, "Women's Trade Union," 130–33.

CHAPTER 27. UNREQUITED LOVE

1. Jennifer A. Lemak and Ashley Hopkins-Benton, *Votes for Women: Celebrating New York's Suffrage Centennial* (Albany: State University of New York Press, 2017), 54.

2. Lemak and Hopkins-Benton, *Votes for Women*, 54.

3. Jason Jones, "Breathing Life into a Public Woman: Victoria Woodhull's Defense of Woman's Suffrage," *Rhetoric Review* 28, no. 4 (2009): 355.

4. Katherine Flynn, "Meet Victoria Woodhull, America's First Female Presidential Candidate," National Trust for Historic Preservation, accessed September 5, 2018, https://savingplaces.org/stories/meet-victoria-woodhull-america-first-female-presidential-candidate#.W6jx8bjphua.

5. Helen Lefkowitz Horowitz, "Victoria Woodhull, Anthony Comstock, and Conflict over Sex in the United States in the 1870s," *Journal of American History* 87, no. 2 (September 2000): 413.

6. Lemak and Hopkins-Benton, *Votes for Women*, 54.

7. Lemak and Hopkins-Benton, *Votes for Women*, 54.

8. Lemak and Hopkins-Benton, *Votes for Women*, 54.

9. Flynn, "Meet Victoria Woodhull."

10. Marjorie Spruill Wheeler, ed., *One Woman, One Vote: Rediscovering the Woman Suffrage Movement* (Troutdale, OR: NewSage Press, 1995), 75.

11. Eleanor Flexner and Ellen Fitzpatrick, *Century of Struggle: The Woman's Rights Movement in the United States* (Cambridge, MA: Belknap Press of Harvard University Press, 1996), 147.

12. Flynn, "Meet Victoria Woodhull."

CHAPTER 28. RAMPANT RACISM

1. Marjorie Spruill Wheeler, ed., *One Woman, One Vote: Rediscovering the Woman Suffrage Movement* (Troutdale, OR: NewSage Press, 1995), 135.

2. Wheeler, *One Woman, One Vote*, 135.

3. Shirley Wilson Logan, ed., *With Pen and Voice: A Critical Anthology of Nineteenth-Century African-American Women* (Carbondale: Southern Illinois University Press, 1995), 30.

4. Kate Clarke Lemay, *Votes For Women! A Portrait of Persistence* (Washington, DC: National Portrait Gallery, 2019), 36.

5. Faye E. Dudden, *Fighting Chance: The Struggle over Woman Suffrage and Black Suffrage in Reconstruction America* (Oxford: Oxford University Press, 2011), 8.

6. Lemay, *Votes for Women!*, 36.

7. Elaine Weiss, *The Woman's Hour: The Great Fight to Win the Vote* (New York: Viking, 2018), 133.

8. William L. O'Neill, "The Fight for Suffrage," *Wilson Quarterly* 10, no. 4 (Autumn 1986): 101.

9. Lemay, *Votes For Women!*, 37–38.

10. O'Neill, "The Fight," 101–2.

11. Dudden, *Fighting Chance*, 3.

12. Terborg-Penn, *African American Women in the Struggle for the Vote, 1850–1920* (Bloomington: Indiana University Press, 1998), 8.

13. Wheeler, *One Woman, One, Vote*, 137.

14. Weiss, *The Woman's Hour*, 136.

15. Weiss, *The Woman's Hour*, 138.

16. Wheeler, *One Woman, One Vote*, 136.

17. Terborg-Penn, *African American Women*, 32.

18. Terborg-Penn, *African American Women*, 12.

CHAPTER 29. A FORMIDABLE OPPONENT

1. "Voting No on Women's Suffrage," New York State Parks, accessed September 10, 2018, https://nystateparks.blog/2017/09/06/voting-no-on-womens-suffrage/.

2. Provenance Note—Charles S. Fairchild owned the pennant highlighted in this chapter. Fairchild was the fourth owner of the estate, which would later become Lorenzo State Historic Site. He was a staunch anti-suffrage supporter and active in the local effort to prevent women from gaining the vote. The collection of Lorenzo State Historic Site includes many anti-suffrage items, such as printed speeches, several issues of *The Woman Patriot*, a button, pennants, books, and handbills.

3. Kristy Maddux, "When Patriots Protest: The Anti-Suffrage Discursive Transformation of 1917," *Rhetoric and Public Affairs* 7, no. 3 (Fall 2004): 283.

4. Susan E. Marshall, "In Defense of Separate Spheres: Class and Status Politics in the Antisuffrage Movement," *Social Forces* 65, no. 2 (December 1986): 327.

5. Aileen S. Kraditor, *The Ideas of the Woman Suffrage Movement, 1890–1920* (New York: W. W. Norton, 1981), 14.

6. Marshall, "In Defense," 330–31.

7. Maddux, "When Patriots Protest," 285,

8. Kraditor, *Ideas*, xi.

9. Kraditor, *Ideas*, 44–66.

10. Marjorie Spruill Wheeler, ed., *One Woman, One Vote: Rediscovering the Woman Suffrage Movement* (Troutdale, OR: NewSage Press, 1995), 188.

11. Maddux, "When Patriots Protest," 187–286–.

12. Cathleen Nista Rauterkus, *Go Get Mother's Picket Sign: Crossing Spheres with the Material Culture of Suffrage* (Lanham, MD: University Press of America, 2010), 27–28.

13. Wheeler, *One Woman, One Vote*, 188.

14. Wheeler, *One Woman, One Vote*, 203.

15. "Voting No on Women's Suffrage."

16. Maddux, "Patriots Protest," 292–93.

17. Kraditor, *Ideas*, 14.

18. Wheeler, *One Woman, One Vote*, 187.

CHAPTER 30. COURTING THE SYSTEM

1. "Her Work," National Susan B. Anthony Museum and House, accessed July 18, 2018, https://susanbanthonyhouse.org/blog/her-life/.

2. Kathi Kern and Linda Levstik, "Teaching the New Departure: The United States vs. Susan B. Anthony," *Journal of the Civil War Era* 2, no. 1 (March 2012): 127–28.

3. Lemak and Hopkins-Benton, *Votes for Women*, 43.

4. Kern and Levstik, "Teaching the New Departure," 130.

5. Eleanor Flexner and Ellen Fitzpatrick, *Century of Struggle: The Woman's Rights Movement in the United States* (Cambridge, MA: Belknap Press of Harvard University Press, 1996), 158–59.

6. Flexner and Fitzpatrick, *Century of Struggle*, 159.

7. Flexner and Fitzpatrick, *Century of Struggle*, 159.

8. Flexner and Fitzpatrick, *Century of Struggle*, 158–59.

9. "Virginia Minor and Women's Right to Vote," National Park Service, accessed August 3, 2019, https://www.nps.gov/jeff/learn/historyculture/the-virginia-minor-case.htm.

10. "Virginia Minor." National Park Service.

11. "Virginia Minor." National Park Service.

12. "Virginia Minor." National Park Service.

13. Flexner and Fitzpatrick, *Century of Struggle*, 162.

14. Kern and Levstik, "Teaching the New Departure," 129.

15. Ann D. Gordon, *The Trial of Susan B. Anthony* (Washington, DC: Federal Judicial Center, Federal Judicial History Office: 2005), v.

CHAPTER 31. THE SOUTH

1. Christina E. Dando, "The Map Proves It: Map Use by the American Woman Suffrage Movement," *Cartographica: International Journal for Geographic Information and Geovisualization* 45, no. 4 (Winter 2010): 221–23.

2. Provenance Note—The map seen here is held in the collections of the Library of Virginia. It is one of many archival items making up the Equal Suffrage League of Virginia Papers, 1908–1938. The Equal Suffrage League of Virginia was organized in 1909 in Richmond. Its primary purpose was to publicize and propagandize women's issues in the state, with the goal to win the political vote. Virginia was one of six states that did not ratify the 19th Amendment. The organization's papers include correspondence, organization records, printed materials, "Votes for Women" buttons, and postcards.

3. Sarah H. Case, "Woman Suffrage in the Southern States," National Park Service, accessed August 4, 2019, https://www.nps.gov/articles/woman-suffrage-in-the-southern -states.htm.

4. Eleanor Flexner and Ellen Fitzpatrick, *Century of Struggle: The Woman's Rights Movement in the United States* (Cambridge, MA: Belknap Press of Harvard University Press, 1996), 221–22.

5. Flexner and Fitzpatrick, *Century of Struggle*, 318.

6. Case, "Woman Suffrage in the Southern States."

7. Elaine Weiss, *The Woman's Hour: The Great Fight to Win the Vote* (New York: Viking Press, 2018), 138.

8. Flexner and Fitzpatrick, *Century of Struggle*, 318.

9. Case, "Woman Suffrage in the Southern States."

10. Marjorie Spruill Wheeler, ed., *One Woman, One Vote: Rediscovering the Woman Suffrage Movement* (Troutdale, OR: NewSage Press, 1995), 317.

11. Case, "Woman Suffrage in the Southern States."

12. Weiss, *The Woman's Hour*, 208.

13. Wheeler, *One Woman, One Vote*, 334.

14. Winifred Conkling, *Votes For Women! American Suffragists and the Battle for the Ballot* (Chapel Hill, NC: Algonquin, 2018), 260.

CHAPTER 32. READ ALL ABOUT IT!

1. David Nasaw, *Children of the City: At Work and at Play* (New York: Anchor Books, 1985), 86.

2. This canvas literature bag is part of the Cornell University Collection of Political Americana. Collected by Susan H. Douglas between 1957 and 1961, the collection includes items representative of American political campaigns and movements between 1789 and 1960. Unlike many suffrage objects produced in the United States that used the traditional American suffrage colors of gold and purple, this bag was printed in green and purple on white canvas. New York, Connecticut, and New Jersey were the few states that adopted the British inspired color scheme of green, white, and purple rather than following the lead of the national American organizations. Printed by Calhoun Show Print of Hartford, Connecticut, this bag was likely used by members of the Connecticut Woman Suffrage Association.

3. Rosalyn Terborg-Penn, *African American Women in the Struggle for the Vote, 1850–1920* (Bloomington: Indiana University Press, 1998), 58–59.

4. "The Revolution," Accessible Archives, accessed June 23, 2018, http://www.accessible -archives.com/collections/the-revolution/.

5. "Suffrage Journals," Woman Suffrage Memorabilia, accessed June 23, 2018, http:// womansuffragememorabilia.com/woman-suffrage-memorabilia/suffrage-journals/.

6. Margaret Finnegan, *Selling Suffrage: Consumer Culture and Votes for Women* (New York: Columbia University Press, 1999), 139–40.

7. Finnegan, *Selling Suffrage*, 142–48.

8. Terborg-Penn, *African American Women*, 60.

9. Finnegan, *Selling Suffrage*, 142–48.

10. Christine Bold, ed., *The Oxford History of Popular Print Culture*, vol. 6. *US Popular Print Culture, 1860–1920* (Oxford: Oxford University Press, 2012), 262.

11. Finnegan, *Selling Suffrage*, 148.

12. Finnegan, *Selling Suffrage*, 150.

13. "Women Turn Newsies for Suffrage Cause," *Detroit Free Press*, April 14, 1912.

14. Advertisement, *Suffrage Daily News*, September 24, 1914.

15. "Plan Election Night Jubilee for Women," *Democrat and Chronicle*, October 30, 1915.

16. Finnegan, *Selling Suffrage*, 167.

CHAPTER 33. SUFFRAGE WITH A SIDE OF SOUP

1. Kenneth Florey, *Women's Suffrage Memorabilia: An Illustrated Historical Study* (Jefferson, NC: McFarland, 2013), 69.

2. Amanda Mackenzie Stuart, *Consuelo and Alva Vanderbilt: The Story of a Daughter and a Mother in the Gilded Age* (New York: HarperCollins, 2005), 310–12.

3. Florey, *Women's Suffrage*, 69.

4. Stuart, *Consuelo and Alva*, 316–19.

5. Ina Bort, "Suffrage on the Menu, Part 3: Alva's Political Equality Association Lunchroom," New-York Historical Society, accessed June 9, 2018, http://behindthe scenes.nyhistory.org/suffrage-menu-alva-vanderbilt-belmont/.

6. Margaret Finnegan, *Selling Suffrage: Consumer Culture and Votes for Women* (New York: Columbia University Press, 1999), 124.

7. Ina Bort, "Suffrage on the Menu."

8. Jessica Ellen Sewell, *Women and the Everyday City: Public Space in San Francisco, 1890-1915* (Minneapolis: University of Minnesota Press, 2011), 150–51.

9. Tove Danovich, "How Restaurants Helped American Women Get the Vote. The History of Suffragist Dining Spaces in the US," accessed June 19, 2018, https://www.eater .com/2018/3/29/17164320/suffragette-restaurant-history-nyc.

10. Sewell, *Everyday City*, 151.

11. Bort, "Suffrage on the Menu."

CHAPTER 34. ON THE ROAD TO VICTORY

1. Richard Kurin, *The Smithsonian's History of America in 101 Objects* (New York: Penguin, 2013), 311–16.

2. Jennifer A. Lemak and Ashley Hopkins-Benton, *Votes for Women: Celebrating New York's Suffrage Centennial* (Albany: State University of New York Press, 2017), 124.

3. Holly J. McCammon, "Out of the Parlors and into the Streets: The Changing Tactical Repertoire of the US Women's Suffrage Movements," *Social Forces* 81, no. 3 (March 2003): 791–93.

4. Sara Egge, "The Grassroots Diffusion of the Woman Suffrage Movement in Iowa: The IESA Rural Women and he Right to Vote," PhD diss., Iowa State University, accessed June 23, 2018, http://lib.dr.iastate.edu/etd/10489.

5. Jessica D. Jenkins, "Marching Shoulder to Shoulder: New Life in the Connecticut Woman Suffrage Movement," *Connecticut History* 50, no. 2 (Fall 2011): 141.

6. Julie Wosk, *Women and the Machine: Representations from the Spinning Wheel to the Electronic Age* (Baltimore, MD: Johns Hopkins University Press, 2001), 126.

7. Virginia Scharff, *Taking the Wheel: Women and the Coming of the Motor Age* (Albuquerque: University of New Mexico Press, 1999), 86.

8. Wosk, *Women and the Machine*, 126.

9. Patri O'Gan, "Traveling for Suffrage Part 1: Two Women, a Cat, a Car, and a Mission," *O Say Can You See? Stores from the National Museum of American History* (blog), accessed June 23, 2018, http://americanhistory.si.edu/blog/2014/03/traveling-for-suffrage -part-1-two-women-a-cat-a-car-and-a-mission.html.

10. Wosk, *Women and the Machine*, 127.

11. O'Gan, "Traveling for Suffrage."

12. Wosk, *Women and the Machine*, 127.

CHAPTER 35. LIFTING AS WE CLIMB

1. David Boers, *Uncovering Black Heroes: Lesser-Known Stories of Liberty and Civil Rights* (New York: Peter Lang, 2017), 57.

2. Marjorie Spruill Wheeler, ed., *One Woman, One Vote: Rediscovering the Woman Suffrage Movement* (Troutdale, OR: NewSage Press, 1995), 38.

3. Rosalyn Terborg-Penn, *African American Women in the Struggle for the Vote, 1850–1920* (Bloomington: Indiana University Press, 1998), 91.

4. Boers, *Uncovering Black Heroes*, 48.

5. Charles Harris Wesley, *The History of the National Association of Colored Women's Clubs: A Legacy of Service* (Washington, DC: National Association of Colored Women's Clubs, Inc., 1984), 16.

6. Debra Michals, "Mary Church Terrell (1864–1954)," National Women's History Museum, accessed August 11, 2019, https://www.womenshistory.org/education-resources/biographies/mary-church-terrell.

7. Terborg-Penn, *African American Women*, 88, 92.

8. Boers, *Uncovering Black Heroes*, 57.

9. Terborg-Penn, *African American Women*, 93.

10. "National Association of Colored Women's Club in Session," *New York Age*, July 24, 1920.

11. "National Association of Colored Women's Club in Session," *New York Age*, July 24, 1920.

12. "Negro Woman's Resolutions for Enforcement of Federal Suffrage Amendments," Tennessee States Library and Archives, accessed August 11, 2019, https://cdm15138 .contentdm.oclc.org/digital/collection/p15138coll27/id/233/rec/8.

13. "Negro Woman's Resolutions for Enforcement of Federal Suffrage Amendments," Tennessee States Library and Archives, accessed August 11, 2019, https://cdm15138 .contentdm.oclc.org/digital/collection/p15138coll27/id/233/rec/8.

CHAPTER 36. LOBBYING FOR THE VOTE

1. Margaret Finnegan, *Selling Suffrage: Consumer Culture and Votes for Women* (New York: Columbia University Press, 1999), 49.

2. "Tactics and Techniques of the National Woman's Party Suffrage Campaign," American Memory, Library of Congress, accessed June 23, 2018, https://www.loc.gov/ collections/static/women-of-protest/images/tactics.pdf.

3. Jessica D. Jenkins, "Marching Shoulder to Shoulder: New Life in the Connecticut Woman Suffrage Movement," *Connecticut History* 50, no. 2 (Fall 2011): 134.

4. Jenkins, "Marching Shoulder to Shoulder," 132–39.

5. "Woman Suffrage Tunic," Wisconsin Historical Society, accessed June 23, 2018, https://www.wisconsinhistory.org/Records/Article/CS2808.

6. Genevieve G. McBride, *On Wisconsin Women: Working for Their Rights from Settlement to Suffrage* (Madison: The University of Wisconsin Press, 1993), 266.

7. "Woman Suffrage Tunic," accessed June 23, 2018, https://www.wisconsinhistory.org/ Records/Article/CS2808.

8. McBride, *Wisconsin Women,* 266.

9. Theodora W. Youmans, "How Wisconsin Women Won the Ballot," *Wisconsin Magazine of History* 5, no. 1 (September 1921): 25.

10. McBride, *Wisconsin Women*, 266.

11. "20,000 Suffragists to March with Petition," *Buffalo Evening News*, June 7, 1916.

12. Anne Firor Scott and Andrew MacKay Scott, *One Half the People: The Fight for Woman Suffrage* (Urbana: University of Illinois Press, 1982), 33–34.

13. Scott, *One Half the People*, 34.

CHAPTER 37. SWIMMING FOR SUFFRAGE

1. Frances M. Abbott, "A Comparative View of the Woman Suffrage Movement," *North American Review*, 166, no. 495 (February 1898): 142–51.

2. Gerald R. Gems, Linda J. Borish, and Gertrude Pfister, *Sports in American History: From Colonization to Globalization* (Auckland, NZ: Human Kinetics, 2008), 212.

3. Patricia Campbell Warner, *When the Girls Came Out to Play: The Birth of American Sportswear* (Amherst: University of Massachusetts Press, 2006), 78.

4. Gems, Borish, Pfister, *Sports*, 251.

5. Linda J. Borish, "Athletic Activities of Various Kinds: Physical Health and Sport Programs for Jewish American Women," *Journal of Sport History* 26, no. 2 (Summer 1999): 258.

6. Borish, "Athletic Activities," 259.

7. Linda J. Borish, "Settlement Houses to Olympic Stadiums: Jewish American Women, Sports and Social Change, 1880s-1930s," *International Sports Studies* 22, no. 1 (2000): 15.

8. Sarah Laskow, "The Surprising History of Swimming's Suffragists," *Atlas Obscura*, accessed July 21, 2018, https://www.atlasobscura.com/articles/women-swimming-pioneers-suffrage.

9. Borish, "Settlement House," 15.

10. "Suffragists in Bathing Suits Make Myer's Lake Their Forum," *Salem News*, July 18, 1912.

11. "Suffragists to Swim the Delaware with Torch of Liberty," *Evening Public Ledger*, August 20, 1915.

12. Mark Dyreson, "Icons of Liberty or Objects of Desire? American Women Olympians and the Politics of Consumption," *Journal of Contemporary History* 38, no. 3 (July 2003): 435.

CHAPTER 38. FALLING INTO LINE

1. "Norwegian Headdress and Vest," Wisconsin Historical Society, accessed July 23, 2018, https://www.wisconsinhistory.org/museum/exhibits/p2p/green/materials_performance.asp.

2. Edith M. Phelps, *Selected Articles on Woman Suffrage* (Minneapolis: H. W. Wilson, 1912), 6.

3. Sidney R. Bland, "New Life in an Old Movement: Alice Paul and the Great Suffrage Parade of 1913 in Washington, DC," *Record of the Columbia Historical Society, Washington, DC*, 71/72 (1971/1972): 657–59.

4. Bland, "New Life," 259–60.

5. Margaret Finnegan, *Selling Suffrage: Consumer Culture and Votes for Women* (New York: Columbia University Press, 1999), 54.

6. Jessica D. Jenkins, "Marching Shoulder to Shoulder: New Life in the Connecticut Woman Suffrage Movement," *Connecticut History* 50, no. 2 (Fall 2011): 135–36.

7. Bland, "New Life," 663–64.

8. "Tactics and Techniques of the National Woman's Party Suffrage Campaign," American Memory, Library of Congress, accessed July 23, 2018, https://www.loc.gov/collections/women-of-protest/articles-and-essays/tactics-and-techniques-of-the-national-womans-party-suffrage-campaign/.

9. Finnegan, *Selling Suffrage*, 52–53.

10. Marjorie Spruill Wheeler, ed., *One Woman, One Vote: Rediscovering the Woman Suffrage Movement* (Troutdale, OR: NewSage Press, 1995), 16.

11. Eleanor Flexner and Ellen Fitzpatrick, *Century of Struggle: The Woman's Rights Movement in the United States* (Cambridge, MA: Belknap Press of Harvard University Press, 1996), 256–57.

12. Eleanor Flexner and Ellen Fitzpatrick, *Century of Struggle*, 256–57.

13. Jennifer A. Lamak and Ashley Hopkins-Benton, *Votes for Women: Celebrating New York's Suffrage Centennial* (Albany: State University of New York Press, 2017), 132.

14. Wheeler, *One Woman*, 269–69.

15. Jennifer Schuessler, "The Complex History of the Women's Suffrage Movement," *New York Times*, August 15, 2019.

CHAPTER 39. JAILED FOR FREEDOM

1. "Tactics and Techniques of the National Woman's Party Suffrage Campaign," American Memory, Library of Congress, accessed July 15, 2018, https://www.loc.gov/col lections/women-of-protest/articles-and-essays/tactics-and-techniques-of-the-national -womans-party-suffrage-campaign/.

2. "Tactics and Techniques."

3. Marjorie Spruill Wheeler, ed., *One Woman, One Vote: Rediscovering the Woman Suffrage Movement* (Troutdale, OR: NewSage Press, 1995), 17.

4. Eleanor Flexner and Ellen Fitzpatrick, *Century of Struggle: The Woman's Rights Movement in the United States* (Cambridge, MA: Belknap Press of Harvard University Press, 1996), 275.

5. Flexner and Fitzpatrick, *Century of Struggle*, 275–77.

6. Flexner and Fitzpatrick, *Century of Struggle*, 277.

7. Flexner and Fitzpatrick, *Century of Struggle*, 277.

8. Wheeler, *One Woman, One Vote*, 286.

9. "Tactics and Techniques."

10. "Tactics and Techniques."

11. "Jail Door Pin," National Woman's Party, accessed July 15, 2018, http://national womansparty.org/collectionitems/jail-door-pin-2/. The pin highlighted in this chapter was presented to Betsy Graves Reyneau, who spent time at the Occoquan Workhouse. As an active member of the National Woman's Party (NWP), Reyneau later painted portraits of many of the leaders of the NWP. When she died in 1964, her daughter gave the pin to Pauli Murray, a famed civil rights activist and lawyer, who was a close friend to Reyneau. The pin was then passed for many years from feminist to feminist. Upon Murray's death in 1985, the pin was donated to the NWP by the last woman to receive the pin, with the blessing of Murray's family.

12. Flexner and Fitzpatrick, *Century of Struggle*, 277.

13. Mary Church Terrell, *A Colored Woman in a White World* (Amherst, NY: Humanity Books, 2005), 356.

14. Flexner and Fitzpatrick, *Century of Struggle*, 278–79.

15. "Tactics and Techniques."

CHAPTER 40. WINNING THE WEST

1. In 1966, Wyoming's 75th Anniversary Commission purchased South Pass City, as a birthday present for the citizens of the state to ensure that the town's storied history would not end up lost to time. Now a state historic site, South Pass City has become one of the most accurately restored and authentically exhibited historic sites in the West. Seventeen of the site's twenty-three original structures have been restored, with many of the site's thirty thousand artifacts exhibited in their original buildings.

2. Eleanor Flexner and Ellen Fitzpatrick, *Century of Struggle: The Woman's Rights Movement in the United States* (Cambridge, MA: Belknap Press of Harvard University Press, 1996), 152.

3. "South Pass City," Wyoming State Parks, accessed May 1, 2018, http://wyoparks.state .wy.us/index.php/about-south-pass-city.

4. "South Pass City," WyoHistory, accessed May 1, 2018, https://www.wyohistory.org/ encyclopedia/south-pass-city.

5. Tom Rea, "Right Choice, Wrong Reasons: Wyoming Women Win the Right to Vote," WyoHistory, accessed May 2, 2018, https://www.wyohistory.org/encyclopedia/right -choice-wrong-reasons-wyoming-women-win-right-vote.

6. Rea, "Right Choice."

7. Rea, "Right Choice."

8. Flexner and Fitzpatrick, *Century*, 152–53.

9. Marjorie Spruill Wheeler, ed., *One Woman, One Vote: Rediscovering the Woman Suffrage Movement* (Troutdale, OR: NewSage Press, 1995), 11.

10. Wheeler, *One Woman, One Vote*, 11.

11. Ann Bausum, *With Courage and Cloth: Winning the Fight for a Woman's Right to Vote* (Washington, DC: National Geographic Society, 2004), 98–99.

12. Rea, "Right Choice."

13. Wheeler, *One Woman, One Vote*, 11, 99–100.

CHAPTER 41. PROGRESSING IN POLITICS

1. The Progressive Party (also known as the Bull Moose Party in comments made by the party's leader, Theodore Roosevelt) was created in 1912 to offer a more progressive perspective on social issues. Items like the campaign bandana seen here were produced as

campaign memorabilia. Sold in support of the party, items like this would have been seen at rallies and other events hosted by the Progressive Party.

2. Jo Freeman, *We Will Be Heard: Women's Struggles for Political Power in the United States* (Lanham, MD: Rowman & Littlefield, 2008), 52.

3. "Centuries of Citizenship: A Constitutional Timeline," National Constitution Center, accessed May 6, 2018, https://constitutioncenter.org/timeline/html/cw08_12159.html.

4. Leroy G. Dorsey, "Managing Women's Equality: Theodore Roosevelt, the Frontier Myth, and the Modern Woman," *Rhetoric and Public Affair* 16, no. 3 (Fall 2013): 424.

5. Doris Groshen Daniels, "Theodore Roosevelt and Gender Roles," *Presidential Studies Quarterly* 26, no. 3 (Summer 1996): 652–56 and "Theodore Roosevelt and Women's Suffrage," American Experience, PBS, accessed May 6, 2018, https://www.pbs.org/wgbh/americanexperience/features/tr-gable/.

6. Daniels, "Gender Roles," 656.

7. Daniels, "Gender Roles," 656–57.

8. Daniels, "Gender Roles," 657.

9. Jo Freeman, *We Will Be Heard*, 51–52, 73.

10. Freeman, *We Will Be Heard*, 51.

11. Daniels, "Gender Roles," 657.

12. Eleanor Flexner and Ellen Fitzpatrick, *Century of Struggle: The Woman's Rights Movement in the United States* (Cambridge, MA: Belknap Press of Harvard University Press, 1996), 255.

13. Freeman, *We Will Be Heard*, 72–73.

CHAPTER 42. A MOVE EASTWARD

1. "Specimen Ballot, 1912," ICHi-14325, Facing Freedom in America, Chicago History Museum, http://facingfreedom.org/taxonomy/term/19/0?page=3.

2. In 1968, this ballot box was donated to the Chicago History Center. At the time, the donor, Sidney T. Holzman, was the chairman of the Board of Elections in Chicago.

3. Adade Mitchell Wheeler, "Conflict in the Illinois Woman Suffrage Movement of 1913," *Journal of the Illinois State Historical Society* 76, no. 2 (Summer 1983): 96–99.

4. Wheeler, "Conflict," 99.

5. "May Get Vote on Suffrage," *Chicago Daily Tribune*, March 13, 1912.

6. "Defeat Spurs on the Suffragettes," *Chicago Daily Tribune*, April 11, 1912.

7. Wheeler, "Conflict," 104.

8. Wheeler, "Conflict," 105.

9. Grace Wilbur Trout, "Side Lights on Illinois Suffrage History," *Journal of the Illinois State Historical Society* 13, no. 2 (July 1920): 150.

10. Eileen L. McDonagh and H. Douglas Price, "Woman Suffrage in the Progressive Era: Patterns of Opposition and Support in Referenda Voting, 1910–1918," *American Political Science Review* 79, no. 2 (June 1985): 417.

11. Trout, "Side Lights," 151–55.

12. Trout, "Side Lights," 155–61.

13. Wheeler, "Conflict," 95–96.

14. Trout, "Side Lights," 165–66.

CHAPTER 43. WALKING INTO HISTORY

1. This evening shoe was donated to the collection of the Montana Historical Society by John C. Board in 2006. Prior to Rankin's death in 1973, Board had been acquainted with the former congresswoman and interviewed her on several occasions. In 1967, Board published an article about Rankin titled, "The Lady from Montana," in *Montana: The Magazine of Western History*. During a visit to her ranch to locate personal papers, Rankin and Board found the shoe among Rankin's personal items. The shoe was later used by sculptor Terry Minnaugh as reference when modeling Jeannette Rankin's figure for a bronze sculpture in the US Capitol rotunda and the Montana State Capitol.

2. Office of History and Preservation, Office of the Clerk, US House of Representatives, *Women in Congress, 1917–2006* (Washington, DC: U S Government Printing Office, 2006), 18.

3. Joan Hoff Wilson, "'Peace Is a Woman's Job . . . ,' Jeannette Rankin and American Foreign Policy: The Origins of Her Pacifism," *Montana: Magazine of Western History* 30, no. 1 (Winter 1980): 30.

4. Wilson, "Peace," 30.

5. Kathryn Anderson, "Steps to Political Equality: Woman Suffrage and Electoral Politics in the Lives of Emily Newell Blair, Anne Henrietta Martin, and Jeannette Rankin," *Frontiers: A Journal of Women Studies* 18, no. 1 (1997): 103.

6. Wilson, "Peace," 30.

7. Wilson, "Peace," 30.

8. Anderson, "Steps to Political Equality," 106.

9. "Jeannette Rankin," History, Art, and Archives, United States House of Representatives, accessed May 18, 2018, http://history.house.gov/People/Listing/R/RANKIN,-Jeannette-(R000055)/.

10. John C. Board, "The Lady from Montana," *Montana: The Magazine of Western History* 17, no. 3 (Summer 1967): 12.

11. Winifred Conkling, *Votes for Women! American Suffragists and the Battle for the Ballot* (Chapel Hill, NC: Algonquin, 2017), 225.

12. Anderson, "Steps to Political Equality," 106.

13. "Jeannette Rankin," History, Art, and Archives, United States House of Representatives.

14. Letter from Gov. Joseph M. Carey to Miss Harriet Noble, 1916, League of Women Voters of Indiana Records, 1908–1920, Indiana Historical Society.

15. Anderson, "Steps to Political Equality," 116.

CHAPTER 44. TIPPING THE SCALE

1. Christine A. Lunardini and Thomas J. Knock, "Woodrow Wilson and Woman Suffrage: A New Look," *Political Science Quarterly* 95, no. 4 (Winter 1980/1981): 656.

2. Elaine Weiss, *The Woman's Hour: The Great Fight to Win the Vote* (New York: Viking, 2018), 79.

3. Lunardini and Knock, "Woodrow Wilson," 656.

4. Lunardini and Knock, "Woodrow Wilson," 555.

5. Lunardini and Knock, "Woodrow Wilson," 657.

6. "Woodrow Wilson," The White House, accessed September 30, 2018, https://www .whitehouse.gov/about-the-white-house/presidents/Woodrow-wilson/.

7. John Milton Cooper, *Woodrow Wilson: A Biography* (New York: Vintage Books, 2009), 171.

8. Daniel J. Tichenor, "The Presidency, Social Movements, and Contentious Change: Lessons from the Woman's Suffrage and Labor Movements," *Presidential Studies Quarterly* 29, no. 1 (March 1999): 15–16.

9. Weiss, *Woman's Hour*, 80–82.

10. Weiss, *Woman's Hour*, 83.

11. Weiss, *Woman's Hour*, 83–84.

12. Tichenor, "The Presidency," 18.

CHAPTER 45. MOTHER KNOWS BEST

1. Ann Bausum, *With Courage and Cloth: Winning the Fight for a Woman's Right to Vote* (Washington, DC: National Geographic, 2004), 98–100.

2. Marjorie Spruill Wheeler, ed., *One Woman, One Vote: Rediscovering the Woman Suffrage Movement* (Troutdale, OR: NewSage Press, 1995), 333.

3. Winifred Conkling, *Votes for Women! American Suffragists and the Battle for the Ballot* (Chapel Hill, NC: Algonquin, 2017), 158–261.

4. Anastatia Sims, "Powers That Pray and Powers That Prey: Tennessee and the Fight for Woman Suffrage," *Tennessee Historical Quarterly* 50, no. 4 (Winter 1991): 209.

5. Conkling, *Votes for Women*, 261.

6. Elaine Weiss, *The Woman's Hour: The Great Fight to Win the Vote* (New York: Viking, 2018), 297.

7. Weiss, *Woman's Hour*, 299.

8. Weiss, *Woman's Hour*, 205–97.

9. Weiss, *Woman's Hour*, 305.

10. Letter from Fenn Burn to Harry T. Burn, August 1920, C. M. McClung Historical Collection, Knox Public Library, Knoxville, TN.

11. Weiss, *Woman's Hour*, 307.

12. William L. O'Neill, "The Fight for Suffrage," *Wilson Quarterly* 10, no. 4 (Autumn 1986): 99.

13. Jennifer Schuessler, "The Complex History of the Women's Suffrage Movement," *New York Times*, August 15, 2019.

CHAPTER 46. UNDER THE WATCHFUL EYE

1. "History of League of Women Voters Texas," League of Women Voters, accessed December 2, 2018, https://my.lwv.org/texas/history.

2. "History of the Women's Movement," National Women's History Project, accessed December 2, 2018, http://www.nwhp.org/resources/womens0rights-movement/history-of-the-womens-rights-movement/.

3. "History," League of Women Voters, accessed December 2, 2018, https://www.lwv.org/about-us/history.

4. Elaine Weiss, *The Woman's Hour: The Great Fight to Win the Vote* (New York: Viking, 2018), 323.

5. Weiss, *Woman's Hour,* 225–26.

6. "History of the League of Women Voters of Texas."

7. "One Hundred Years Ago Today, Texas Women Votes in a Primary Election for the Very First Time," League of Women Voters, accessed December 2, 2018, https://my.lwv.org/texas/article/one-hundred-years-ago-today-texas-women-voted-primary-election-very-first-time.

8. "El Paso Woman Is Honored by Voters' League," *El Paso Times,* October 14, 1919.

9. "League of Women Voters Entertain with Poll Tax Tea Saturday at Khaki Club," *El Paso Times*, January 8, 1920.

10. "Pointing Zero Hour for Texas Voters," *Austin American-Statesman*, January 20, 1924.

11. "History of League of Women Voters Texas."

12. Weiss, *Woman's Hour*, 332.

13. Eleanor Flexner and Ellen Fitzpatrick, *Century of Struggle: The Woman's Rights Movement in the United States* (Cambridge, MA: Belknap Press of Harvard University Press, 1996), 320.

CHAPTER 47. BRIDGES OF HOPE

1. "Voting Rights Act (1965)," Our Documents, accessed December 5, 2018, https://www.ourdocuments.gov/doc.php?flash=old&doc=100.

2. Marjorie Spruill Wheeler, ed., *One Woman, One Vote: Rediscovering the Woman Suffrage Movement* (Troutdale, OR: NewSage Press, 1995), 153–54.

3. Elaine Weiss, *The Woman's Hour: The Great Fight to Win the Vote* (NY: Viking, 2018), 328.

4. Wheeler, *One Woman*, 153–54.

5. Faye E. Dudden, *Fighting Chance: The Struggle Over Woman Suffrage and Black Suffrage in Reconstruction America* (Oxford: Oxford University Press, 2011), 198.

6. Ann D. Gordon et al., *African American Women and the Vote, 1837–1965* (Amherst: University of Massachusetts Press, 1997), 10.

7. Eleanor Flexner and Ellen Fitzpatrick, *Century of Struggle: The Woman's Rights Movement in the United States* (Cambridge, MA: Belknap Press of Harvard University Press, 1996), 323.

8. "Voting Rights Act (1965)."

9. "Selma-to-Montgomery March: National Historic Trail and All-American Road," National Park Service, accessed December 5, 2018, https://www.nps.gov/nr/travel/civilrights/al4.htm.

10. "Edmund Pettus Bridge," National Park Service, accessed December 5, 2018, https://www.nps.gov/semo/learn/historyculture/edmund-puttus-bridge.htm.

11. "Selma-to-Montgomery March."

12. "Voting Rights Act (1965)."

13. "Voting Rights Act (1965)."

14. Weiss, *Woman's Hour*, 328.

CHAPTER 48. TAKING THE NEXT STEP

1. "ERA Charm Bracelet (I)," National Museum of American History, accessed December 10, 2018, http://americanhistory.si.edu/collections/search/object/nmah_1066419.

2. Elaine Weiss, *The Woman's Hour: The Great Fight to Win the Vote* (New York: Viking, 2018), 238–40.

3. Eleanor Flexner and Ellen Fitzpatrick, *Century of Struggle: The Woman's Rights Movement in the United States* (Cambridge, MA: Belknap Press of Harvard University Press, 1996), 321.

4. Allison K. Lange, "The Equal Rights Amendment Has Been Dead for 36 Years. Why It Might Be on the Verge of a Comeback," *Washington Post*, June 18, 2018.

5. Flexner and Fitzpatrick, *Century of Struggle*, 322.

6. Flexner and Fitzpatrick, *Century of Struggle*, 324.

7. "History of the Women's Rights Movement," National Women's History Alliance, accessed December 10, 2018, http://www.nwhp.org/resources/womens-rights-movement/history-of-the-womens-rights-movement/.

8. "History of the Women's Rights Movement," National Women's History Alliance.

9. Lange, "Equal Rights Amendment."

10. Susan Ware, *American Women's History: A Very Short Introduction* (Oxford: Oxford University Press, 2015), 107.

11. Kristina Peterson, "Equal Rights Amendment Could Soon Be Back in Congress," *Wall Street Journal*, July 3, 2019.

12. Gayle Lemmon, "Now's the time to ratify the Equal Rights Amendment," CNN, accessed December 10, 2018, https://www.cnn.com/2018/11/24/opinions/time-to-ratify-the-equal-rights-amendments-lemmon/index.html.

13. Lange, "Equal Rights Amendment."

CHAPTER 49. GOING GLOBAL

1. "Full Tape with Lewd Donald Trump Remarks" (*Access Hollywood* footage), YouTube, October 21, 2016, https://www.youtube.com/watch?v=NcZcTnykYbw.

2. Karl Vick, "Perhaps the Largest Protest in US History Was Brought to You by Trump," *Time,* January 26, 2017, http://time.com/4649891/protest-donald-trump/.

3. "Our Mission," Women's March, accessed December 15, 2018, https://www.womens march.com/mission/.

4. "Our Story," Pussyhat Project, accessed December 15, 2018, https://www.pussyhat project.com/.

5. Tove Hermanson, "Knitting as Dissent: Female Resistance in America since the Revolutionary War," Textile Society of America, September 2012, https://digitalcommons .unl.edu/cgi/viewcontent.cgi?article=1695&context=tsaconf.

6. Kristen Jordan Shamus, "Pink Pussyhats: Why Some Activists Are Ditching Them," *USA Today*, January 11, 2018.

7. "The Pussyhat," Victoria and Albert Museum, accessed December 15, 2018, https://www.vam.ac.uk/articles/the-pussyhat.

8. "Knitting the Resistance: Crafting Political Protest from the 2017 Women's Marches," Department of Art, Art History, and Design, Michigan State University, accessed December 15, 2018, http://www.art.msu.edu/galleries/union-art-gallery/knitting -resistance/.

9. Vick, "Perhaps the Largest."

10. Shamus, "Pink Pussyhats."

11. Shamus, "Pink Pussyhats."

12. Anna Russell, "The Victoria and Albert Gains a Pussyhat," *The New Yorker,* accessed December 15, 2018, https://www.newyorker.com/magazine/2017/04/24/the-victoria-and -albert-gains-a-pussyhat.

CHAPTER 50. RECKONING WITH THE PAST . . . AND FUTURE

1. "The Portrait Monument," *Atlas Obscura,* accessed December 8, 2018, https://www .atlasobscrura.com/places/the-portrait-monument-washington-dc.

2. Sandra Weber, *The Woman Suffrage Statue: A History of Adelaide Johnson's Monument to Lucretia Mott, Elizabeth Cady Stanton and Susan B. Anthony at the United States Capitol* (Jefferson, NC: McFarland, 2016) Kindle edition, chap. 7.

3. Maggie Esteves, "Adelaide Johnson: Artist with Flair," *United States Capitol Historical Society Blog,* accessed December 8, 2018, https://uschs.wordpress.com/tag/portrait -monument/.

4. Weber, *Woman Suffrage Statue,* chap.9.

5. Weber, *Woman Suffrage Statue,* chap. 9.

6. "Portrait Monument to Lucretia Mott, Elizabeth Cady Stanton and Susan B. Anthony," Architect of the Capitol, accessed December 8, 2018, https://www.aoc.gov/ capitol-hill/other-statues/portrait-monument.

7. Weber, *Woman Suffrage Statue,* chap. 9.

8. Lorraine Boissoneault, "The Suffragist Statue Trapped in a Broom Closet for 75 Years," *Smithsonian Magazine,* accessed December 8, 2018, https://www.smithsonianmag .com/history/suffragist-statue-trapped-broom-closet-75-years-180963274/.

9. Jennifer A. Lemak and Ashley Hopkins-Benton, *Votes for Women: Celebrating New York's Suffrage Centennial* (Albany: State University of New York Press, 2017), 216–17.

10. Weber, *Woman Suffrage Statue,* chap. 9.

11. Weber, *Woman Suffrage Statue,* chap. 9.

Index

About the Author

Jessica D. Jenkins has worked in museums and cultural institutions for more than ten years specializing in collection and exhibition curation. After receiving a bachelor of arts in history at Quincy University, she completed a master of arts in public history from Central Connecticut State University. As a graduate student Jessica undertook the study of the women's suffrage movement, continuing to deepen her knowledge and study of the subject since. Her previous publications on the topic include articles for the journal *Connecticut History* and the magazine *Connecticut Explored*. In addition to her work on suffrage, Jessica co-authored the 2015 book, *House of Worth: Fashion Sketches, 1916–1918* and has written on other historic topics such as World War I poster art. She previously served as curator of collections for the Litchfield Historical Society, Litchfield, Connecticut, where she was responsible for the management of the institution's museum collection and exhibition program of its two museums, the Litchfield History Museum and the Tapping Reeve House and Litchfield Law School. In her current role as director of collections for Minnetrista, Muncie, Indiana, Jessica plays a key role in the care of the institution's historic collection and the telling of its stories.